D1600877

A family's search for the truth in the face of deception, infidelity and murder

A MEMOIR BY

LORI AND CINDY HART

Cover artwork by Terisa Davis

ISBN 978-0-9977077-1-7
Printed in the United States of America.

Dedication

Just when you think you finally understand your family,

Just when you think your family members are under control,

Just when you think you can leave your childhood family behind, some unanticipated event will rock you to your core, shattering all of your carefully constructed perceptions of family.

The magnitude of family will sweep through you and you will know with irrefutable certainty that everything you are and will be, can be attributed to your family.

This book is dedicated to our large, crazy, chaotic family and especially to our Mother. She always said you can pick your nose but you don't pick your family. We miss her every day.

Contents

Prologue

"Who but the mad would choose to keep on living? In the end, aren't we all just a little crazy?"
— Libby Bray

(February, 2013)

"Maybe we have the day wrong."

I'm tired of sitting in the car. The cold is making my nose run as I cradle my fingers around the coffee cup to keep them warm. My sister, Cindy, is scrunched down in the front seat texting furiously on her phone. She looks up occasionally and wipes away some of the fog from the window as she peers back towards the entrance of the cemetery.

"I'm sure it's going to happen today," she snaps. "Be patient!"

I lean back in my seat and roll my window down a few inches to get a clearer view. The unwelcomed cold air rushes in and within seconds I can feel it stiffening the leather seat. Even under more pleasant circumstances this would be a miserable way to spend an afternoon. But these were far from pleasant circumstances.

From my vantage point, the grave is barely visible. The headstone is engraved only with her name: *Noreen Rudd*. The grave next to Noreen's is adorned with the name of her mother, *Irene Kumeta*, who died only recently.

The wind picks up, blowing the last of autumn's leaves across the two graves. It makes me shiver and I roll the window back up and lean back in the car seat, sipping intermittently from the coffee that seems to grow cooler by the minute. From the corner of my eye I can see Cindy's profile. She is frowning at her phone, probably texting back and forth with her youngest son, Matt. Matt is 16 years old and was not born when this story began. Occasionally, she anxiously glances in her rearview mirror determined not to miss anything or to be caught off guard. Cindy is my rock. She keeps me focused. I can't think of anyone else I would rather be here with than my sister. I close my eyes, lean back, and lose myself in a myriad of thoughts and questions — and the unlikely journey that has brought us to this place.

"Someone's coming!" Cindy whispers, excitedly jarring me back to reality. Her phone tumbles to the floor as we both scramble to look toward the cemetery entrance. A line of cars drives slowly down the winding entrance road.

"You were right," I whisper breathlessly as the cars slowly come to a stop near Noreen's grave.

I can see the emblem on the side of one of the police cars. *Arlington Heights*. Closely following the police car is a black hearse. I am transfixed as the convoy stops and the doors start opening. A variety of people step out into the chilly Chicago air. One sets up a tripod with a camera pointed towards Noreen's grave. A small truck with the name of the cemetery pulls up and several men jump out and lift numerous orange construction horses and set them close to the headstone. The men retrieve shovels from the truck and begin to position themselves around the grave. Someone gives a signal and the men slip black masks over their faces as the cameraman appears to begin filming the event.

"Why are they wearing masks?" Cindy whispers.

"I don't think they want their faces on the film," I answer. I don't realize at the time that the wearing of the masks is actually for sanitary and protective reasons, as an environmental health officer — who was undoubtedly one of the many men who were present around the gravesite — usually supervises the workers as well as the entire process.

For what seems like eternity, the men painstakingly remove the last vestiges of earth around the casket and jostle it from its vault enclosure. As the rusting box is lifted from the ground, it swings backwards, striking the headstone and splitting it in two. One of the men tried valiantly to prevent the casket from hitting the stone, but it was too late. The tombstone cracked evenly between her first and last name, an eerie sign.

The casket carrying the body of young Noreen Kumeta Rudd is moved slowly towards the hearse. It is slid into the back and the large back doors slam shut, blocking our view.

Forty years ago, 19-year-old Noreen was laid to rest in this small cemetery plot wearing the white wedding dress she was married in only 27 days before her death. The recent court order allowing her body to be exhumed has disturbed her eternal sleep as the authorities, awash with fresh and potentially incendiary information, grope to find answers to her untimely death.

The small procession of cars drearily winds its way out of the cemetery leaving only the cemetery workers to place orange construction horses around the now-empty grave. Eventually, the workers also retreat from the empty grave leaving only Cindy and I still staring transfixed on the hole in the ground.

"What do we do now?" I ask.

"I guess we'll wait to see if Noreen can shed light on what happened," Cindy carefully answers.

I start the car and move toward the exit. It is almost anticlimactic to think we will now just head for home. I know it is another stop in the journey that started so many years ago. It is another piece in the puzzle that will help us know what happened in our childhood suburban house.

I clearly remember the day Noreen died, although I was only a junior in high school. It seems like her shadow has always been in our lives. The uncertainty of her death, and the way it has interwoven its way into our lives hovered over us for more than four decades. Perhaps the exhumation of her body will finally uncover the truth, bringing along with it peace and rest … not only to her, but also to us.

I glance over at Cindy, who's deep in thought. Her phone keeps beeping, but she appears not to hear it. I want desperately for her to say something. But she isn't saying a word as we sit in the middle of this garden of death. The open grave can be seen in the rearview mirror as we slowly head towards the cemetery entrance. I can't help but think about the man who brought Cindy and me to this small cemetery on a cold, blustery Chicago day. It has been more than forty years since we first met our stepfather, Donnie Rudd.

What you're about to read is a journey into the mind and life of a man who built his life on a foundation of lies and deceit. With a path of destruction always in his rearview mirror, he'd drive on to his next destination intact. But he left survivors who would always remember the impact he had on their lives. Survivors like Cindy and me.

There's an old saying that time will either promote you or expose you. After more than four decades, we believe Father Time has shown up — replete with hourglass in hand — to do what he does best. And the top bulb of the hourglass is nearly empty.

Cindy turns and asks me the familiar question:

Do you think he did it?

CHAPTER ONE
The Question

I still can't get Cindy's question out of my head. I am sitting at a table in the back corner of a Starbucks and it's driving me crazy. I hate the fact that this haunting question caused my sister and me to take on the role of amateur sleuths and stalk an exhumation at a local cemetery. In some strange way, this might be the price for peace.

I pop open my computer and Google the word that's been stuck in my head for some time now: *Sociopath*. The results are quick — and dead-on.

> *"A person with a psychopathic personality whose behavior is antisocial, often criminal, and who lacks a sense of moral responsibility or social conscience."*

Or maybe this one:

> *"Sociopaths have little regard for the feelings of others and use manipulation to get what they desire."*

But Google definitions aren't working for me. At least not today. Google's sociopath seems orderly. Clinical. Almost boring. There's no hint of the madness, destruction, and chaos we endured from living with a real sociopath. It's the difference between reading about a tornado and watching it barrel toward your home, spitting dirt, plants, and debris, leaving a path of destruction in its wake.

For more than 25 years, our lives have revolved around the life and actions of one real, live, breathing, crazy sociopath. A man who felt no guilt. A man with ice coursing through his veins and a passionless heart beating in his chest. I think he was our stepfather — but even as I write the words, I can't be sure. Because you can never, ever, be sure anything a sociopath says is true — even when it is about something as simple as whether he was married to your mother when she died.

Do you think he did it?

The question drags me reluctantly to the past. Closing my eyes helps me focus. So with eyes closed tightly, I begin the kaleidoscope of memories that always follow the question. After years of languishing in the back roads of my mind, I have an overwhelming desire to figure out what really happened at our childhood home. To find some peace in the truth surrounding our family. The past cannot be laid to rest until the truth is told.

That search for truth — or at least understanding — has been difficult. It is undeniably complicated and the passage of years doesn't make it any easier to solve the mystery, even if time has brought some clarity to events that occurred so many years ago. Most mysteries have common denominators that are premised on strong emotions. Emotions like love, passion, jealousy, or revenge. But Donnie Rudd was incapable of that type of feeling. That lack of emotions makes it harder to understand the man.

Over the years, I read books about famous sociopaths and tried to compare their lives with what we knew about Donnie. There is a certain familiarity in many of the stories. The lies. The schemes. The manipulation of family and friends. The selfish, egotistical acts. But none of these stories really tell you what it is like to be on the inside of living with madness. To be in the eye of the storm every day. To eat breakfast each morning with a man under suspicion of multiple murders. To have the normalcy of life in the suburbs interrupted by murder, infidelity and violence.

Donnie was president of the District 54 school board when I graduated from middle school. He handed me my diploma after they called my name. When I got back to my seat and unrolled the diploma, he had drawn little hearts around my name. Again, a conflicting flood of emotions at the memory.

We despised the crises that followed him, but found the adrenaline rush that came with his escapades, addictive and intoxicating. We knew he was a liar, but found ourselves believing the incredible things he said. We accepted Donnie as normal, only to be dragged back to the reality of his insanity by some totally unpredictable, senseless act.

Right now you are probably wondering about me and Cindy. It is true that our lives were surrounded by madness, but we are remarkably sane — most of the time. I am the mother of two grown girls. I have been married for 30 years and work as a professional for the same company for the last 15 years. Cindy has been married almost as long and has two boys. We talk about what we would be like if Donnie had not been part of our lives. But neither of us can imagine a childhood without him. "No regrets" is what we tell each other. We even wore T-shirts one summer a couple of years ago with that saying emblazoned on our chests. No one can change the past. But every now and then, Cindy and I decide we are going to try and figure things out. Two middle aged women trying desperately to put their unusual childhood into perspective. Are we who we are because of what happened or in spite of what happened? It is during these times, we know that we have not really left Donnie behind.

I believe this is a true story. But all I can really say is that it is our truth. It is what we saw and what we felt during the difficult years when Donnie was the focus of our family life. When you live with the devil, it is not always easy to figure out the truth. About anything.

The smoldering of my hot coffee dissipates by the time it reaches my face, I resign myself to the fact that the story — no matter how strange and convoluted — needs to be told. Did he do it? I'm still not sure. But I do know why I am finally sitting down at this computer.

It is because I think they are going to arrest him.

CHAPTER TWO

The Beginning: The Hart Family

It's hard to tell the Hart family story and even harder to know where to start. It has always been difficult for others to see what we saw. Eventually, we retreated from the passion of wanting outsiders to know about our previous crazy life. To solve the enigma, there would need to be an understanding of the man. To see the whole picture. And to do that, we have to start at the beginning.

My mom, Dianne Hart, was a complex, brilliant, difficult, obsessive, conflicted, hard-to-understand individual who was the lynchpin of our family. She parlayed her intelligence into a peculiar kind of creativity. She would make my Girl Scout troop cook without utensils on our weekend camping trips. She forced us to use orange peels as pans to cook eggs and soup. She would hang small cereal boxes and bananas on the bushes in the back yard and make us "pick" our breakfast from nature. She organized the fun fair at our elementary school, spending days building the haunted house. There was something indefinable that drove Mom to prove she was different. She was constantly looking for ways to distinguish herself. It was like she knew she was an extraordinary person trapped in the life and body of someone who lived an ordinary life. She was always looking for a way out of her suburban lifestyle. She desperately sought an escape from the dregs of commonplace that held her back and obliterated her dreams of the nirvana of exceptionality that would make her something and someone special.

Mom was a pretty woman, even though she struggled with her weight. Her prototypical '60s hairdo was fashionable and well maintained. Each week, she would get her hair done at the local beauty shop and then sleep on her stomach with her face between the crack of two pillows to try and keep the hairdo in place as long as possible between appointments. She would meticulously put on her false eyelashes when she went out at night.

While things were attractive and well-kempt on the outside, the inner workings were a bit less glamorous. We lived in a small northwestern suburb of Chicago called Hoffman Estates. Our parents bought a beautiful tri-level home there for $23,000. In the early 1960's, this was considered to be quite an accomplishment. We had an above-ground pool with a fenced-in backyard. Everything about this neighborhood was perfect. At least from the outside.

At an early age, I remember coming home and finding Mom lying on the couch looking lethargic and bored. Discontentment was evident in the way she moved, the way she spoke, and the perfunctory actions she laboriously and unenthusiastically performed. The dishes were piling up in the sink and the laundry would go undone until it reached critical status. Our grandparents (Mom's parents) started coming over every Tuesday to bring us doughnuts and work all day to clean the house and do the laundry. Mom would periodically have bursts of energy during which she would undertake initiatives as diverse as starting a catering business to redecorating the entire house. Eventually, though, she would lose interest and return to her magazines or books, looking for a more significant meaning to her life.

Hindsight being 20/20, I look back now at all the signs that something was not quite right. But in my wildest dreams, I could never have dreamed how wrong things could go. Chronic unhappiness and discontentment plagued Mom for most of her marriage and her life. Dad always said Mom wanted more than he could give her. Turns out she wanted more out of life than being a mom and a wife. She just didn't know how to get there. Until Donnie.

I was born in 1957, the oldest of the four Hart children. Cindy came two years later and Jack was born the following year. Glory is the baby and came along in 1963. The four of us are products of a dysfunctional family reared in an era of time we call "The Donnie Years." We survived, but there is undeniable collateral damage. You can see it in each of our personalities, our idiosyncrasies, and how we react to stress. We are a family obsessed with solving problems and fixing the unfixable. It's a role we took on early in life, necessitated by the vortex of tribulations brought on by The Donnie Years. For Cindy, there is no problem too big to solve. From the mundanities of figuring out your bank account or your vacation issues, to managing your love life and your family problems, Cindy is well suited for the role. She will also do anything to keep peace. She never raises her voice and never seems angry — even when she is. She always hated the confrontations and struggles that were part of our childhood. I can still see her small figure with her hands over her ears and her eyes wide open as she processed the unfolding drama of The Donnie Years. She was fiercely protective of our father during the divorce and still shares a special bond with him.

Mom called me the "Queen of Harts." Cindy and Glory called me "The Boss." I think they mean the same thing. I don't apologize for it because someone needed to be in charge during years of family crises. It was usually me. I always have a mental agenda of what needs to get done before I go to bed. Life is one big list of chores when you are in charge. I am also a bit of a fixer myself, but on a less personal basis than Cindy. I tend to be more distant and am almost always in control of my emotions. I have the ability to manage mind-numbing stress and act like it has no effect on me. But, of course, it does. Cindy continually tries to "fix" me, but it only frustrates her.

Jack is the family mechanical fixer. He would fix our cars when Donnie would disable them, check our phone lines, and help us track down phone taps. Mom pushed him to join the Navy from the time he graduated elementary school. He enlisted in the Navy by the time he was 17 years old. I don't think he thought he had a choice. Jack is incredibly stubborn and hates to follow rules. He acted up quite a bit during the divorce, his rebellion manifesting itself in things like setting fires, going to family counseling drunk, and driving before he got his license. But thankfully he settled down after his years in the Navy.

My youngest sister, Glory, is an eternal optimist. She is the one to have with you when things go really wrong. Her sense of humor could crack us up in the midst of the most tragic situations. Once when I was directing what needed to be done after Mom died, she said, "Who died and left you boss?" I was horrified at first ... until we both started laughing about the irony of her statement and our lives. Glory was too young to really remember the worst of the Donnie years. But she has heard our stories for so many years, I sometimes forget that she was just a baby.

Dad, John Hart, was a tall, handsome man who thrived on the security of the family routine he established when he married Mom. He was an excellent provider and an extremely hard worker. The "typical" all-American family was very important to him because he did not have that type of childhood growing up. His father died suddenly of pneumonia when my father was just four years old. Dad remembers very little about his father, but recalls he was a peddler during the Depression years. Grandma Pauline had my dad when she was only 16. She was a beautiful woman who owned a dress shop, but really wasn't equipped to take care of her young son after her husband died. So Dad was raised by his grandmother. Great Grandma Hart only had a third grade education, but she loved Dad and wanted him to be successful. College was never an option in Dad's world. Grandma Hart's greatest wish was that he'd someday get a job with the Chicago Transit Authority.

Grandma Pauline went through a succession of boyfriends after her husband died until she finally married Grandpa George, a long distance truck driver. Life didn't get much better for anyone after they married, although it was always interesting to visit them. All of the closets, cabinets, and crawlspaces were filled with products and appliances George said "fell off his truck." As kids, we would get to "shop" for our Christmas presents in the many closets and storage spaces at Grandma Pauline's apartment.

If you haven't caught on to the beginnings of family dysfunction yet, you will. I sometimes think it is that dysfunction that allowed Donnie to sustain his relationship with our family for more than 20 years. The Hart family struggled with the definition of a normal family. Dad's half-brother, George Jr., was murdered when I was 10. There were whispers he was involved in drugs. Dad's half-sister was raped by a Chinese man and had a child … at least that's how Grandma Pauline explained her Chinese-looking grandson. As Dad got older, Grandma Pauline was confined to a wheelchair. She would seldom get dressed and took steroids that made a couple of hairs on her chin grow quite long. It made her look like she had a scraggly beard.

George, Pauline, Dad's half-sister, and her son all lived in a small Chicago apartment. Grandma was taken care of by a young man named Pauly who was mentally challenged. Grandma Pauline claims that they found him at the local grocery store and brought him home along with a gallon of milk and three large steaks. He slept on the porch of the apartment. Pauly would cook dinner when we would visit.

Dad found out Grandma Pauline died when he called to wish her a happy Mother's Day. George told him Pauline had died the previous month and gave him the name of the cemetery where she was buried. A little impersonal, yes, but the Hart family tended to be like that. Dad always wanted the security of the family he never had. It probably was one of the reasons he had such a hard time letting go of Mom.

My parents met when Dad was 19 and Mom was 15. He was playing basketball in the Leyden Church league in the Northwest Chicago suburbs in May of 1953. Mom and her girlfriend came to watch the game and needed a ride home. Dad carefully maneuvered his way to make sure Mom was the last one dropped off and managed to get her phone number. A month later, he bought her a silver compact for her 16th birthday from the currency exchange where he cashed his paychecks. I still have that compact he bought for her more than 60 years ago. It represents the love that comes when you are too young to know what is best for you ... the kind of love that only happens in fairytales. By the time Mom was 17, they were engaged. Although there were hopes of attending college, she was married just three weeks after her 18th birthday. My grandmother signed the consent for a marriage license because Mom wasn't old enough. I was born before Mom's 20th birthday.

Dad was also a fixer. He had a talent for fixing cars and purchased his own Standard Oil gas station not too far from O'Hare Airport in the early 1960s. He would get up early and work late at the gas station. When it would snow, he would be out all night snowplowing local businesses. He would get home dead tired and usually be asleep in his favorite armchair by 8:30 each night. He knew Mom hated the fact that he was too tired to talk to her at night, but the long days in the cold Chicago winter put him right to sleep despite his best intentions.

Mom yearned for someone she could talk to about politics, strategies, and other sundry ideas. She was busting to be free. Mom convincingly pushed Dad to go to trade school at night. After working all day at the gas station, he would go to DeVry Technical Institute for classes three nights a week. These were difficult years for the Hart family. It took all of Dad's strength to complete the courses while working full-time at the gas station. He finally got his FCC communications license and sold the gas station when I was in 6th grade. He started a more "professional" job at a company called Aeronautical Radio and performed technical work on airline communication systems.

After the gas station was gone, things got better at home. The Hart family had money in the bank. For the first time, a family vacation was an option. The summer before Dad started at his new job, we took our first real vacation, a three-week driving odyssey to California, visiting the obligatory tourist sites along the way; Grand Canyon, Mount Rushmore, Yosemite, the Redwood Forest. We did them all in one big, monster family vacation, with the four of us kids in the back of our purple station wagon, fighting, arguing, and hitting each other for 21 straight days. The trip was fun, but we were ready to be home by the end of the three weeks. Dad and Mom were making up for lost time. Dad was able to get home earlier and spend more time with us. He liked working at Aeronautical Radio and thought the best days for our family were ahead of us. Things were looking up for our family. At least Dad thought they were.

But the devil, as they say, is in the details.

In March 1970, Mom announced her candidacy for the local District 54 school board. There were 10 candidates total, including one Donnie Rudd. The newspaper headline on April 13, 1970 announced that "Mrs. Hart Leads District 54." She was elected to the board along with Gerald Lewin and Donnie Rudd. In 1970, she was the president of the fastest growing school district in the United States. Her transformation from slightly overweight stay-at-home mom to a rather powerful community leader was almost inevitable. She was so happy to be doing something productive and making a difference in the school system. The growth of Hoffman Estates made her position as president of the school board a very powerful one. Local builders negotiated with Mom regarding land contributions and new schools. She was the lead negotiator with the teacher's union during salary negotiations. But things were also changing with our family. Mom's position in the community was keeping her away from home more and more. She had less and less to talk about with Dad. It was the beginning of the end of our normal life.

Sometimes I wish Mom had not been so smart. Her dissatisfaction with her life seemed to be directly attributable to her IQ. She was a Mensa member, which put her IQ in the top 2 percent of the population. Although, as the years passed, it became clear Mensa may be a great measure of intelligence, but it certainly said nothing about a person's common sense or good judgment. Another question that always haunts me is "*What might have been?*" What would our lives be like today if Mom could have found happiness in being just a mother? What if she could have found the personal satisfaction she craved in making Halloween costumes and being the most creative mom on the block? What if the simple things that make some moms so interesting and normal had similar appeal to her? Maybe she wouldn't have joined the damned PTA and school board, which signaled the beginning of the end. Maybe we would have just been the typical slightly dysfunctional all-American family.

But her choice in the relentless pursuit of "higher purpose" led her — and us — into a plummeting descent that would forever intertwine our lives with the family of Donnie Rudd.

CHAPTER THREE
The Rudd Family

About two miles from the Carleton Road house where we lived, Donnie Rudd and his family moved into a small ranch tract home across from St. Hubert's church in Hoffman Estates. The Flagstaff ranch house was actually very small and quite homely. Donnie turned the garage into a spare room. "Do-it-yourself" was not what he did best. Instead of a regular wall on the outside of the house, he put up some jumbled, crooked cedar shingles making that side of the house look like a badly built wooden shack. There was a rickety screened porch in the back. A family room with an additional bedroom were eventually added onto the back of the house. The walls in the back bedroom were just wood paneling nailed roughly six inches apart, the finished sides facing each respective room they created. Donnie was not good at plastering so he minimized the work by nailing the panels directly to the wooden studs. It didn't make for very good insulation, but it created the sense of a room as long as you didn't lean on the walls which would bend inward with any applied weight.

Donnie had a very distinctive decorating style which influenced the décor inside the small Flagstaff house, and reflected his unique personality. The front door opened to the living room, which had red shag carpeting. Two black, shiny vinyl couches graced the room. The wall opposite the front door was wallpapered with a faux zebra fur. The tiny "master bathroom" walls were covered with one-foot carpet tile squares of a checkerboard red and blue pattern. Donnie and his first wife, Louann, had wallpaper in their bedroom made of shiny metallic paper with an overlay of velvety-flocked trees, which looked like weeping willows. You could touch the willows, which were fuzzy and also cold and shiny. The bedspread was a thick, black, faux fur. The kitchen had wainscoting on the bottom half and on the top a wallpaper of bright red flowers and hearts with equally bright green vines. The last room was a big "family room" and also the part of the addition to the house. This room had shag carpeting that looked a bit like a calico cat, except the colors were greens and browns and oranges. The couch was yellow vinyl with a wood back. There were big picture windows out to the back yard. The décor in the place was visually assaulting and definitely had the Donnie touch; he favored loud and tacky. It was a very '70s décor, but louder and more flamboyant than any of the other homes. [1]

Donnie was born in Winnie, Texas, in 1942. He was the son of Eddie and Vita Mae Rudd. Donnie's identical twin brother, Ronnie preceded him into life by only a few minutes. His brother, John William, was born 10 months before the twins. Donnie always said he and Ronnie were born on the kitchen table, but I haven't been able to verify that because Eddie and Vita Mae are dead, and Ronnie isn't sure about the kitchen table thing, although he did say they were born at home.

The Rudd family moved to Liberty, Texas, when the boys were small. Eddie and Vita Mae were both school teachers in Liberty for many years. Eddie and Vita Mae were known as strict disciplinarians both in school and at home. All three Rudd boys excelled at academics. It would not surprise anyone in Liberty to hear that all three Rudd boys had done very well in their

---

1 This wonderful description of the Rudd house was provided by my step-sister Terisa.

post high school academic pursuits. Both Ronnie and Donnie fought for valedictorian rights as seniors at Liberty High School. Ronnie came out the winner on that one, but Donnie was close behind.

Ronnie would become one of the most successful Certified Public Accountants in Houston, Texas. With a loving wife and family, Ronnie lives a comfortable life without drama in a beautiful home overlooking the Texas mountain country. He is almost the alter ego of his twin brother. An interesting contradiction: The good twin and the bad. The older brother, John became a well-known Texas minister and later a successful businessman. Donnie enrolled at Texas A&M in the chemical engineering program. The Rudd boys were on their way to professional success.

Donnie met his first wife while attending Texas A&M University in College Station, Texas. Louann attended A&M's sister college, Texas Women's University, in nearby Dallas. She was 19 when she met Donnie on a blind date arranged by a friend for a college mixer between the two schools. The two became engaged a short time later. During these early years, Louann saw little of the craziness in Donnie that would define him in later years. She would later reflect that he was emotionally volatile when faced with situations he could not control. At one point, Louann started questioning her decision to marry Donnie so quickly. However, when she started talking about delaying the wedding date, Donnie responded by threatening to drive off a bridge. Eventually, Louann and Donnie did get married in a small wedding ceremony in Dallas, near Louann's family home.

Shortly after their marriage, Donnie graduated from Texas A&M with his degree in Chemical Engineering. He claimed he was the salutatorian of his high school class behind only his twin brother, Ronnie, and valedictorian of his engineering class when he graduated from college. Shortly after graduation, he landed a job as a chemical engineer at the US Gypsum Company, which was owned by Quaker Oats and located in Barrington, Illinois. So the Rudd family moved to Illinois not far from our home on Carleton Road. Shortly after the move, Donnie began attending night school at Chicago Kent College of Law. Eventually he would get his law degree and move into the patent department at the Quaker Oats Company.

I first met Donnie when I was in middle school and he was around 29 years old. Mom asked if I could babysit for a friend. She dropped me off to watch Donnie's three small children. Mom was animated as she talked about how smart Donnie was as we drove to the house. She turned her station wagon into the driveway of the small ranch house. Louann was sitting on the couch briskly pulling each of her daughters' hair into tight ponytails. Donnie drove me home later and gave me a big tip. There was nothing about that meeting that would hint at what would come or the role Donnie would play in my family's life.

Donnie and Louann were much different than other adults. I attributed it to the fact that they were from Texas, which seemed like a foreign country for a Midwestern suburban child. Unlike most of the men in our working class neighborhood, Donnie was a professional and wore suits during the week. He was particularly partial to brown suits which he wore with a wide assortment of ties, all with a link to Texas. Sometimes he even wore a cowboy hat. His favorite after-work clothes were pastel-colored leisure suits that looked a little like safari outfits. Sometimes he would wear a turtleneck under the jacket of the leisure suits. He had the same outfit in several different colors but regardless of whether he was wearing a suit, a yellow leisure suit, or blue jeans, he *always* wore his cowboy boots.

Louann was attractive, but extremely loud. She spoke with a strong Texas accent and would look up at the ceiling and close her eyes when she would talk about Donnie. She had ever-changing hobbies, which were always scattered around the house and would dominate her conversation. Around this time, she became pregnant with her fourth child.

Louann loved crafts and creative projects. She would focus on stained glass making, then she moved on to Native American folklore and would make beaded headbands, feather headdresses, and loincloths, and teach all of the kids native dance routines. She was also a Mary Kay sales representative and really wanted to win the coveted pink Cadillac by selling loads of makeup, which was stored floor-to-ceiling in her closet. My Mom was one of her biggest clients.

At some point, the Rudd family joined our church, a conservative Southern Baptist congregation called Bethel Baptist. Bethel Baptist was one of the largest churches in Hoffman Estates. It was founded by Pastor Frank Bumpus. Both Mom and Dad were founding members of the church — Mom would play the organ for Sunday services and Dad was a long time Deacon. Every Sunday, the two families sat in the pews of the church and listened to Pastor Bumpus while he pounded away at the pulpit with his hellfire and brimstone messages. The animated preacher would raise his voice to full crescendo with sermons about the wrath that would befall sinners and those who did not commit to having the Lord Jesus Christ as their personal Lord and Savior. The two families would go out for a buffet luncheon afterwards like so many other Hoffman Estates families. Mom and Louann became friends working on PTA projects, Girl Scouts, and craft projects with the pack of children from the two families. Life seemed idyllic and no one suspected that the burgeoning friendship between the two families would be the catalyst for what happened next.

Mom and Donnie also became friends and confidants through their positions on the local school board. The local newspapers screamed their names as they maneuvered through high profile, political issues such as separating the large district from oversight by the County School Superintendent. Both Mom and Donnie would trade off on serving as president of the board. In July 1970, Donnie was also nominated to serve as a member of the Hoffman Estates Planning Commission. Their important positions on the school board also required a certain amount of travel, much to my dad's chagrin. Dad really struggled to adjust to Mom's transformation from stay-at-home wife and mother to local socialite. Mom was spending a lot of time with Donnie, so she constantly reassured Dad everything was OK. She also became friends with Louann, which seemed to make everything a little better. We were just two suburban families that enjoyed each other's company and spent a significant amount of time together.

I was in eighth grade the first time I saw something unusual in the Rudd household. Mom dropped me off to help Louann with the three girls during a shopping trip. When I arrived at the small ranch house, Louann was getting her things together in the kitchen. Lying on the floor of the kitchen, just a short distance from one of the bedrooms, was Donnie. He didn't have a pillow under his head and was motionless on the cold, hard floor. Louann seemed to be oblivious to the prostrate body of her husband as she put items into her purse and talked to me.

"Is Mr. Rudd OK?" I finally asked.

"Don't mind him," she answered. "Sometimes he just does that." She stepped over his feet to pick up her car keys and motioned for me to get the girls so we could leave. I looked over my shoulder as I left the kitchen and saw him lift his head. Louann didn't mention the incident again.

The Hart and Rudd family were spending more and more time together, yet tension was building between the spouses. Mom and Dad argued frequently behind closed doors after they came home from dinner with Donnie and Louann. One particular argument occurred when Dad objected to Mom attending an educational conference in another state. He seemed particularly disconcerted that Donnie would also be attending. It just didn't look right to him. Still, everyone continued to go to church on Sunday and the two families started talking about taking a vacation together during the summer of 1971.

But trouble was brewing … and it would all come to a head in late summer right before I started my first year of high school.

CHAPTER FOUR
The Break Up

Friday, August 13, 1971, was the end of our family as we knew it. And it was the beginning of the "Donnie Years" for the Hart family. How appropriate that Friday the 13th was the day Mom announced she wanted a divorce.

I had just attended high school orientation and was going to start school in a couple of weeks. Cindy was also getting ready for junior high and already had her schedule and books. Glory and Jack were still in elementary school. It was a characteristically hot and sticky Chicago summer day when Dad received a call from Mom in the late afternoon. She sounded upset and told him that she had something important to tell him. After getting off the phone, the more Dad thought about the conversation, the more concerned he became. He finally jumped in the car and headed for home. *Cancer*, he thought. *She must have cancer for her to summon me home in this manner*. He pulled into the driveway and jumped out of his truck.

Mom was in their bedroom sitting on the bed waiting for him. The important news was blunt and totally unexpected. In a flat, emotionless voice, the woman he married more than 15 years ago coolly blurted out:

"I want to marry Donnie. I want to leave. I don't want anything but Donnie. You can have the house. You can have the kids. You can have the money. Just let me leave."

"You're having an affair?" he asked incredulously. "You're having an affair ... with *Donnie*?" Without waiting for an answer and too stunned to fully take in the information he had just ingested, Dad added, "Does Louann know?"

Mom was calm and unequivocal about her decision.

"Donnie told Louann this afternoon. We want to be together."

Dad's next impulse was unexpected. He picked up the telephone sitting on the dresser near Mom and promptly dialed Louann's number.

"Louann, this is John Hart."

Louann was puzzled. Although the two families were friends, Dad had never called the Rudd house before.

"Has Donnie talked to you?" he asked politely. Louann would later say as soon as she heard Dad's voice she instantly knew why he was calling.

"Talk to me about what?" she asked.

"Never mind," he answered and quickly hung up.

"Are you sure Donnie wants a divorce?" Dad calmly asked my mother. "It doesn't seem as if he told Louann."

For the first time since she made her bold decision, Mom looked a little uncertain.

"I am sure he told her," she answered. "Donnie said he would tell her this afternoon at the same time I told you."

A couple of miles away, Louann sat looking at the phone in her hand for several minutes. Finally, with steely resolve, she dialed Donnie's office number at the Quaker Oats Company.

"Donnie, do you have something to tell me?" she asked.

Donnie smugly denied there was a story to be told.

"John Hart just called me and asked if I talked to you," Louann told him. "Why would John Hart be calling *me*?" Still, Donnie feigned ignorance.

"Donnie, you need to come home right now and tell me

what is going on!" Louann insisted. But Donnie hung up on her. She tried calling him back repeatedly but he wouldn't answer his phone. He stayed at the office long enough to make sure Louann would get her information from Dad, absolving Donnie of the manly duty of having to own up for his actions.

It has never been clear what initially attracted Mom to Donnie. She couldn't articulate what she saw in this man whose actions and emotions never matched what he said in his love letters. Donnie was admittedly smart and confident, although "arrogant" was the modifier most people used to describe him. It's possible she was impressed with the fact that he was a lawyer. Maybe her life with Dad was just not enough for her or maybe she really didn't want to be a mom to four kids. Dad would say Mom and Donnie "fell in love with each other's brains" when he tried to explain it to us. But most of the time, I think Donnie just sucked her in. She really had no control over the situation. Donnie told her she was the smartest woman he had ever met. He told her she was beautiful and special, and she wanted to believe everything he said was true. He wrote poems for her and told her he could not live without her. The love he wrote about was different than the love she had known and grown up with. It was intense and passionate and not based on the reality of married life. Donnie's world of adventure, soul mates, and endless love was different from the saccharine Girl Scout meetings, backyard barbecues, and suburban sameness that defined our family life.

During this time, nothing mattered to Mom except for her infatuation with Donnie. But Dad was not going to let his marriage end without a fight. Although Mom seemed adamant that all she wanted was Donnie, it wasn't quite as clear that she really wanted to leave her old life behind. Although she was seeing Donnie, she came home each night and slept in her bedroom with Dad next to her. During one after-dinner discussion, Mom suggested maybe an arrangement could be negotiated. She would stay and continue to act as wife and mother, but only if Dad gave her Tuesdays and Thursdays off for visitation with Donnie.

Dad looked at her disbelievingly. "You want a *date* night?" he asked. "What am *I* supposed to do on Tuesday and Thursday?"

"Join a bowling league," was Mom's terse resolution. One thing was becoming clear about Mom. The only thing stronger than her infatuation with Donnie was her fear of being alone. It was something that would never change for as long as she was alive. Right now she needed Dad at home, waiting for her, in case things with Donnie did not work out. But she was not going to give up Donnie.

The Donnie obsession went way beyond anything in the realm of *normal*. Mom loved us, but we knew Donnie was first in her heart. I used to say that I hoped I was never in a sinking boat with Mom, Donnie, and two life preservers because I knew who would be swimming. That may sound terrible, but Mom wasn't mean. It's not that she didn't love her children or try to be a good mother. She just never managed to quite hit the mark, but each of us loved her unconditionally. Her fantasy life was in overdrive, and Prince Charming had arrived to take her to the ball. Reality, however, was waiting around the corner.

Unfortunately, when you dance with the devil, things don't always turn out the way you planned.

CHAPTER FIVE

Divorce Wars

The next six months can only be characterized as open warfare between the two sets of parents. Although Mom seemed steadfast when she announced she wanted a divorce, nothing was clear after the first couple of days. Donnie was the only one who seemed resolute that he would not be staying with Louann. Dad would discretely follow Mom to try and catch her with Donnie. He would conspire with Louann on signals they could send to each other when either Mom or Donnie left home. Louann's report would help him know if there was a scheduled rendezvous.

Mom actually had the nerve to ask Dad not to call Louann and talk about Donnie and their relationship. Interestingly, she thought this somehow was not "fair" behavior. Dad reluctantly agreed but continued to exchange information with Louann anyway. Although she continued to live at our house with Dad, Mom would frequently leave for days at a time as she thought about what she was going to do. When she was with Donnie, she did not care about us, Dad, her parents, our house, or our life. Dad tried desperately to change her mind, but there was nothing he could do to break through the spell that seemed to have been cast over her. Mom wanted to be with Donnie more than she wanted to live. She was selfishly committed to finding a way to be with him. On the other hand, just in case things didn't work out, she wanted Dad to wait around. It was difficult for Dad to know what to do.

"I'm tired of lying," Mom confessed to Dad one day. She was sitting in her favorite green chair next to the fireplace she oiled each Saturday morning. "I won't lie anymore. Ask me anything and I will tell you the truth. My heart can't handle the lies."

Dad thought he wanted to know. He took a moment and began the interrogation.

"Where would you meet him?" he asked.

Mom methodically began to name the hotels, the trips, and the places she had been with Donnie.

"In our house?" Dad asks.

"Yes," she answers.

The heartbreaking game went on for several minutes until Mom stood up.

"You don't want to know anything more," she said, and walked out of the room. She was probably right.

Even these dangerous games of truth or dare did not force a resolution of the family issues. Mom and Dad continued to live in the house, sleep in their bed, and argue about the future. Then Donnie would call and Mom would be out the door. Dad struggled immensely with the change in Mom's personality. She could not explain it to him — probably because she did not understand it herself — and likely because it really had nothing to do with him. There was nothing he could do to change himself or our life that would be sufficient to change her mind. She was drawn to Donnie with a kind of herculean magnetism no one who knew her understood.

Donnie, on the other hand, did not seem to go through the same emotional upheaval as the other three participants in the doomed marriages struggled to find solid footing after the affair. Donnie never cried, did not yell, and seemed quite unconcerned as to the effect the affair was having on any of the children. His youngest child was still a baby. During most of the drama, Donnie would sit quietly in the background, blowing smoke rings into the air as accusations flew and divorce, property, and the welfare of children were discussed.

Before the final split could occur, the fight for our mother's soul would have to take place. In the beginning, Dad was convinced he could stop her from leaving. Our grandparents prayed, Dad cried, her brother threatened her, and the noise rose to a deafening crescendo as the first real Donnie battle raged on in the house on Carleton Road. All four of us kids sat on the bed with our hands over our ears hoping it would end soon. We prayed for a silence to the chaos in our previously happy home.

Finally, Mom agreed to try and break it off with Donnie. Dad was elated, but knew it would be difficult to keep her from talking to Donnie. Dad's only hope would be to send Mom away to a place where Donnie could not find her. This self-administered exile would act as a "detox" of sorts. For Mom, Donnie was like a drink to an alcoholic. And just as an alcoholic goes through the rigors of withdrawal, it would be even harder to break the spell cast by Donnie over our mom.

Mom drove to Rockford, a city about an hour northwest of where we lived, and checked into a hotel. My father was the only one who knew where she was. He drove there every night as soon as he got off work. He'd spend the night and leave every morning to make the two-hour drive back to work. Once he was at work, he'd call her every hour to make sure she was still there. He was hopeful for the first time. After five days, it appeared that Mom had not been in contact with Donnie. If Dad could keep her from him long enough, the reasoning went, there might be some hope. Maybe Mom's addiction could be cured.

After the fifth day, Mom decided it was time to come home. Dad called her every hour the first day she was back. She promptly picked up the phone each time, and with that peace of mind, Dad was able to go back to working. But when he called at 2:00 p.m., there was no answer. He frantically dialed again and again. He jumped in his car and drove home only to find that Mom was gone. No note. No call. Just gone. He was disconsolate.

Donnie made contact. Mom was on a binge.

She didn't return for several days. Ashamed, sad, unable to explain her actions, she retreated again to her bed. It would be a pattern that would repeat itself throughout her life. She wanted to leave but could not actually pack her bags. She hated being in the house but was too afraid to leave, so she went to bed and closed her eyes hoping something would change when she woke up. Each afternoon when we would get home from school, she would be in the same place; in bed, lights turned off, curtains drawn, and the blanket over her head.

One afternoon, Mom's withdrawal took a frightening turn. Cindy came home from school and sat on the bed talking to Mom about her day, but Mom appeared to be groggy and confused.

"Mom's not acting right," she came and told me.

We went downstairs only to find Mom's bed empty. Cindy looked around the room. I looked in the bathroom. We heard a noise from the room we called our "utility" room. This room had a washer and a dryer but was used primarily for storage. Cindy stopped at the door, completely transfixed and gripped by what she saw. Mom was standing in front of the washing machine with a bottle of pills in her hand. She was taking them out methodically one by one and lining them up on top of the washing machine. The line of pills stretched across the entire washing machine door.

"Lori!" Cindy was able to finally yell.

I pushed her aside just as Mom started systematically putting the pills in her mouth one by one. I struggled with her and pushed the pills towards the edge of the washing machine. Some fell to the floor and some become lodged in the crack in the washer door. Mom dropped to her knees with the pill bottle in one hand while trying to pick up the pills that fell to the floor with the other. I pushed the pills with my foot under the washing machine while trying to pry the pill bottle out of her hands.

To my right, I saw Cindy's small, thin frame in her blue plaid pants and blue shirt standing with her hands over her mouth. Her eyes behind her glasses were like saucers.

"Help me!" I yelled.

She looked at me in terror and began shaking her hands. By then I had the pill bottle in my hand, but Mom was working frantically to pry my fingers off of it.

"Help me!" I yelled again.

Still no response from Cindy. Not knowing what else to do, I let go of Mom with one hand and reached over and slapped Cindy hard on the cheek. She was stunned, but it did the trick as she finally reached over to help me pull Mom away from the pills.

We dragged our crying mother back into the bedroom and got her into bed. Cindy stood at the end of the bed with the red imprint from my hand still freshly etched on her cheek. We locked eyes with each other in a moment of sheer disbelief. Cindy returned to the utility room and meticulously picked each pill up from the floor. I could see a tear stain on the red hand print on her face. I was heartbroken in the moment but too occupied to think about it for long. She put each of the pills she collected into the pill bottle and flushed all of them down the toilet.

I called Dad at work and told him what happened. His job is almost a half hour away, so he called Louann who was just a few minutes away. Louann made the short trip to our house in about 10 minutes. She headed straight for the bedroom and pulled the covers off of Mom, who was passed out.

"You are *not* going to do this!" she said. She pulled Mom out of bed. "Help me!" she demanded.

Together we got Mom to a sitting position on the bed and slipped a nightgown over her head. We each took an arm and began walking her back and forth down the hall.

"No man is worth this, Dee," she said, using the nickname Mom's friends sometimes called her. "Especially not Donnie! I am *not* going to let you do this!"

Louann and I walked Mom back and forth holding her up, dragging her feet along the floor. Finally, Louann turned on the bathroom shower. We helped her get Mom into the shower and turned the water on cold. The shock of the cold water finally woke her up.

When Dad arrived home, we were still walking Mom, soaking wet, with a towel over her head. We continued to walk and walk as she recurrently repeated, "Just let me sleep." We weren't hearing any of it. We kept walking with her until the effects of the pills started to wear off.

I think the stark realization finally hit Dad that he was going to lose the battle for his marriage. Mom was not going to stay married to him and there was nothing he could do. She was going to eventually wake up, pack her bags, and leave the Carleton Road house. Dad was a hard-working, honest man. He really never lived a life apart from Mom. He didn't know what he was going to do. But the night of the pills, Dad submitted the final mea culpa of his marriage; he let Donnie come over to the house to be with Mom. He gave up his fight to save her — and maybe himself as well. He went over to Louann's for dinner because he didn't want to be alone.

I was 14 years old and still having trouble comprehending the entirety of what was happening in our family. That night, Donnie sat on the couch with me in front of the fire because Mom was still sleeping off the pills. Slowly, I started to relax and my head, tilted toward his shoulder as I dozed off. The events of the day had finally caught up with me. I woke to find Donnie kissing my hair. I jumped to my feet and glared at him. I refused to flinch and he finally looked away. I walked upstairs without saying a word. Donnie never tried to touch me again. I was never quite sure why, and it is scary to think about, but I felt Donnie and I came to an understanding that night.

CHAPTER SIX

The Switcheroo

Although Dad was devastated by Mom's affair, he also felt very sorry for Donnie's wife. Louann was a homemaker with four kids under the age of 8. He also felt comfortable talking to her as she was going through the same problems. As the battle to keep Mom from leaving began to wind down and the battle for property and money heated up, Dad and Louann often commiserated with each other. They ate dinner together and began spending a substantial amount of time trying to figure out what they were going to do. At some point, Dad and Louann figured out there was no turning back. There would be no miracle to save their marriages. Dad and Louann started to accept divorce as an inevitability and started finding some comfort in each other. It wasn't planned, but it seemed to fill in some of the loose ends. Mom was going to leave. Louann had many attributes that were important to Dad. The pendulum of the divorce began to shift. At some point, Dad and Louann went to a movie and the friendly relationship built on the infidelity of their spouses began to change. Dad and Louann became a couple. They started "dating" even as they both hoped something would change and their marriages could somehow be saved.

Dad and Louann's relationship changed the playing field for everyone. At least no one was going to be left alone. In fact, it appeared everyone was going to end up with a house, a car, and even four kids. Mom did not like the idea, but she really was not in a position to protest.

The decision was made to reset the Hart and Rudd families. Each house would still have two parents. The eight kids would circulate back and forth between the two houses. Everyone pretty much had the same thing as before. It was definitely weird, but it seemed like a better solution than the indecision that had been plaguing us thus far. Still, the whole thing was very confusing to us. We found out about this new arrangement when one Sunday Mom came into our rooms and said we were all going to church. We got dressed and the Rudd and Hart families all went to church and sat in their usual front pews. Our very religious, Republican, suburban, prototypical family had just pulled a switcheroo of biblical proportions. The whole idea may have made sense to the parents, but it was a hard sell at church.

Dad was the first to discuss the situation with Pastor Bumpus. It must have been difficult for our conservative fire and brimstone pastor to figure out what to do with the two struggling families. The church was not as clear how to handle the relationship between Dad and Louann. Then Mom met with Pastor Bumpus. Mom wanted to make sure her soul was secure even with the affair. She believed that once your name was in the Book of Life, you were set. Your place in heaven was secure. She was adamant that Pastor Bumpus should not be able to erase her name from that Book no matter how significant her recent sins appeared to be. But Pastor Bumpus was equally adamant; if she continued to stay with Donnie, Bethel Baptist was not the church for her. Needless to say, Mom was not in the repenting mood. So the deal with the devil was in place. She chose Donnie and walked away from more than 30 years of religious beliefs.

It was understandable our parents' actions would not be sanctioned by the church, but it was hard understanding how the decision was made to kick Mom out. Not that Dad was at fault, but there did appear to be a move afoot for him to be with Louann. The Bethel Baptist Church spent years preaching to the congregation that if you believed in God you would go to heaven. Everyone was a sinner. If you sinned, it didn't mean you wouldn't go to heaven. In my fourteen year old mind, Pastor Bumpus went against the thesis of all his sermons by not allowing Mom to continue to attend church. It was difficult to understand how the church could abandon her for her sins. The church was abandoning our family with their sanctions.

Shortly afterwards, Dad moved in with Louann, and Donnie appeared at our Carleton Road house with his suitcase. Dad, ever mindful of social propriety, moved into a small guest room on Flagstaff with Louann and the four Rudd children. Donnie packed a few things into the back of the new Ford Pinto he bought and moved into the downstairs bedroom with Mom. The whole thing was incredibly awkward for the eight children. It seemed like there was this constant flow of children, parents, and belongings that surged through each of the houses. It was like a big game of musical chairs. Then the music would stop and everyone would try and find a bedroom. Terisa, Donnie's youngest daughter, said we reminded her of a struggling NFL team, always trading quarterbacks and team members to try and fix a particular problem. There was a false assumption that by simply changing spouses it would somehow bring some peace to the families. But actually the opposite occurred.

No one adjusted easily to the new living arrangements. Suddenly, instead of four kids and two parents at the Flagstaff house, every other weekend there were eight kids. When the Hart kids were at the Flagstaff house, we represented Mom, who was now a hated figure for Louann. Conversely, when we were at the Carleton Road house, we represented Dad to Donnie. The same was probably true for the Rudd kids. Each of the parents couldn't help but be angry at what had transpired. The constant flow of children back and forth made it difficult to forget the situation that had forced this change. Louann might have liked to think she could put Donnie's infidelity aside and start her new life with Dad, but it was difficult to do under the circumstances. The four Rudd kids started calling our father "Dad" the day he moved into the Flagstaff house. Donnie was referred to as "Daddy Rudd." From our perspective, it didn't seem right that these unrelated children were calling our father "Dad." The Rudd children also enrolled in school under the last name Hart. This was not a legal name change, but it did make the situation even more confusing. The local school was suddenly overrun with Hart children. It was a crazy situation and it seemed like no one was happy.

Mom didn't feel quite so guilty now since Dad was sleeping at the Rudd house. It was during this time the divorce got ugly on every side. Donnie started to exhibit some of the behaviors that would become increasing problematic in years to come. He was determined to portray Louann as the one who was troubled in their marriage. He would sneak back to his old house and move Louann's car from where she parked it. Louann would come out of the house to pick up her kids from school only to find her car was gone. She would get hysterical and call Dad at work and tell him her car was stolen. By the time Dad got home, the car would be back in the driveway. Louann would cry and swear the car had disappeared and then reappeared. About once a week, Donnie would also make an early morning stop and let the air out of her tires. He would take mail out of her mailbox, not pay bills, and do everything possible to make Dad and Louann's life difficult. The car wars were also a harbinger of things to come. Donnie fascination with disabling automobiles would wreak havoc in our family for years to come.

Donnie controlled every situation to the maximum degree possible. Dad and Louann's relationship gave him less control, which he clearly did not like. He worked harder to make sure Louann was not happy. And his arsenal was plentiful: Lies, deceptions, manipulations, you name it. And he was just getting started.

CHAPTER SEVEN
The New Normal

In the middle of changing the houses and the increasing divorce hostilities, Donnie's parents, Eddie and Vita Mae Rudd decided they were going to visit Donnie and their grandchildren. The elderly Rudds knew nothing about Mom or the divorce. Once Eddie and Vita Mae made up their mind, there was no stopping the visit. So as the elderly couple began the long drive from their retirement home in Marble Falls, Texas, to Hoffman Estates, Illinois, Donnie was frantically trying to figure out how to keep his new living arrangement a secret. To this day, no one could ever explain how he did it, but Donnie was able to convince Mom, Dad, and Louann that everyone had to change back to their original houses for the elder Rudds' visit. In the middle of the angry divorce proceedings and the child custody challenges, Donnie moved back into the house on Flagstaff and Dad returned to Carleton Road.

"This is really weird," I muttered to Cindy as we watched the preparation for the visit. But Cindy was just happy to see Dad back at our house. I still was not sure that the smaller Rudd children would be able to keep a secret. When Eddie and Vita Mae pulled into the driveway of the Rudd house, everything looked exactly the way it had looked during their last visit. Astonishingly, none of the Rudd children mentioned any changes during the four-day visit, although Vita Mae did wonder aloud why the children were referring to their father as "Daddy Rudd."

When Eddie and Vita Mae pulled out of the driveway to return to Marble Falls, they still had no idea of the turmoil occurring in the two families. And if it hadn't been for the threatening thunderstorm, they probably would have left town without a clue. But fate has a funny way of catching up to you. It will hunt you down, set the most unlikely people in your path, and yell your secrets from the highest rooftops.

As Eddie Rudd was approaching the tollway, he saw the clouds in the distance and decided to stop at the local Ponderosa for dinner until the storm passed. What are the chances that the man sitting at the next table knew Donnie and what was happening with the two families? What do you call that? Karma? Fate? Providence? Whatever it was, Eddie and Vita Mae found out at the Ponderosa that their son, Donnie, was divorcing Louann and that he was involved in an extramarital affair with Mom. Eddie and Vita Mae immediately turned around and headed back to the Flagstaff house to confront Donnie.

Donnie always avoided confrontations, but was unable to evade his father. So, Donnie did what he does best. He lied. Donnie told his parents he had cancer and was undergoing chemotherapy. The effects of the treatment were clouding his mind and his judgment, he told them. He needed time to get his strength back and to figure things out. Vita Mae broke down in tears over her son's "illness," her thin figure shaking as she wept for her son. Eddie's anger started to melt as he understood the stress his son was under. Cancer changed everything. It turned out that cancer would become another weapon in Donnie's arsenal that he would brandish again and again as it suited his purposes over the next few decades. Cancer always seemed to trump bad acts. It was a great excuse for actions that could not otherwise be explained. Donnie craved pity. Not because he wanted people to feel sorry for him. Pity *empowered* Donnie. Pity made Donnie's family, friends, and victims more vulnerable to him. It weakened those around him, making it easier to manipulate the emotions of those close to him. Eddie and Vita Mae's anger turned to sorrow at their son's made-up illness.

After they returned to Marble Falls, they would write letters to Louann begging her not to complete the divorce until Donnie's treatments were over and he was back in his right mind. Donnie was no longer the "bad one." In Eddie and Vita Mae's mind, Louann was the villain who wouldn't understand the challenges Donnie was facing as a result of his "illness."

By August, 1972, both families were starting to finalize the terms of their respective divorce agreements. The charges and accusations between the two families were starting to lessen. The round of custody hearings, psychologist visits, and angry confrontations started to wind down. Mom and Dad finalized their divorce early in August. Donnie and Louann finalized their divorce later that same month. Donnie and Louann signed a written property settlement agreement and agreed Louann would keep custody of their four children, all between the ages of 1 and 8. Donnie was ordered to pay Louann $500 per month in child support, which was based on his relatively low earnings of $20,000 per year. Louann received the majority of marital property with the exception of a small 1972 Ford Pinto that Donnie had recently purchased.

Louann married my father the following Saturday in a small ceremony at the church. There was no turning back. Donnie and Louann's children were now officially our stepsiblings. Donnie told Mom that he would throw out any of Dad's personal property that was still in the house three days after the divorce was finalized. Although Dad already had the majority of his clothes at Flagstaff, he moved the last of his tools, lawn equipment, and clothes from Carleton Road right before his wedding to Louann. As the weeks passed, it became apparent that despite the urgency of their affair, Mom and Donnie did not seem to have any immediate plans for marriage.

As 1972 came to an end, most of us kids still went to the same church, lived in the same community, and — except for the fact that none of the neighbors would talk to us and we had swapped out a parent — there was still enough left of our life before Donnie to feel like maybe everything would be OK. The familiarity of the Carleton Road and Flagstaff homes as well as their proximity to each other, made it a little easier to adjust to the new living arrangements.

Donnie and Mom had some difficulty making ends meet. The Carleton Road house was bigger and Mom was not gainfully employed. Shortly after the divorce, she got a full-time job as a legal secretary at a small law firm in Wood Dale, Illinois. She also started taking night classes at the local junior college.

Mom struggled with what she had done to our family. She had what she yearned for — Donnie was now her living partner. But she continued to be morose and depressed about what had happened over the past year. For the first time, she saw some of Donnie's unusual behaviors. Shortly after the divorces were finalized, he resigned from the District 54 school board, citing health problems.

"I have had five surgeries over the past year," the newspaper quoted him as saying.

"Is Donnie sick?" I asked Mom one morning after looking at the article.

"I'm not sure what that is about," she answered.

Both of us knew that Donnie had no surgeries and seemed to be in good health. He denied telling the reporter that he had five surgeries and suggested that the reporter had "lied" about his health. Mom seemed puzzled about the misrepresentation of Donnie's health but could find no reason for it. Donnie would use the "health" weapon over and over as the years went on to extricate himself from any uncomfortable situation.

Mom wrote Glory a "Christmas memory" about the first Christmas after the divorce.

> *"In my whole life, I never felt as desolate as I did that Christmas of 1972. I had just finished ripping my entire life into shreds and I wonder if anyone noticed how little of me was left. I was determined to make that first Christmas as a single mom a memorable one. I dressed up in my fanciest dress, the lavender heather-colored sweater dress. I wore a pendant with a purple stone. I decorated the house, bought the presents I could afford, and wrapped them up to look like a castle. I used shirt cardboard and the inside of waxed paper rolls to make the turrets and drawbridges of the castle, I covered everything with foil and glitter and it made a pretty presentable castle.* "

Unlike Donnie who left his previous life behind quite easily, Mom suffered from overwhelming guilt from the divorce. Nothing was like she thought it was going to be. Donnie worked a lot and she was left to ponder whether she had made the right decisions. Donnie's primary emotion during this period seemed to be contempt for Dad and Louann. It angered him to see Louann happy in her new marriage.

Donnie liked to tell stories about Louann and why he felt it necessary to divorce her. Even though Donnie was the partner guilty of infidelity, he was not interested in taking the blame for the divorce. He spent a great deal of time creating the perception he was the victim in his first marriage and he made the only rational choice in divorcing Louann. I was still in high school, and while these conversations sometimes made me uncomfortable, I also became less sure as to who the bad guy was in the whole divorce situation.

Although reluctant to admit it, I found Donnie to be quite interesting during this time. I hated waking up in the morning and smelling the smoke from his cigarettes or pipe in our house. It didn't seem right. But he would tell me stories about his life as a CIA agent and the secret missions he carried out in Vietnam.

"I jumped out of helicopters in the jungle," he would say. He claimed he earned several medals but because his missions were top secret, he was not able to keep them at home. His medals were stored in a secret vault at CIA headquarters in Langley, Virginia. He also said he graduated number one in his class at Texas A&M with a major in chemical engineering. He hinted he was involved in several government investigations due to his past military service. But he couldn't tell me the details because I would "need security clearance" before he could talk freely. There were always veiled references to government corruption and his role in almost any story that hit the newspapers. I felt guilty for listening to his stories, but it was a little bit exciting to think we lived with someone so important. Donnie was a lot different than our hard-working blue-collared father.

Donnie seemed almost gleeful engaging in small destructive acts such as moving Louann's car, although it did not appear to accomplish anything significant. While he never seemed to personally participate in any confrontation or heated discussion, his actions were often the precipitating events for such encounters. He relished the role of observer as the people around him argued and fought about what he did. He almost reveled in the attention the maliciousness brought to the two households. It was starting to become clear Donnie did not think the same way as most people, but no one was sure how he did think.

Mom started saying there was a thin line between genius and madness. And Donnie had one foot on each side of the fence.

CHAPTER EIGHT

The Month of Noreen

By early summer 1973, it seemed everyone was starting to settle into the new living arrangements. Money continued to be an issue in the two families, especially between Donnie and Louann. In early spring, Louann filed a petition to modify the Decree of Divorce. She stated that Donnie had refused to pay certain bills and that he also received a substantial increase in his income, which should require an increase in the amount of his child support. I frequently heard Donnie and Mom talking about money. On March 1, 1973, the court entered an order restraining Donnie from taking the minor children during his custody visitation to the premises or in the company of Mom. Although he continued to live at our Carleton Road house with her most of the time, Donnie entered into an apartment lease at a nearby apartment complex which further stretched the budget. Donnie said the small apartment in The Hilldale Apartments in Hoffman Estates would be where he would take his kids for visitation, even though he rarely exercised his rights to visit and seldom kept the Rudd children overnight.

Donnie would disappear at times telling Mom he was working. Although Donnie continually reassured Mom nothing had changed, she could sense something was different. She started driving by the Hilldale apartment when he was late coming home. Donnie and Mom argued in the downstairs bedroom with the door locked on numerous occasions. The fact that Dad married Louann so quickly left Mom quite conflicted. This was *her* love story. It was about finding *her* soul mate. She wanted the security of marriage to Donnie now that returning to Dad was no longer an option. *She* was supposed to be the one who left everything behind for love. This was not supposed to be about Dad. Dad and Louann were establishing a new life and Mom was spending an increasing number of nights at our home alone. It was not supposed to be this way.

It was about this time that Mom became aware of Donnie's relationship with a young woman. For the first time, Mom started to see how easy it was for infatuation to make a person blind to another's person's faults. Donnie's faults were starting to become visible and it was clear he was not who he seemed.

In 1953, Noreen Kumeta was born in the northwest suburbs of Chicago. She was one of three girls born to Alfred and Irene Kumeta. She graduated from high school in 1971 and began to look for a job right around the time Donnie and Mom were breaking up their respective marriages. When Noreen first met Donnie at her job at Quaker Oats, she had no idea of the events that were unfolding in his life and how those events would impact her own life. Noreen was deeply impacted by the death of her high school boyfriend in an automobile accident. It may have made her more open to the charms of the older man who practiced law at the same company. Noreen was 19 years old and Donnie was 31. It was the summer of 1973. It had been about nine months since the respective Hart and Rudd divorces were filed. Everyone assumed that Mom and Donnie would get married sometime before the end of the year.

What did Donnie Rudd tell Noreen about his life before he met her? Did he tell her about the breakup of his marriage or about the affair? One thing is for sure, he didn't tell her about us — or about where he spent most of his nights. It is not clear whether Noreen knew anything about Mom, but our family knew of Noreen. It was inevitable that Donnie's different worlds would eventually collide. Mom saw Noreen for the first time at Donnie's apartment one summer night in 1973. She had taken to cruising through his apartment parking lot when he was late returning home from work. This night, she found his car parked two buildings away from his apartment. Mom became emboldened to find the truth. At first, Donnie did not answer her knock, but Mom was not deterred. The lights were on and she saw movement through the windows. Her knocking became increasingly insistent and she also began yelling for Donnie to open the door. Finally, Donnie came to the door and stepped out onto the balcony, carefully closing the door behind him but not before my Mom saw there was a young, blond woman in the apartment sitting on the couch.

Donnie spoke in a low whisper assuring Mom the woman was a client and he was only working. He flattered Mom and told her how much he loved her. He said she changed his life and that she was everything to him. He couldn't live without her. The charm assault continued as he slowly started moving her away from the apartment door and the woman sitting inside.

At first, Mom began to succumb to his pleadings. Mom wanted desperately to believe him. But something stopped her. Instead, she became increasingly insistent that she was going to talk to the woman in the apartment. Mom tried to push her way past Donnie to enter the apartment. Donnie became more physical as he pushed her away from the door. His demeanor changed from charming and manipulative to angry. There was a look in his eyes Mom had never seen. Her legs began to tremble and fear overcame her. Mom started to believe that this man she had given up everything for, intended to do her harm. Donnie was pushing her away from the apartment door, and towards the edge of the balcony. During the altercation, both ended up on the ground. A neighbor opened the door and yelled that he was calling the police. Mom extricated herself and made her way to her car yelling at Donnie and telling him to never contact her again. Donnie followed her to the car assuring her that he loved her and that she needed to listen to him.

"You don't have to be afraid of me, she is just a client," he pleaded. He stood in front of the car as she tried to pull away. "I'll kill myself if you leave," he shouted as he ran next to her car window. "I'll kill you … and your kids!"

Mom sped away as Donnie stood in the parking lot shaking his fist. As Mom's car disappeared around the corner, he headed back up the stairs to do damage control with the young woman in the apartment. He probably told her the same thing he told Mom. Some crazy client was stalking him. It was an excuse that always worked for him. It must have worked this time, because Noreen stayed.

Mom burst into the house as all four of us were lying on the floor watching TV that evening.

"Get in the bathroom!" Mom ordered. She locked all of the doors, turned off the lights and brought a small flashlight into the adjoining bedroom. We sat in the dark, huddled on the floor watching the small sliver of light coming under the bathroom door.

"Is this a tornado drill?" I hear Glory's voice coming from the side nearest to the door.

"I think we would be in the bathtub if it was a tornado," Cindy answered.

"If it's a tornado, we should go to the basement," Jack added

"It's probably a Donnie thing," I finally said.

"Why do we have to sit in the dark for a Donnie thing?" Cindy innocently queried.

"It's *always* a Donnie thing," was the only answer I could come up with.

In the bedroom, Mom dialed Dad and breathlessly told him that "Donnie is coming to kill us." Of course, she wanted Dad to come and save us. Back at his house, Dad was not so sure. He sat on the edge of the bed trying to decide what to do.

"How do I know it isn't a trap?" he asked Louann. "I'll go there and Donnie will shoot me, claiming he thought I was a burglar."

But the call from Mom is hard to ignore.

Finally, Dad called the Hoffman Estates Police Department and asked them to meet him at Carleton Road. Back in the bathroom, I heard the doorbell ring and opened the bathroom door a crack but couldn't see anything.

"Where are you going?" Cindy whispered. I could feel her hand on my foot. She was right behind me.

"Shhhhh! I'm going to go see what is happening," I whispered back.

We crawled slowly down the hall until we could see around the corner, down the stairs. The flashing lights from the police car reflected off the light in our front foyer. The door was open and Mom was talking to Dad and two police officers. Glory and Jack were following us down the hall to get a look.

"Dad's here," I whispered, just in case they couldn't see. The four of us lay on the floor peeking down the stairs as Mom cried and tried to explain what happened. Mom stood at the door as one of the police officers came in and went downstairs. I could hear him checking the patio doors that led to the back yard. The officer seemed to be checking the bushes outside the front door. I could see his flashlight through the sidelights of the front door.

After an exhaustive search of the yard, a check of the locks on the door, the police were ready to leave. It was not clear whether this was a domestic disturbance between Mom and Dad or if there was something else going on. But there was no evidence that Donnie was on the premises or in any place where he was a real threat to our family. Finally, it seemed that the situation had been diffused. We were hustled off to bed and the Carleton Road house went dark.

The next morning, it was like nothing happened. We were surprised to find Donnie was sleeping in the downstairs bedroom next to Mom. The woman, the police, and the threats had completely dissipated with the bright sun of morning. No one talked about the night before. As a kid, there is a brief moment where you wonder if the night before was a dream, but eventually you are just so glad everything is over that you forget about trying to figure out what happened.

These periodic blowups and then reconciliations without explanation would become commonplace with Mom and Donnie. But this time, the peace would not last long. Donnie continued to disappear, much to Mom's chagrin. He insisted she was imagining things. He weaved stories about crazy clients that followed him and thought they were in love with him. Meanwhile, his love letters and poems to Mom increased. But Donnie and Mom were coming to the proverbial fork in the road. There would be only so many excuses Donnie could make about the young blond woman. The month of Noreen was about to start for the Hart family.

On Friday, August 17, the truth regarding Noreen finally came out. I knew there was a problem as soon as I walked in the door that Friday afternoon. The tension in the room was palpable. Donnie and Mom were sitting at the kitchen table. Mom was crying. But both moved quickly into the downstairs bedroom and although I could hear muffled voices and crying, it was hard to make out any words. Cindy hovered behind me as I knocked on the door but got no answer. I tried the doorknob, but the door was locked.

"Go away!" Mom yelled. But finally, she came to the door.

"Donnie is leaving," she announced. "He is getting married."

"*You're* getting married?" I asked, not quite comprehending what I just heard. At first I thought he was marrying Mom. It didn't make sense.

"He is marrying Noreen this weekend." she answered.

I could not believe it. Who was Noreen?

Up until now, everything was equal. Each family had two parents, kids, a house, and two cars. Although it was different, we could go on kind of like before. But this would change everything. Dad couldn't come back, he married Louann.

Once again, Donnie was ruining our lives.

Mom and Donnie retreated back into the bedroom with the door locked. I pounded unsuccessfully on the bedroom door. The hours passed and the sun started to set. By 10:00 p.m., it was clear Donnie was not leaving. I couldn't control myself any longer.

"Get out of our house!" I yelled as I pounded ferociously on the bedroom door. "You can't let him stay the night," I screamed at my mother.

"Are we invited to the wedding? Can I be a bridesmaid? What is the matter with you?!"

For a minute, I thought about breaking down the door. I took off my shoe and pounded again. Finally, I heard Mom's voice.

"Go to bed," she said.

That is all.

"Go to bed."

I headed back to my room livid and slammed the door while sinking to the floor. *How could he do this to us?*

The next morning, I watched from my upstairs window as Donnie pulled out of the driveway in the Pinto. I wondered aloud if we would ever see him again.

But Donnie had assured Mom he would be back. He was going to Mexico for a CIA mission, but he would call her and they could talk about things. Maybe things can still be worked out, he promised. This promise of a conversation was enough of a lifeline for Mom to grab. She was hopeful she could change his mind.

Although Donnie tried to tell Mom he would put off his planned wedding, he left our house and married Noreen the next day in a modest wedding with guests, cake, and dancing. The marriage took place on August 18, 1973 … just over two years from the date that Mom announced she was leaving Dad. Donnie's twin brother and his wife attended the wedding. Donnie had been approving invitations, making guest lists, and choosing wedding cakes while living at our house. He was making honeymoon reservations and planning his new life while he sipped coffee and read the newspaper at our kitchen table. Less than a year after finalizing the divorce from Louann, Donnie was now a married man. But incredibly, he was not married to our mother.

Mom would find out later that Donnie did, indeed, make the trip to Mexico. But he was not there on a secret CIA mission, but on a honeymoon vacation with Noreen. There were no secret drops or clandestine meetings. Only piña coladas by the pool. Later, she would find out he had been seeing Noreen for several months. In fact, they were scheduled to get married earlier that summer, but had changed the wedding date after a family death. The fact that he had been able to balance the demands of both Mom and Noreen while still working through his divorce was really difficult for Mom — and for all of us — to grasp. It's as if we had been the victims of a gigantic scam.

A rational person would think the Hart family had seen the last of Donnie. He made his choice. He chose the pretty young blond woman over Mom and her four kids. But as I said before, nothing about Donnie was rational. Nothing happens as expected when it comes to figuring out Donnie. I started to fear for Mom. It had become clear over the past year that she desperately needed Donnie. What were we going to do if he was really gone? Do we really want him back? It was the start of our love/hate relationship with Donnie's existence in our lives. It was indisputable we would have preferred to never see or hear from Donnie Rudd again. But the situation with Mom was tenuous and made us wonder if there was any chance of their reconciliation.

As the weeks progressed, no one was sure about the situation between Donnie and Noreen. Donnie continued to call Mom almost every night. When Donnie returned from Mexico, notes appeared on Mom's windshield. Childish notes, really, some with nothing more than XXX's from top to bottom. One said, "I really, really love you" with the word "really" repeated 50 times. Mom heard that Donnie married Noreen, but incredibly, he vehemently denied the marriage had taken place during every call. But reality was starting to set in with Mom. Despite the letters, the phone calls, and the professions of love, Donnie had not spent the night at Carleton Road. She was too afraid to face the truth, but deep down she knew. Although she was the "other" woman for most of her relationship with Donnie, she justified it all, knowing that eventually she would be *the one*, his wife.

Noreen changed the dream.

"I made a bargain with the devil and Donnie is out marrying Noreen," she wept. She would live partway in a dream world of sleep in which there was no Noreen and everything with Donnie turned out as planned. The other half of her waking hours was spent with the stark reality that she had destroyed our family and was alone.

Less than a month after Donnie left our house to marry Noreen, the Noreen situation took a devastating, unexpected turn. No one could have foreseen the news that Donnie told Mom in a terse phone call that came in the middle of the night. "Noreen is dead." That is all that Mom said. Mom's words after this call were shocking, even in our less-than-normal life.

Mom left the house immediately after she received the call. She returned to the house weeping and was completely unresponsive to my questions. She turned and walked away, back into her bedroom retreat, and closed the door. I could hear the curtains being drawn and the mattress creak as she withdrew to the safety of her bed. Later, I would read the newspaper article about the accident she left on the kitchen table.

> *"Mrs. Rudd, a librarian for Quaker Oats in Barrington was pronounced dead on arrival Friday evening at Sherman Hospital in Elgin apparently from injuries sustained in a car accident on Illinois Route 62 near Bateman Road in Barrington, Illinois."*

The phone started ringing off the hook at our home the day after the article appeared in the newspaper. Most of our friends and family still thought Donnie was living with Mom. Mass confusion ensued because people thought Mom died in the car accident, or in some cases, maybe Louann. The source of the confusion was the unexpected phrase, "*Mrs. Rudd.*" No one understood the "Mrs. Rudd" in the car accident was Donnie's new 19-year-old wife. The confusion abounded because no one knew about Noreen or Donnie's recent marriage to the young woman.

Years later, we would learn the facts of the accident. On Friday, September 14, 1973, police responded to a call regarding a motor vehicle accident on Route 62 at or near its intersection with Bateman road in Barrington Hills, Illinois. When police arrived, the Pinto wagon was located in a grassy area that contained light shrubbery. Donnie was sitting in the passenger seat with a mortally wounded Noreen lying with her head in his lap and her feet on the driver's side. The officers pulled Noreen out of the car and began performing mouth-to-mouth resuscitation. She was not breathing. The officer giving aid noted that the back of her skull appeared to be gone. Noreen was transported to Sherman Hospital in Elgin where she was pronounced dead on arrival. The reporting officer noted that the weather was clear and there were approximately 165 feet of skid marks in the grass leading to the Pinto's location. The car appeared to have hit a barbed wire fence and had only minor damage. When interviewed at the scene, Donnie told the officers that another car veered into his lane, causing him to leave the road. He stated that the passenger door came open and Noreen was thrown from the car. He pointed to a rock that appeared to have blood and hair on it located near the car, suggesting that this was the rock that killed Noreen. A witness from the funeral home remembered the extensive damage to Noreen's skull and the need to fill the holes in her head during the burial preparation. No autopsy was performed, and the death was designated an accident.

The day after Noreen died and Mom met Donnie to hear the details of the accident, she wrote Donnie a note.

> *Dear Donnie,*
> *I'm sorry I was unable to be of any help to you tonight but I did not know for sure that you were married and learning of it under these circumstances was more than I could bear. You must know how sorry I am. We will be glad to keep Kitty for you for a while but I think when some time has passed she should be with you. I wish there was some way I could help. Donnie, please find someone to talk to, someone who can help you and please try and forget the things I said to you tonight. — "D"*

Mom would later tell close friends that she slept with Donnie the night immediately following the accident. His blood-soaked clothes were still in a plastic bag in the corner of the room. Noreen's clothes were still in his closet. Did the police give him her purse after the accident? If they did, it would probably be sitting on the kitchen table. Mom was back in his bed in the small Hilldale apartment. But this time it was also Noreen's bed. Her letter implies she was angry with him and unable to sympathize over the death of Noreen. Did he whisper in her ear what happened? Did he tell her the details of the accident? Did he cry and ask her to take his cat? Did Mom feel some small sense of relief or hope? Ashamed at her thoughts, did she return home wondering whether she now had a chance to renew her relationship?

The funeral took place on a September morning; not even a month after Donnie married Noreen. Donnie decided to bury her in the white wedding dress she wore just weeks before. Donnie wanted his young children to attend the funeral. He called Louann and asked to have them dressed nicely when he picked them up. It was so confusing for everyone because no one knew he was married. It enhanced his image as a grieving widower with the four small children standing by his side. No one in our house was invited. Mom sat silently in her chair the morning of the funeral. But after Donnie dropped his children off, he returned — to our house. At first, I thought he was merely seeking comfort and would leave soon. But hours stretched into days and we finally had to accept the fact that Donnie was back.

Once again, Mom and Donnie resumed their tortured relationship.

Donnie had returned less than a month after he left. An eerie sameness settled into the Carleton Road house.

We never met Noreen, but she impacted our lives greatly and we felt like we knew her. For one month, it seemed as if the world stopped while she unknowingly became the focal point of everything happening in our family. At the end of the month, we chose to ignore the obvious elephant in the room and joined the dysfunctional conspiracy of silence regarding Mom's shortcomings and Donnie's deceit.

And so the month of Noreen ended.

CHAPTER NINE

After Noreen

For the first few days after Donnie's return, Mom was quiet. The desperation she felt to keep Donnie in her life was difficult to distinguish from true happiness and even harder to distinguish from her fear of being alone. There was little conversation about Noreen or why Donnie had returned to our house. But a few days after the funeral, she asked me if I wanted to go with her to look at the car ... the car that Noreen died in. It was parked in the corner of the auto shop where it was towed after the accident.

There seemed to be little damage to the car itself. From a distance, it was impossible to tell whether it was damaged at all. I got out of the car with Mom but hung back, unsure of what we were looking for. As I slowly approached, I could see through the side window into the interior of the car. There was blood on the front seat and something else that I couldn't identify. A feeling of nausea swept through me as I thought of the young blond woman who had lost her life in the car. Mom continued her own inspection of the car. She circled the car first and then stopped to look into each window. She tried the door handle of the passenger's side, but it was locked. After a few minutes, she turned to leave. The tears were streaming down her face as she returned to our car. We drove home in eerie silence.

Finally, as we pulled into the driveway of the Carleton Road house, Mom broke the silence by saying quietly, "I think the gray stuff was part of her brain." There didn't seem to be an appropriate response, so I sat silently. I had never come that close to death before.

I had heard Noreen's name so many times over the past month that I felt like I knew her. I could not comprehend how a beautiful, blond young woman who looked like she was my age would marry Donnie. The dizzying rollercoaster of emotions I felt for the past month had left me discombobulated and uncalibrated. It became almost impossible for me to relate to anything that was happening around me. With a steady stream of affairs, anger, sadness, divorce, and death, it became nearly impossible to know whom I should be mad at or whom I should feel sorry for. I lost track of who the good guy was and who the bad guy was. All I knew is that since Donnie came into our lives nothing had been right.

But slowly, life started to return to normal ... not the "normal" we had before all this began, but the *new normal*. Donnie and Mom went out to dinner on the weekends. There was talk of taking a vacation early the following year. But there was no talk of Noreen.

"Is Donnie sad about Noreen?" I finally asked Mom a few days after the visit to the car. "When Uncle Alvin died, I cried for days. Donnie never says anything."

Mom was slow to answer.

"Of course he is sad," she said. "He just hides it." Mom rarely talked about Noreen again.

A couple of weeks after the accident, I worked up the nerve to ask Donnie what happened the night Noreen died. I was driving with him to pick up a pizza. Surprisingly, he didn't seem reluctant to talk about it.

"How did you get in the accident?" I finally asked.

"It wasn't an accident ... I was forced off the road. I think it is related to an investigation I am working on," he said with a straight face, obviously alluding to his James Bond alter ego that indulged in covert CIA operations.

"How do you know it was on purpose?" I innocently asked.

"The car stopped after it ran us off the road. A man got out and looked down at us and then drove away. If it was just an accident, he would have helped."

"Who would run you off the road?"

Donnie proceeded to talk about an investigation he was working on regarding corruption in Hoffman Estates. He spoke about his involvement with Jim Thompson and the fact that people were angry about the role he played. Donnie said that he felt the driver who ran him off the road had done so intentionally and at the request of someone in the investigation.

"Who is Jim Thompson?" I asked, the name sounding vaguely familiar.

"He is the attorney general [who would later become the governor] for Illinois." This was entirely new information. He had just added a new category to his resume. Let's see ... he was a Vietnam veteran, Special Ops operative, corporate lawyer, part-time covert CIA agent, and now he was running secret operations for the Illinois attorney general. Even at 16, I was starting to have doubts about what was true and what was not.

"Noreen was sleeping," he continued. "The door opened and she fell out. The car door hit her in the head and she bled to death."

It was one of the few times I heard Donnie actually say Noreen's name.

Noreen was buried at a small cemetery not far from the apartment she shared with Donnie for the short month of their marriage. A small tombstone marked the final resting spot for Noreen Kumeta Rudd.

After her death, Donnie received life insurance payouts on two policies that were taken out on Noreen. The first policy was an employee benefit that all employees of Quaker Oats received. It included an initial lump sum plus 25 percent of the employee's salary for five years. The second policy was a Voluntary Accident Life Insurance Policy that the employee had to purchase. The available coverage ranged from $10,000 to $100,000. Noreen had purchased the maximum coverage of $100,000 and named Donnie as the beneficiary. Mom showed me the insurance check Donnie received as a result of Noreen's death shortly after he moved back into our home. At that time, $100,000 was a very significant amount of funds. Our immediate financial issues appeared to be resolved with Noreen's death.

Cindy and I started talking about following Donnie soon after he moved back to our house. While not privy to all of the details of Noreen's death, Donnie's return to our house so quickly generated plenty of speculation both within and outside of the family.

Initially, Cindy and I thought he might find another girlfriend and leave us again. We talked about getting spy equipment to listen in on his phone calls and practiced putting an empty wine glass against the door of the bedroom to see if we could hear any conversations. We started keeping track of his absences in a small spiral notebook that was hidden under the mattress. As fans of Nancy Drew, we fancied ourselves as a crack team of detectives who could figure out the mystery behind our enigmatic stepfather. We hoped more proof of Donnie's bad character might convince Mom to leave him before he left her again. As the years passed, our detective work would become motivated more by our desire to be prepared for the next inevitable crisis rather than hope that Donnie would be out of our life. We became more realistic about Mom's relationship with our stepfather over time.

One night, Donnie left his briefcase in the corner of the

living room. After he went to bed, Cindy and I crept down the stairs to look through it. There were pictures of the Pinto in an envelope. There was also a brief summary of the inquest into Noreen's death. It was noted that Noreen died from a massive head wound. Her weight before and after the accident showed a significant amount of blood was lost as a result of the head wound. The letter from Mom to Donnie that she wrote the day after Noreen died was also in the case. I pushed the papers back into his briefcase and sat on the couch thinking about what I had just read. I had questions. But who do you talk to about something like this when you are 16 years old? I took one of the pictures of Donnie and Noreen at their wedding, the letter from Mom to Donnie, and a copy of Noreen's inquest. I slipped it into a shoebox and carefully placed the box in the far corner of my closet.

Donnie continued to visit Noreen's sister for years after her death. Four or five times a year he would go to her house and have dinner with her family. Noreen's sister felt sorry for him. She would ask him when he was going to find someone to share his life with. They were never aware of all the inconsistent stories Donnie told of the accident that killed Noreen. He played the part of the grieving widower, something he clearly was not.

After Noreen died, an uneasy peace settled in at Carleton Road. It was easy to forget the cataclysmic residual effects resulting from Donnie's affair, the wedding, and then Noreen's car accident, because no one talked about it. It was impossible not to sometimes wonder if it really happened. At some point, the Hart family learned to step away from painful events. There was no changing what happened with the divorce or with Noreen. Mom let go of her anger regarding Donnie's relationship with Noreen when he was back at Carleton Road, sleeping next to her in the downstairs bedroom. Donnie showed no sorrow regarding the tragic death of Noreen, preferring to settle back into his familiar routine with Mom and work. It was as if Noreen never existed. There were no pictures, no tears, and no memories. Donnie's occasional mention of Noreen's name was designed to engender pity from family, friends, and business associates.

There were whispers outside our home, of course, regarding what happened to Noreen; murmurs in the neighborhood about the one-car accident that killed her. Questions as to how she bled to death so quickly. And general unease regarding the inappropriateness of Donnie's return to Mom's bedroom. But the enormity of what happened and the tragic nature of the accident resulting in her death made it hard to push Donnie for answers to obvious questions. After all, he was still a "grieving" widower. The status earned him a certain respect, allowing him to avoid any discussion of what happened.

Donnie's return to Carleton Road started a different type of craziness. Again, he would tell the same stories. Clandestine meetings, investigations, and incredible stories of courage and heroism. This time around, the stories were not as interesting as they were when we first met him. There was something not quite right about Donnie's endless descriptions of life before us. Dad would ask questions about Donnie during our Tuesday night visitation dinners at Barnaby's Pizza. All four of us would excitedly tell Dad what Donnie said and the unusual things he did.

"He leaves the house in the middle of dinner without saying a word," I'd tell Dad. "He just gets up and walks out. He says he was in the war and is in the CIA."

"He jumps out of helicopters," Cindy chimes in to the discussion. "He goes on missions."

"He was never in the war," Louann would laugh. "I would have known if he was in the war. He was in college. Why would he say that?"

Dad would just shake his head. But dinner almost always ended where it started.

"I don't understand why she [Mom] left us for him," he would say in a sad voice.

There was no doubt Donnie Rudd was not quite right. No one knew to what extent or what to do about it.

"Is Donnie going to leave again?" I finally asked the question one evening as Mom was driving me to a school event. As the words slipped out, I wished I could take them back. While I wanted to know, I wasn't ready to hear Mom talk about him.

"I hope not," was all she said, but she seemed worried.

Mom was happy Donnie returned, but not unaware their relationship was different. Donnie was no longer her soul mate. During the divorce, she believed she was meant to be with Donnie. He was the love of her life. After Noreen, she knew that wasn't true. But she was determined not to be alone. An exceptionally smart woman, she started thinking about ways to solidify her position to prevent Donnie from leaving again … or at least make it more difficult for him to leave her for yet another woman. Donnie chose the young, beautiful Noreen to marry. Mom couldn't do anything about the age issue, but she *could* level the playing field on some of her other "disadvantages." Mom saw her responsibility for four children as a reason Donnie might leave again.

Donnie was not interested in his role as a father — and especially not a stepfather. The animosity of the divorce changed the way all four of us interacted with the adults in our life. We were exceptionally independent and not afraid to challenge decisions made on our behalf. Both Jack and I became quite belligerent and angry regarding the actions of our parents. Donnie had very little to do with his own four children and wasn't going to modify his life to accommodate four very strong-willed adolescent stepchildren. Mom was increasingly torn between her role as a mother and her need to keep Donnie.

Although life was returning to some semblance of "normal," there were new signs that storm clouds of change were continuing to gather on the horizon. It would be only a matter of time before another event would challenge the stability of the Hart family still living on Carleton Road.

The Christmas after Noreen died and Donnie collected his insurance money was an exceptional gift year for the family. There was money for the first time in years. I received a car as an early Christmas gift, a green 1969 Chevy Bel Air with three gears on the steering wheel. My siblings got an assortment of dolls, small electric toy cars they could plug into the wall and drive around, and even pet spider monkeys. *Real live spider monkeys!* They named their monkeys Skippy and Zonk. The monkeys were dirty and loud but definitely amusing. Cindy's monkey lived for just a short time. Dad and Louann were less than happy that Donnie was sending home expensive toys and live animals back to the tiny Flagstaff home. There were still four kids, two dogs, and two adults living in the small tract home … and now spider monkeys joined the family.

Donnie loved to place Dad and Louann in difficult situations. He liked being the Disney Dad with no responsibility for the children besides taking them to an occasional dinner. He found some particular pleasure in putting Louann in the position of telling the Rudd children there was no room in the house for their new toys or pets. "I think I'll buy Terisa a pony for her birthday," I remember him saying one evening. "They can keep it in the backyard." Although the pony never materialized, Donnie was always thinking of ways to make Dad and Louann's life more difficult.

The divorces were final, but the war waged on between the four adults in the two families. It really wasn't easy to live at either house. The Hart children continually moved back and forth between the two houses as we struggled for some type of peace and normalcy to our lives.

But "normalcy," as we would soon find out, was a myth in this blended troupe we called a family.

CHAPTER TEN

Mom's New Course

From our perspective, we first noticed things were going to change after Donnie returned home was the appearance of the large "Garage Sale" sign in the front yard of Carleton Road on a Friday afternoon in early spring. There were numerous other signs on the garage saying "Everything Must Go." Mom cut little pieces of pink paper and marked prices and stuck them on items she wanted to sell. Everything in our house had a small pink sticker on it. The sticker on our living room couch said "25 cents." Mom was determined to liquidate our entire household furniture inventory in one weekend. It wasn't about the money; she was purging the past. It was a statement about her life and what she would do to keep Donnie. By the end of the weekend, we were shocked to be standing in our empty kitchen with no place to sit. But Mom was cheerful ... at least she wanted us to *think* she was cheerful and everything was going as planned. She said we were going out to celebrate the garage sale results. She took some of the money she made from the garage sale and took us all out to McDonald's for dinner.

Selling your furniture for pennies did not leave much of a profit but it was a pretty good strategy for getting rid of everything quickly. Next, it was the dogs. Our German Shepherd was shipped to Dad's house. Last, I came home from school to find my dog, Gwen, was also gone. There was no explanation and no discussion.

"I found her a good home," was all Mom would say. "You are busy in school and I can't take care of her." No amount of crying or yelling could change her mind. When it came to what she thought she needed to do to keep Donnie, Mom was not in a negotiable mood.

I desperately sought to be independent from the ongoing drama of our family situation. By taking extra classes and summer school, I obtained sufficient credits to graduate from high school in June 1974 after completion of my junior year. A couple of weeks before my graduation ceremony from high school, Donnie and Mom took a long weekend and flew to Las Vegas. Although they told no one, they got married at a small chapel during the trip. After the drama of the divorces and Noreen's death, the wedding was probably anticlimactic. It probably took place to assuage Mom's fears that Donnie was going to leave her again.

For the second time in less than 12 months, Donnie was saying "I do," exchanging rings, and making a lifelong commitment to a woman … in sickness and in health, till death do them part.

It's impossible to say why Mom thought keeping the marriage a secret was important. It might have been because of the inappropriateness of the marriage so soon after Noreen's death. Maybe she wanted to keep this small victory to herself. And maybe she was afraid someone would talk her out of it if she told anyone. The marriage would remain a secret from everyone, including her own children for years. Several months after the wedding, Donnie and Mom took a belated honeymoon to one of Donnie's favorite vacation spots. Mexico. The fact that he honeymooned in Mexico with Noreen was not a deterrent to a honeymoon vacation with Mom.

At my graduation ceremony, I sat on the football field waiting for my name to be called so I could step up and accept my diploma. Up in the stands were the four people that now constituted the parenting segment of my extended family. Dad and Louann, and Mom and Donnie. It was hard to believe how drastically life had changed from that August night right before I started high school — when Mom announced she wanted a divorce — to this day. Looking up into the stands, it was impossible not to feel conflicted about the whole family situation. But there was also a slight sense of relief that I was starting to leave my childhood and my crazy family behind.

Not long after my graduation, a "For Sale" sign went up in the yard of our beloved Carleton Road house. Mom was covering all her bases. The wedding ring was not enough. Donnie was more likely to stay when bound with a contractual obligation. Besides, Mom explained to us that moving would be an adventure and we could all just start over. Everything was going to fall into place and we would all be better than before. Cindy, Glory, Jack, and I listened, but I don't think anyone thought the move would be easy or happy.

The physical changes associated with things like where we lived were obvious. The quiet changes taking place as each Donnie event unfolded were not as easy to see at the time but would actually have a greater impact on our lives. Mom was changing. She recognized her own vulnerability and weakness in the vortex of struggling with decisions involving both Dad and Donnie and Donnie and Noreen. She didn't like feeling weak and susceptible. And she certainly didn't like herself. As she pulled herself out of the despair of almost losing Donnie, she started to take a little more control of her life. There was more to her agenda than just the furniture, dogs, and the house; Mom was going to transform *herself.* Although, she always struggled with her weight, this time she was going to do something definitive. Meager personal savings were used to have a balloon inserted into her stomach so that she could finally lose the weight that dragged her down. Within months, she lost 30 pounds. Mom decided she wanted to be *somebody* … and it wasn't "Mrs. Hart" or "Mrs. Rudd."

"There are already too many Mrs. Rudds out there," she once said. "I don't want anybody to be confused about who I am."

She took back a shortened version of her maiden name, which had been Markowski, and became Dianne Marks. And finally, she decided she wanted to channel her natural intelligence — which dragged her down in the past — and do something positive with her talents. Donnie was not going to be the only lawyer in the family. Mom announced that she was going to go to law school.

It was not the first time she talked about law school. Mom dreamed of becoming a lawyer before she even met Donnie. But after Noreen died, she started to actively plan the path to eventually achieve a law degree. In a letter she wrote shortly after Noreen died, Mom said this about her dream to become a lawyer:

> *"Why a lawyer? When I was young I thought law consisted of dusty old law books and desert dry discussions. Somewhere along the way I realized law is a social science as well as an institution. It is a way to help people with problems which threatened to overwhelm their lives."*

As her world disintegrated during the divorce and the battles with Donnie continued, it was very appropriate she understood she would need tools to keep these problems from overwhelming her life. Ultimately, the law degree would help her compartmentalize problems and work to formulate solutions. Her law degree would one day replace her overwhelming natural tendency to go to bed and pull the covers over her head when things went wrong. It was one of her learned life lessons that I always felt she passed on to me.

But going to law school was not going to be easy. Although she had never attended college, she took some courses at the local junior college. She enrolled in her first junior college class shortly after she started her relationship with Donnie, a historical geology class. Why would she take a geology class and not something more practical? She would say, "Somewhere in the dark days of the divorce, I made up my mind to be a lawyer and someone said it was a good idea to study science if you wanted to practice law."

By the time Mom really started thinking seriously about law school, she realized she was going to be a very old, white-haired lady before she ever obtained a college degree. She refocused her efforts and starting taking and passing "CLEP" courses. CLEP allowed you credit for traditional college classes if you could show proficiency in the subject matter. She also joined the college's speech team, which was unusual. There were not many older women on the team.

It was in 1974, right after her marriage to Donnie, that she discovered DePaul University's School for New Learning, a nontraditional adult degree program that based its requirements for a bachelor's degree on competencies rather than hours present in the classroom. All Mom had to do was to demonstrate that she possessed the competencies of an educated person and DePaul would give her the piece of paper that would be her passport to law school. So she started to strategize. You need a science competency? How about her private pilot's license? You need a humanities competency? How about a tape of her playing the piano as an accompanist for the community chorus? You need organizational competencies? How about the nature center program she developed for the school district?

Even though Mom finally married Donnie, all of her actions were geared toward obtaining a level of self-sufficiency. Her plan was very ambitious for a woman who married at the age of 18, became a mother by 19, and lived as a housewife for so many years. But Mom was smart and motivated. Although female lawyers were not common in the 1970s, I don't think anyone doubted she would eventually become a lawyer.

The four of us were still bewildered by the continuing changes in our family. I found refuge in my friends and stayed away from both houses as much as possible. Cindy still gravitated between the two families, constantly pulled into whatever direction she felt was the fairest. She worried about Dad all the time, but felt I needed a partner in the chaos at Mom's house. When she was at Dad's house, she would sit on a small stool next to Dad's workbench watching him work. Glory was so young she was starting to forget the normal days. And Jack was more and more angry at the ever-changing family relationships. Sometimes there were eight kids in one house and sometimes there would be just one. Most of the time even the parents were confused as to which kids were supposed to be living at which house. And there didn't seem to be an end in sight.

CHAPTER ELEVEN

After Carleton Road

The Carleton Road house sold the summer of 1974. Mom and Donnie started house hunting in earnest. Finally, they announced a new home had been found and we went to see it on a bright Saturday morning. Like everything else in our lives, our new living arrangement was going to push the boundaries of what was normal.

First, it wasn't a house. It was a townhouse in a townhome association called Barrington Square. Second, it was not one townhouse ... it was two! There were two row townhouses set immediately next to each other. The four of us kids stood in front of the two houses looking confused as Mom talked about Barrington Square. None of us really understood exactly what the plan was.

"Who is going to live in this one?" I asked as we walked up the stairs of the first townhome. I was starting classes at a local junior college and knew that I would be living at home at least for a while.

"Donnie and I," Mom said casually. "You kids will live next door."

It was a typical Mom solution. She could live with Donnie like she had no children, all the while still meeting her parental responsibilities.

"Will we still eat together?" Jack asked.

"Sure, you will just come over to our house to eat."

Mom had all the answers. Cindy and I looked around at the two houses.

"What are we going to do about breakfast when it rains?" Cindy finally asked.

Mom looked around and without pausing a second, said, "I guess we will cut a door between the two houses."

It didn't seem right, but the kids couldn't really articulate why the situation seemed worrisome. At the time, our ages were 17, 15, 14 and 11. So we packed up the remainder of our belongings and moved to Barrington Square. Most of our friends thought it was awesome. It was like living in a college dorm without leaving home. There were never any parents watching TV in the living room or yelling about the music being too loud. The two townhouses were quite nice. Neither of them had a garage, but each had a small fenced-in courtyard. The kids' house was on the right. It had a nice living room when you walked in, with two bedrooms upstairs and two in the basement.

Glory and Cindy chose bedrooms upstairs, and Jack and I moved to the basement. Mom tried her hardest to make our bedrooms unique and make us excited about the move. She had carpet installed on one of Cindy's walls. I got a waterbed in the basement. She let one of my friends paint a mural of the album cover of Yes' *Tales From Topographical Oceans* on the wall of my bedroom.

Finally, Mom hired a carpenter to put a door between the two houses. It made it easier to get back and forth when it got cold out. It was a beautiful, decorative door with wrought iron carve-outs. The door was in our kitchen and lead into their living room. Donnie and Mom always locked their side during the day after they left and at night.

Eventually, we adjusted to this new concept of family and our new two-house life. Mom attended night classes almost every night downtown. I enrolled in college classes, and

Cindy and Jack continued with high school. The "new normal" was continuing to evolve into an even "newer normal." But we would all learn quickly that there was really nothing close to normal in family life with Donnie Rudd.

The next few years would be called Donnie's Crazy Years. Crazy even in our abnormal family life. No one can ever really explain all that happened. Some details are just too painful and some simply got lost in disbelief. Friends who lived through those years with us share a special bond. Trying to explain Donnie to an outsider is next to impossible. There is no place to start. Every story leads to a question that leads to a story. You had to be there to understand.

Our family was now spread out between two townhouses. Donnie and Mom were in 2058 W. Sutherland Place and the kids' place was at 2056 W. Sutherland. Each townhouse had its own particular style. Neither of the homes were suited for a family. Mom appeared to have adopted Donnie's Texas style of home decor in the parent house. There was a fancy wine rack with rather expensive bottles of wine that sat next to the door between the two houses. Donnie's new couches were soft brown plush and made you sink into them when you sat down. The coffee table and dining room table were rustic looking with rough-hewn wood planks.

Donnie had an extensive gun collection, now prominently displayed in the living room. He had cane guns, pen guns, and guns that looked like cannons on wheels. They were distributed all around the house. He also had a carved ivory pipe collection that sat on top of the TV and on the windowsills. The pipe heads were white and carved to look like a person's head. He had artwork with pictures of mice with wings, naked ladies, and clown-like lawyers hanging on the walls. A stuffed rattlesnake sat in a corner as well as a stuffed armadillo. The master bath had black faux fur wallpaper and was located in the hall outside the master bedroom. There was a large painting of a half-naked lady hanging on the bedroom wall.

"Do you think it's Mom?" Cindy whispered to me the first time we saw it.

"I hope not," I answered. I looked at the picture over my shoulder as we walked out of the room. "I hope not," I said again.

After the first couple of months, there was a growing realization that having our own house was not as glamorous as it first seemed. None of us were very good at cleaning, cooking, or fixing things that broke. Still, it had some advantages. At one point, I was able to get a dog and kept it in the basement for three months without Mom knowing. Cindy managed to have one of her friends from school live in her bedroom for two weeks after running away from home. Mom never found out about that one. Mom checked on us each night at about the same time. We could hear the lock turning and knew she was coming. It gave us an opportunity to make sure that any obvious contraband was hidden.

Although we were living separately, Donnie still found us to be a burden. Gradually over time, the little skirmishes between him and us started becoming more regular and more pointed. His focus turned to us as Dad and Louann became less reachable since their marriage. Donnie was as determined to make us miserable as we were to make sure he was not successful.

The war between Donnie and the Hart kids started slowly at first and gradually gained steam. It was hard to understand how Mom observed what was happening and did nothing. Donnie did not communicate directly with us. Problems were determined by his actions. Everything was an action and a response to that action. That was our way of talking in the Donnie Rudd dictatorship. There was no yelling in this house. There were no demands. There was a silent war where the combatants circled each other and worked silently to make their points.

I liked the windows open because I hate to be hot. After I'd leave for school, Donnie would head to our house with hammer and nails in hand and would nail my bedroom window shut so I couldn't open it at night. When I got home, Cindy helped me pry the nails off with a pair of pliers she found in the basement. Finally, the window opened. Cindy hid the pliers on a fencepost in the backyard in case we needed them again. Cindy tends to like it warmer, but she was always willing to help me thwart Donnie. He returned the next day and super glued the windows shut. It took Cindy several days to saw through the super glue with a collection of nail files, knives, and a screwdriver.

Another time, someone left the oven on after cooking a pizza, so Donnie took the knobs off the stove. Jack countered by using the pliers to turn the stove on and off.

On and on it went.

I was working as a waitress and would often come home late. My feet hurt and I wanted nothing more than to go to sleep. I slipped into the sheets to find Donnie poured water in my bed to ensure I didn't have a comfortable bed to sleep in. I got up and slipped into bed next to Cindy. I was looking for revenge when Cindy motioned to me that the door between the houses was unlocked. I snuck up to the master bathroom while Cindy kept watch and I cleaned the toilet with his toothbrush, put oil in his shampoo, and hid one of each of his socks that he neatly folded in his dresser drawer. We slipped quietly back to the kids' house.

The psychological war was on. We would find pepper in our favorite cereal box. There were always things missing like schoolbooks or a favorite pair of jeans. Sometimes he would mutilate our clothes by putting glue in the pockets or simply ripping a hole in a hard-to-repair place. When something was missing, you could never be sure whether it was lost or whether

Donnie had taken it. There were never accusations or questionings. Just silent war.

We didn't think of ourselves as victims. We were combatants. I'd see his briefcase sitting by the front door when I was at the parent house. I'd move it behind the couch so it was difficult to find. A pair of boots could be separated by taking one boot and putting it in a different closet. We were learning how to cope with the stress of living with Donnie by convincing each other that this was a game that was winnable. Donnie didn't think the lock between the doors was keeping us out of his townhouse, so he used railroad spikes to hammer into the door to keep us out. Glory found a way to get into the parent house through the backyard window well. During one outing, Glory casually picked up what looked like a pen sitting on a shelf. The pen fired and a bullet lodged in the ceiling. Glory set the pen gun back on the shelf and scooted out the window well and back into our townhome.

Donnie was becoming more frustrated by our ability to overcome his obstacles and by our steadfast refusal to become unnerved by his antics. Slowly, the war between the kids and Donnie started to become more physical and more dangerous.

One afternoon, I headed down the stairs to my basement bedroom only to be met with the rising waters of a basement flood. The water was about a foot high throughout the basement. I grabbed some boots from the hall closet and decided to wade through the water to see where it was coming from. As I put my foot in the water, I smelled a slight electrical odor. The water through my rubber boots seemed warm. I hastily retreated upstairs, called Mom, and waited for the repairman to come. Someone had poked a fairly large hole into the hot water heater to flood the basement. The drain in the floor had also been plugged. The repairman said the situation was dangerous because my plugged-in stereo was placed on the ground in the water electrocuting the water as it crept up the basement walls. "Someone could have been electrocuted," the repairman said as he looked quizzically at our blank faces. No one responded to his obvious questions so he shrugged and returned to his work.

Mom watched in horror as Donnie's games got more and more dangerous. Deep down she blamed herself for the chaotic way we lived. Still, she couldn't bring herself to leave Donnie or even confront him. At times, she hated Donnie for her inability to leave him. Frustrated with the escalating violence, I packed my bag and moved to the Flagstaff home. After a week of sleeping on the family room couch and living out of a suitcase, I crept back to my basement bedroom in the townhome.

Jack started out living with Dad. However, he started to drink heavily and had several altercations with the police. Dad set up family counseling only to have Jack show up drunk. Jack started gradually spending more and more time at the townhome where he had more freedom and wasn't under the accountability or supervision of responsible adults. Generally, Glory stayed with Mom. And Cindy, ever in the middle, gravitated between the two houses trying not to take a side.

I finally decided to move from the junior college to a four-year college. I was accepted into Northern Illinois University, in DeKalb, about an hour away, and realized for the first time that I might be able to finally leave some of the drama behind. Cindy graduated from high school and settled into her own townhome a few miles away from the chaos. Eventually, she married a man she met while she was bartending, as her search for a normal family and the white picket-fenced home continued. Jack joined the Navy the next year. By 1977, only Glory continued to live with Mom and Donnie.

By this time, Donnie had been in our lives for almost five long years. We all knew there was something not right about him. He was different than us in so many ways. Although I attended college and lived in a dorm more than an hour away, there were still things that happened at home that created a great deal of stress for me. I hated that my youngest sister, Glory, was still living at home and that we were not there to help when something happened.

Most of Donnie's bad acts during this time could be best characterized as devious. But occasionally, Donnie would show a burst of violence that was very scary. One evening, I got a frightened phone call from Glory. I was just coming back from the cafeteria dorm where I had eaten dinner. "He put a hammer through my TV," she sobbed. Apparently, Donnie was angry she left the TV on. He took a hammer and smashed the TV screen, walking away without saying a word. Over the phone, it sounded like pandemonium at the townhome. Mom was yelling and Glory was crying. "I think he is going to kill us," Mom yelled in the background. "Maybe I should call the police."

At that point, snow was starting to fall as a storm began in DeKalb. I frantically called my friends and finally located a car that I could borrow. It took me more than two hours to make the drive home in the snow. It was after 11:00 p.m. when I finally pulled into the parking lot at Barrington Square. The townhome was dark as I walked up to the front door. Mom and Donnie were asleep in their bedroom. Glory was asleep in her bedroom. The broken TV was pushed to the corner of the room and someone had swept up the broken glass into a pile. It was as if everyone just moved on from the angry outburst. It was the first time I realized these periodic outbursts had become the norm in our house. It was a discomforting thought. Angry that I came all this way to join the fray, I turned around and made the long drive back to my college dorm.

Next time, I would not be so quick to react, I promised myself. The rules were different when it came to dealing with my stepfather.

CHAPTER TWELVE

Engaging with the Devil

Donnie decided to leave Quaker Oats and start his own law practice. Although he had been married to Mom for several years, no one at his work was aware of his personal life, including the fact that he remarried. He attended company functions alone and would occasionally stop for dinner by himself at a co-worker's home. Mom seemed ambivalent about the fact she was not included in his professional work life. It made it easier for her to focus on school when she did not have to accompany him to any work functions. Donnie worried that his co-workers would find out he was married to Mom. This would have hurt his image as the grieving widower. Donnie received a substantial amount of money when Noreen died which gave him the liquidity he needed to make changes in his professional life. Noreen was not in his life for long, but she made a significant financial contribution towards his professional growth and lifestyle.

Donnie rented out an office in Hoffman Estates and hired a young attorney to help him. Mom filed corporation papers in 1976 for the new law firm, which was called Rudd and Associates. Donnie used his contacts from the school board and local politics to start the business. He had been courting potential clients for a few years on a part-time basis while employed at Quaker Oats. Mom was still working days and going to school at night, but would help Donnie on the weekends. This new job suited his personality. He never liked the corporate rules. He was now unfettered by the restrictions of corporate work and life. He reported to no one. Although he still talked about various litigation cases he worked on while at Quaker Oats, he preferred the attention of being a practicing attorney. He was smart and very different. People were attracted to him. The new business was appearing to be profitable.

In his own practice, Donnie was free to manipulate and control the people who looked to him for help. He was no longer responsible for reporting back and was accountable to no one. Donnie's law firm began concentrating on unusual or difficult cases — cases few other lawyers would touch. Some of the cases would stretch on interminably for years with no end in sight. Cases in which Donnie could make promises he would not keep, but kept him in control and made him look invincible.

While we battled at home with Donnie, Mom continued to work her way through school. When she started her foray into higher education, she only had a high school diploma. Although it took several years of night school, she finally received her college diploma. True to her word, she enrolled in the Kent College of Law to become a lawyer in the fall of 1977. She went to night school because she continued to work full-time as a legal secretary at a small law office. By carrying a full load and attending summer school, she could complete law school by January 1981. Mom was a full-time legal secretary, a full-time law student, and a full-time mother. She loved this period of her life. She would say, "It is a wonderful feeling to know that each day you have taken on one more step on your journey to attain a worthwhile goal."

Chicago Kent College of Law was the same school Donnie received his law degree from. It would also be the law school I would eventually attend. Mom's last year of law school was my first year of law school. Although she went at night, we were able to say we attended law school together for a short time. The path to get her J.D. (Juris Doctor degree) was not easy. It took her close to 10 years of night school to get her college diploma and her law degree. But Mom was determined to finish everything she said she was going to do.

Donnie was not a man who struggled to live by any rules but his own. The practice of law is a profession governed by adherence to strict rules. It was not a good combination. One of the first cases that would eventually result in litigation against Donnie involved a client Donnie began representing in November of 1977, right after he started his own law firm. The board members at Las Haciendas Village initially contacted him regarding an issue at their Homeowner's Association. Eventually, Donnie was retained to represent the Homeowner's Association in a dispute against the builder for faulty construction work. Donnie filed several lawsuits against parties involved in the dispute. Besides the actual filing of a bona fide lawsuit, Donnie did little on behalf of the clients. The Board of the condominium association would pay Donnie for 10 years under the belief that Donnie was aggressively pursuing the lawsuit. It would take the client almost 10 years to discover the case had been dismissed shortly after it was filed. Las Haciendas was just one example of what would become a pattern with Donnie. He loved to tell clients he could win cases. He always acted like a hero. The cowboy who saved the day. Clients loved him. His law practice continued to grow despite occasional blowups with some of his clients.

Towards the end of 1979, Donnie made the decision to merge with another real estate lawyer. Although the new law firm appeared to be successful, no one really knew what Donnie was doing when he would walk out the door of his law office. By 1980, the firm was making a name for itself in the northwest suburbs of Chicago. Both lawyers appeared to get along and worked to increase their client base during the first two years of the young business. For the first year-and-a-half, the decision to partner proved to be a good one. But as Donnie careened out of control, the partnership also began to change.

Suddenly, the 1980s were upon us. Ronald Reagan became president, the web was born, *Raging Bull* was at the movies, "Celebration" by Kool and the Gang was playing on the radio, and offices still used carbon paper to make copies. Donnie got his first cell phone in the 1980s. It came in a shoebox-sized case and cost $1,200. He was exceptionally proud of the fact that he was a pioneer in cell phone use. Donnie's law firm continued to grow even as controversy continued to swirl around his representation of certain clients.

Donnie had been part of our family for more than a decade now. No one would have guessed Donnie would still be in our lives, but he was. And he was larger than life. Although I still waited for the knock at the door and the blue lights flashing outside, no one ever came to arrest him. No angry client or scorned woman showed up with a gun to kill him, even though there were an increasing number of people who seemed to suspect Donnie might be dangerous ... or at least a very skilled liar. On the personal side, my siblings and I were no longer startled by what Donnie said or did. He was part of our family life, but we were wary of his promises and his claims. It was easier to allow him to expound on his business dealings and relationships than to confront him with his known lies. In some ways, we became complicit in his schemes as we smiled and listened to stories we knew were not true. Donnie was a necessary evil, a necessary participant to a continuing relationship with Mom.

Donnie's behavior became more bizarre during this period. There was something not normal in his behavior and reaction to situations. There was a tone in his voice and a look in his eyes that indicated the betrayal or lack of truth in what he said. The average person would not see it unless they knew him.

He started drinking more during these years, which seemed to intensify some of his grandiose beliefs and statements. It would generally start after dinner. After a few drinks, Donnie would do something almost like holding court. He would smoke, blow smoke rings in the air, laugh, and tell outrageous stories. Sometimes, he would name drop famous people he claimed to know. He had a few favorites that would come up over and over again like Michael Eisner, who would become the president of Disney in 1984. There was never any record that Donnie ever met Michael Eisner, let alone that he was friends with him, but he would talk about him as if he knew him well. Later on, he would become fascinated with Bill and Hillary Clinton, talking about Hillary and the Rose Law firm as if he worked there. He had outrageous ideas. At one point he was explaining how the United States could take all of their garbage and waste and send it on planes to Jamaica, effectively turning Jamaica into a garbage dump. He seemed to believe these ideas would actually work.

Although Donnie was not involved with these famous people, there was something almost charismatic that would occur when he talked about his relationships. People wanted to believe him, and sometimes did, all the while knowing what he said could not possibly be true. There was a certain fascination with some of the stories, and particularly the promises he made. Donnie had a way of pulling you into his world and making you believe — or at least hope — there would be some truth to his madness. Even though instincts told you he was not really friends with the president of Disney, a part of you wanted it to be true. I hoped that for once I would be wrong and that I might find myself at Disney World as the guest of the CEO. The logical part of me knew it was not going to happen.

Donnie was a master at finding some fact he could prove was true that would lend an air of legitimacy to some truly crazy story. Some years later after Mom started working with failed banks at the FDIC, his fascination with Hillary Clinton and the Whitewater deal became very focused. He understood enough about failed banks to pull you into his stories because he was knowledgeable about the banking system. He read about the Whitewater investigation and used that information when he talked about his role.

There is a book called The *Diagnostic and Statistical Manual of Mental Disorders* that I read the first time I started researching the word "sociopath." This manual listed several characteristics of a sociopath including callous unconcern for the feelings of others, failure to conform, deceitfulness, manipulativeness, impulsivity, irritability, aggressiveness, and reckless disregard for the safety of others, very low tolerance to frustration, and a low threshold for discharge of aggression including violence, consistent irresponsibility, and lack of remorse. There were also other signs of abnormal behavior including his frequent bouts with "cancer." Donnie started telling people he had cancer back in the early 1970s. Different cancer diagnoses would pop up over the years, usually corresponding with a stressful event in his life. Cancer was a way for him to avoid the consequences of his actions. It helped him avoid being held accountable for something he did.

Researching sociopathic characteristics was more unnerving than a bipolar diagnosis. If Donnie *was* a sociopath, it would mean he had no conscience. A sociopath had more tendencies toward violence, which could be very scary. The more I read about what it meant to be a sociopath, the more I equated Donnie with evil. His ability to simply pick up after Noreen died was very disturbing. There were still so many unanswered questions to what the police determined was an accident. The beautiful picture of Noreen was still tucked away in the shoebox. How could he forget her so easily? Within days of Noreen's death it was as if she never existed.

Mom and I were both law students at Chicago Kent College of law as 1979 ended and the decade of technology advancement started. It was her last year. I hardly ever saw her because she was a night student and I was a full-time day student. We talked about teachers, classes, legal writing, and taking the bar on the weekends when we would both be studying for tests. Mom was an excellent student despite her day job. She won the Moot Court Competition at Chicago Kent and maintained a B average in her classes. She continued to work as a legal secretary for the small law firm in Wood Dale, Illinois, which specialized in real estate. The principal of the firm became her mentor and also a good friend. Over time, Mom became an indispensable member of the firm. Although not yet a lawyer, clients immediately sensed she had the ability to solve their problems and found her easy to talk to about legal problems. Her confidence grew as she worked her way through law school.

The skills she developed during those years started slowly becoming the glue that held Mom together in the increasingly bizarre relationship she had with Donnie. As an almost-graduate of law school, Mom was able to help Donnie. She would draft the documents needed to keep his clients happy. She could sense a potential problem in his office and step in to try and work things out. She was the voice of reason, the beacon of light, the person in charge of damage control, as Donnie careened recklessly out of control in his career as a lawyer.

Although Donnie continued to have difficulty in his representation of clients, his law firm continued to thrive. Meanwhile, Mom's law firm started representing condominium associations and Mom would talk about its potential as a new, growing area of law. Donnie agreed and his competing firm began to solicit condominium, townhome, and homeowner's Associations in the Chicago market area. The representation of these boards became a growing area of business. To Mom's chagrin, Donnie was now competing for the business with the law firm she worked at as a secretary. It put her in a difficult position.

By the 1980s, Donnie was marketing himself as "Mr. Condo." He published articles on representing condo associations in the Chicago Daily Law Bulletin and began writing several small instructional books for condominium board members. He started teaching a class at the local junior college for board members. Donnie loved the condominium business. Eventually, he would represent several-hundred condominium associations, each with its own board. His car license plate said "MR CONDO." He drove around with his weird Texas outfits in his small car with the fancy license plates. He was surrounded by admirers. Many of the boards were controlled by women and he spent evenings at dinner with his clients. These boards were an audience for Mr. Condo. He could go out at night — "with clients," "at a meeting," and "client dinners." Probably, if she thought hard, Mom would have realized the freedom Donnie exercised might not be the best thing for their marriage. But with work, school, and everything else, she just looked the other way.

Mom's law school commencement ceremony was scheduled for January 1981. She was getting ready to take the Illinois Bar exam in the spring. All of us were planning a large family party to celebrate Mom's graduation from law school. She finally was achieving her goal. It took her 10 years of night classes, but she obtained her college diploma and now a law degree. It was quite an accomplishment and everyone wanted to be part of the celebration.

Not surprisingly, just as Mom began to study for her bar exam, an incident occurred that caught us unprepared. Eventually, we would come to realize a lot of these "incidents" happened when the attention was on another family member and not on Donnie. Mom's graduation from law school clearly fell into that category. Somehow, Donnie always pulled the attention right back to himself.

In early January 1981, right after the holidays, Donnie and Mom took a short trip to attend a condo conference out of town. Glory was left at home to feed the cats and take care of the house. On January 17, I had just gotten into bed, when the telephone rang. It was Glory.

"There's someone in the house," she whispered. "I can hear them walking around upstairs."

"Call 911!" I exclaimed. "Right now. Don't wait!"

"It sounds like a woman," Glory retorted. "She's wearing high heels. I'm going to go see who is upstairs."

Although I tried to talk her out of it, Glory crept quietly up the basement stairs and came face to face with a woman in a fur coat standing in the kitchen.

"Are you the maid?" the startled woman demanded.

"No, I am not the maid. Who are you?" Glory sassily responded.

"I have a right to be here," the woman answered. I can hear voices in the background as I waited for Glory to return to the phone.

"You will never guess who it is," she said when she returned to the phone. I can only describe her voice as gleeful. "Guess," she said again. "Here, listen … "

In the background, I could hear someone crying. Loudly.

"It can't be true," I heard the sobbing woman say.

"Glory, put the phone back to your ear! Who is there?" I demand. "Who is crying?"

Glory is laughing. I can hear it in her voice.

"It's Donnie's fiancée," she finally said. "*It's Donnie's fiancée!* He actually got engaged!"

Glory tried to comfort the woman by telling her, "Don't feel bad, he does this all the time." This didn't help the distressed woman or the situation.

It was hard to believe Glory had it right as the story finally started spilling out. It turned out this woman, was one of Donnie's clients. Not content to simply have an affair, Donnie actually proposed marriage to the poor woman. She had no idea Donnie was living with Mom. A large diamond engagement ring was on her finger. "Probably, a cubic zirconia diamond," Cindy would later say.

Donnie and his "finance" had been planning a relatively large wedding. Donnie met her friends and relatives. Donnie told her he was remodeling his house so she would have a nice place to live after they got married. It gave him a reason to never take her there. He told her truthfully that he was a widower, but neglected to mention the woman he was living with was very much alive.

Justifiably, the woman was distraught and couldn't believe Donnie had lied. She finally gathered herself together and left the house, but she had left us with one very big problem. Cindy, Glory, and I spent hours trying to decide whether to tell Mom about the fiancée. She was studying for her bar exam in two weeks. The timing was terrible to tell her that Donnie was planning to get married.

We had become enablers for Donnie over the years. Maybe the correct word is *codependents*. It was inevitable that Mom would stay with Donnie. So what value does the truth bring to the situation? Mom would be miserable. All of her work and dedication would be minimized because we would all be talking about Donnie.

The path became evident; revealing the truth about the fiancée was the only answer. It had to be done. The decision was made to confront Donnie first.

On Monday morning, I headed to Donnie's law office to ask him how he could become engaged while he was married to another person. As I pulled into the parking lot, I noted his car was in its assigned parking space.

"I need to talk to Donnie," I told his secretary. She disappeared into the back offices for a minute and came back to announce, "Donnie can't see you now; he is with one of his clients." As she spoke those words, another lawyer came from the back and I slipped behind him and headed down the hall, past the oblivious secretary.

Donnie's law office was decorated in his usual loud Texas style. He had two rifles mounted on the wall behind his desk. He had a bear head and a deer head mounted on the wall. There were various other stuffed animals, including stuffed armadillos, scattered around the office. There was also a cedar-lined steam room that Donnie had added to the bathroom that adjoined his office. This is where he hid as he heard my voice outside his door. He locked the door behind him and sat in the empty cedar steam room, hoping I wouldn't find him.

"Are you engaged?" I yelled as I pounded on the door. The flashback is not lost on me; several years earlier, I was pounding on the bedroom door of our home yelling, "Are you getting married?" right before Donnie married Noreen.

"I'm telling Mom!" I finally yelled before I turned to leave past the startled secretary.

So what would have happened if Glory had not stumbled into the fiance? Would Mom again have to find out the hard way that Donnie went off and married someone else? Donnie never knew how to extricate himself as he transitioned from one woman to the next. But he also never went down without a fight. Most people, when clearly cornered, would throw their hands up and cry, apologize, feel bad, admit to a terrible mistake, and try to move on. Not Donnie. There was no admitting an affair, let alone a fiancée. No remorse, no tears, no despair, no conflicted emotions. Nothing. Just lies.

"There is no fiancée," he adamantly exclaimed later. He questioned Glory, getting a description of the woman as if he didn't already know who she was. "It's a client," he finally said. A crazy client he was representing.

We have been here before.

We were the handlers charged with searching out the truth. Cindy and I decided to follow him, switching cars and making notes. We tracked him to an apartment in Mount Prospect where I verified the name on the mailbox. But an address and a name were still not enough for us. Cindy searched the house, his briefcase, and the files he left in the back seat of the car to try and make sense of what he claimed and brace for the next inevitable problem. We kept files on what we knew and made notes as we listened to his lies. We wanted to be sure we would not be caught by surprise by anything Donnie Rudd did.

On January 23, Mom received a subpoena from Donnie and a check for $30. Mom threw both on the kitchen table yelling all the while to Donnie that she was not going to appear in court. I looked at the paperwork and slipped them off the table. I swiftly deposited them into the shoebox in the corner of my closet. The subpoena stated:

> *"You are commanded to appear to testify before Judge Holzer on January 27 and bring the following:*
> *Any and all records and all notes relating to conversations between your daughter, Glory Hart, and an unnamed woman at your home on January 17, 1981, between the hours of 7:30 pm and midnight. You are to produce a list of all expenses incurred by you as a result thereof and the names and addresses of all witnesses to the discussion...."*

Donnie claimed he filed a petition for a temporary restraining order against the supposed "crazy client." He was papering his story with the law to give it an air of authenticity.

On January 27, he picked up Glory from the house and told her she was going to court as a witness. She would need to identify the woman she saw at the house. Glory rode to the downtown courthouse with Donnie, but he told her to wait outside. Donnie did not have her enter the court, instead, he asked her to look through the glass doors and see if she could identify the woman she saw at the house.

Glory was not sure, but thought she saw the woman in the courtroom. Donnie left the courthouse with a court order stamped by Judge Holzer stating the defendant "is permanently enjoined and restrained from talking to Plaintiff's family and from going near the home of Plaintiff."

Donnie was smug. He believed the court order would convince Mom that he did not have a personal relationship with this woman. We spent the next few days following him as he went back and forth between home, his law office, and the home of his fiancée. We got her address and her phone number, and I checked the court file. Although Donnie had a stamped order, there was no original order signed by the judge in that file. There was no restraining order. Donnie had lied regarding the court proceedings.

However, the fiancée was real, the engagement was real, and the affair was real. Mom was understandably devastated. She was getting ready to take the bar exam and this should have been a time of excitement and achievement for her. Reluctantly, she agreed that a separation from Donnie might be the right thing to do.

Cindy and I moved quickly. A local real estate broker located a vacant townhome near Mom's work. The townhome could be bought quickly on contract. Mom half-heartedly signed the papers and began preparation for the move. Everyone held their collective breath wondering if this time Mom could truly extricate herself from Donnie. The decision was made to move

Mom out of the Barrington Square townhouse she shared with Donnie and into the Wood Dale condo while he was at work. He would not know of the move until he returned home to find Mom gone. No one wanted a confrontation with Donnie. There were planning sessions, stealthy late night meetings, and detailed arrangements that were made to make the move. Every detail was planned and a contingent of friends and supporters agreed to make a frantic one-day move to try and release Mom from Donnie's grip (an event that would eerily be repeated several years later).

The day of the move came quickly. We waited at a local doughnut shop for the signal that Donnie had left the house before we'd move in. Each person was assigned a list and a room to pack Mom's personal belongings. She had made the decision to leave all of the furniture, artwork, and property of any value to reduce any possible trouble with Donnie. But there were a significant number of client files, paperwork, and pictures that Mom didn't feel she could leave behind. The move would be daunting.

At first, the move was organized and followed the prescribed plan. By 3:00, it was apparent that it would be difficult to be done before 5:00. Mom's clothes were thrown into black garbage bags in order to allow more efficiency in the small truck we rented to complete the move. At 4:45, just as planned, we rolled out of the parking lot on the way to the new condo. By 10:00, everything was unloaded and we were quickly unpacking, trying to make Mom feel at home in her new house.

Mom was unable to help. She sat in a chair with her sunglasses on to hide her eyes. It's as if she didn't want us to see inside of her. Still, we were hopeful as we bought pots and pans and little flowerpots to try and make the condo comfortable. We didn't know how long it would take Donnie to find Mom, but we figured we had a day, maybe two, at the most.

Donnie was out of control when he found out Mom moved out. He called her at her job every 15 minutes. He called me. At first, it almost looked like the move to Wood Dale would stick. At the same time, we knew Donnie called her constantly. He left notes, he followed her, and he sat outside her house. He called and left a message on her answering machine telling her "Purr" had died. Purr was Mom's beloved cat. Still, Mom seemed to be holding firm.

Donnie was professing his undying love for Mom at the same time he was preparing to make sure Mom would get nothing if she left him. He inventoried their assets and methodically began transferring them into the name of his friends. He drew up contracts, filed deeds, and did everything possible to ensure Mom would not receive anything if she left him. Mom had no idea Donnie was willing to risk everything to make sure she got nothing.

We would take turns cooking meals and making sure Mom was never alone. We made schedules and did everything we could to reinforce the positive nature of the move. We treated her like she had an addiction. We attempted to purge her life of Donnie the same way that the family of alcoholics attempts to purge their home of all temptations, dumping liquor down the sink. We tried desperately to intercept the notes, take her out of the house, and not allow her to be alone as she struggled to get through each day without him.

Six weeks after the move, I stopped at the store to buy some groceries for Mom. I had taken to dropping things off once or twice a week on my way home from work. I opened the door to the condo and smelled cigarette smoke. I knew he was there. I didn't say anything. I set the groceries on the table and walked out. I got into the car and drove towards the entrance of Mom's subdivision, finally pulling to the curb about three blocks from her condo. I put my head on the steering wheel and wept bitterly for Mom, for my family, and for myself. I thought of my poor father and how he must have felt that day almost 10 years ago when Mom did not answer his phone call and he knew he lost her again to Donnie.

Within days, Mom moved back in with Donnie, leaving the Wood Dale condo empty. Despite everything we tried to do, Donnie continued to be in our lives. He and Mom returned to the status quo that existed before the discovery of his affair. However, Donnie's "friends" did not have the same desire to give up what transpired during those few weeks. No one wanted to return Donnie's assets, which were transferred during the battle between Donnie and Mom. Eventually, Donnie had to tell Mom that all of their assets were gone. Mom and Donnie were effectively broke. All of the real estate, buildings, and savings now belonged to someone else. Mom was furious. The war regarding the lost assets would rage for years.

During this time, Donnie's law practice dissolved and Donnie returned to practicing law by himself. Once again, the firm of Rudd and Associates was resurrected and Mr. Condo began to work to direct his former clients to his new firm. Donnie would practice law under this name for approximately five years.

I graduated from law school in 1983 and started practicing law at a small firm on Michigan Avenue in Chicago. Jack met and married his wife in 1984 while still in the Navy. I met and married my husband, Ron, in 1986. Glory met and married her husband, Chris, in 1987. Cindy's first marriage ended quickly and she (now divorced) met her future husband, John, in 1986. All of us had new families. There was an acceptance of the fact that nothing could be done about Donnie. There was nothing Donnie did that seemed to convince Mom to let him go. At least the four of us kids felt we would be able to put some distance between us and the Donnie problems as we started our new families.

We were wrong.

CHAPTER THIRTEEN
Legal Shenanigans

"The law, my boy, puts us into everything.
It's the ultimate backstage pass.
It's the new priesthood, baby!"

— Al Pacino's character, John Milton (a.k.a Satan), in *The Devil's Advocate*

Donnie was becoming an increasingly popular lawyer even though the details of the law bored him. He was charming in an offbeat, eccentric type of way. With his cowboy boots and Texas drawl, he had the appearance of a Texas gunslinger that appealed to his Midwest audience. Donnie was becoming a star in the field of representing condominium associations. It allowed him to do what he did best — talk about himself. As good as Donnie was with marketing, he failed miserably at handling the actual *details* required in the field of law. He did not have the patience to work through the details of a case, write briefs, research issues, or perform the type of analysis that usually typified a very good attorney. Young attorneys he employed at his firm performed these details. Donnie focused the majority of his time on selling himself. He would attend condo meetings and talk to condominium boards almost every night. He taught condominium classes at Harper College during the evenings. He would tell potential clients what they wanted to hear. Donnie talked about who he knew and what he would do for you.

Donnie's unabashed opinion of his own abilities sold audiences on his skills as an attorney. He was not afraid to make promises as to what he could do for a client. He was confident, even arrogant, about what he could accomplish. Unlike the tempered presentations of many attorneys, Donnie told clients they were right and would win. He didn't feel it necessary to stay within the bounds of normal attorney/client relationships, either. He supported clients, established personal relationships with many, and told them everything they wanted to hear. He told his clients they were smart, inventive, and that they would be rich one day. Donnie's clients loved him much the same way many women did. But it seemed when things started to go bad, he would lose control over multiple things at the same time. It would leave the impression there were periodic blowups in his business career when the reality was that there were always problems.

Mom made an alarming discovery in the early 1980s. Donnie was paying clients their "award money" rather than admit he did not win their case. In fact, in some instances, he was telling clients he had won their case even though he never even filed the case. The discovery came after Mom found several checks written to Donnie's clients from her personal checking account. Apparently, Donnie did not have sufficient funds in his firm's bank account. Once he told a client he won their case and a judgment was entered, the natural expectation was that money was coming. Rather than admitting he had not won, Donnie started paying the client the amount of the purported "settlement." Most of the initial checks were small. A $2,000 check here, a $5,000 check there. Mom was furious that Donnie was using their joint funds in this way but eventually decided these small checks were probably a good price to prevent malpractice lawsuits. Although the checks were generally less than $5,000 and seemed to be intermittent, Mom was still justifiably concerned.

She started to strategize on ways to gain a little more control over Donnie's business dealings. She encouraged Donnie to take on a partner in the law firm. She hoped that a partner might be able to control some of the issues that were arising with these clients.

In late 1985, Donnie finally agreed to take on a partner in Rudd and Associates. A young associate who had already been working at the firm for several years was chosen. The lawyer had started to build up a substantial number of condominium clients and was a logical choice for partner. Donnie's new partner was an excellent businessman, and in early 1986 he began looking for larger space that would accommodate the growing firm. The firm made a substantial investment in a brand new office suite located near Woodfield Mall, one of the nation's largest, in Schaumburg, Illinois. The design for the space went on for more than six months. Mahogany desks, workspaces, and moldings set the tone for the law firm that both partners were sure would have significant growth over the upcoming years. The new space was scheduled to be completed by the end of 1986.

What Donnie's new partner did not know was that Donnie had a growing number of clients that he was representing "offline" from the firm's condominium practice. These clients were becoming increasingly frustrated with Donnie's inability to deliver on promises and now became part of the new firm's client base. The continued success of the firm was going to be severely challenged as these clients began looking for answers and threatening to go public with their complaints. Several of them had reached their boiling point, and it was all leading to a spectacular business blowup in late 1986.

Clients wanted to believe Donnie. Even when faced with almost indisputable evidence that he was not what he said he was, clients tended to hold onto the hope that he would do what he said. Donnie's clients believed in him much the same way his various women did. Donnie was willing to make promises he would deliver on things he absolutely knew he could not do.

For instance, who would tell a client he won their case and that a check for millions of dollars was in the mail, when no case was even filed? Who would get engaged to a woman without telling her that he was already married? Donnie would. It is impossible to explain, but Donnie seemed to have unlimited power over his relationships.

Donnie was particularly fond of representing smart, powerful men. The smarter the client, the easier it was for Donnie to convince them that he would be the best attorney to handle a difficult case. Smart clients were easy to fool because there was no rational reason for Donnie to lie. Smart men did not see it coming. Donnie didn't receive anything for the lie. If the client really never got the million-dollar check, Donnie could not get his percentage of the settlement. Donnie's lies had nothing to do with money. It was hard for smart, powerful people to understand him because it was not all about the money. There was another element involved in Donnie's representation that was not rational, logical, or reasonable.

In June of 1981, shortly after reopening Rudd and Associates, Donnie agreed to represent a client named Joseph related to a contract dispute with a company. The dispute involved an agreement for the development and patent of an electronic pulsimeter. However, the company was dissolved in December just a couple of months after Donnie filed the lawsuit. In 1983, Donnie entered a judgment in the amount of $40,000 in favor of Joseph. However, the order provided that the judgment could only be satisfied through assets of the corporation, which no longer existed in 1983. None of the assets formerly owned by the corporation or distributed as part of the dissolution of the company could be used to pay Joseph for his judgment. The agreement also provided that Joseph could not pursue the individual defendants or any assets that had been transferred to them as part of the dissolution of the corporation. Donnie may have entered judgment on the case, but it was a worthless judgment and guaranteed Joseph would never receive a dime on the claim.

Donnie was able to tell his client he won a judgment and created the perception he did what he said he was going to do. The Joseph case was almost five years old and still had not seen any resolution. He was becoming increasingly perturbed with Donnie just as a new partner entered into the partnership.

At the same time Joseph was trying to collect his money on the invalid, uncollectable judgment, Donnie started to represent a group of clients in regard to a failed real estate transaction. The Whitehall was a luxury condominium project that got underway in 1986. The $17 million development involved converting a former Franciscan seminary into luxury condominiums. It was located in the upscale community of Oak Brook, Illinois. The initial developer, Milton Zic, purchased the property from the Franciscan Order for more than a $1 million and financed the construction through First South Bank, an Arkansas Savings and Loan bank. In 1986, First South Bank failed like many other banks as part of the growing savings and loan crisis that swept across the nation. Ultimately, a $25 million lawsuit was filed against First South and the Federal Savings and Loan Insurance Corporation, the Federal Deposit Insurance Corporation, and the Resolution Trust Corporation. The foreclosure of the construction loan and the failure of the bank resulted in the bankruptcy of the Whitehall development entities.

Multiple investors invested in the proposed condominium property, including several high-profile Chicago businessmen such as John, the former officer of a large department store. Donnie agreed to represent this group of investors in a lawsuit against First South and the failed Whitehall development. Donnie's expertise and reputation in the condominium field probably was a factor in the investor's use of a small firm rather than the typical large legal firms routinely used by well-known businessmen. Lawsuits are inherently risky business. Even the best cases can go south quickly. Lawsuits that involve multiple businesses, government entities, bankruptcies, and a group of monks are a gamble at best. The court file reflects that Donnie filed a complaint on behalf of the businessmen in 1986.

Undaunted by the bankruptcies and unable to tell his admiring crowd of high-profile clients that the lawsuit was a loser, Donnie went ahead and filed the Motion for Summary Judgment without serving the motion on any of the named defendants. At this time, court records were not electronic. A lot of court proceedings were handled manually by writing orders and handing them to the court clerk who sat next to the judge. The original order was generally retained by the clerk and entered into the court file. It was relatively easy to step up to the clerk, get your orders stamped, but fail to leave the original in the box sitting on the corner of the clerk's desk. By all accounts, this was what happened with the Whitehall case. Donnie entered an order granting judgment on behalf of his clients against the defendants who had not been served and who were protected by the bankruptcy court.

For almost two years, Donnie put off Joseph by claiming he was seeking to collect on the judgment. By 1986, Joseph was becoming increasingly insistent regarding his case. Donnie offered to purchase the worthless judgment from him for $29,000 and gave him an initial payment of $4,000. The problem was that Donnie did not have the additional $25,000 he promised. Joseph became increasingly impatient waiting for his money from Donnie. At the same time, pressure from the Whitehall clients was also building. Donnie's representations to both Joseph and the Whitehall group could not be fulfilled. Donnie started avoiding Joseph, but chose to handle the more savvy Whitehall clients in a different way.

Donnie reported to his clients that he won the Whitehall

lawsuit. He gave them a copy of the order granting summary judgment and advised them that he had a judgment of more than a million dollars entered on behalf of the fellow plaintiffs. It was impossible for Donnie's clients to know that Donnie was not telling the truth. He had not won a Motion for Summary Judgment and no judgment for monetary damages was actually entered. Donnie never served the defendants. There was no record of proper service in the court file. Even if Donnie had properly served the complaint, the bankruptcy filings by the various entities involved in the development would have prevented proceedings in the state court.

It was not surprising that the Whitehall clients believed that they would be able to collect on the judgment. Unlike many of the previous cases where Donnie had entered his Motion for Summary Judgment and Monetary Judgment order, there was no way Mom and Donnie could cover up his deception by simply paying. No one had the million dollars necessary to satisfy the nonexistent judgment. The Whitehall case was becoming increasingly problematic for Donnie as he struggled to give reason after reason for the delay in collecting funds. At the same time, Joseph initiated a collection action against Donnie to collect the balance of *his* judgment that Donnie had purchased to hide the fact that the original judgment was unenforceable.

At some point, the Whitehall investors became suspicious. At first, the thought was that Donnie stole the million-dollar judgment he claimed to have received. What other reason could there be for the delay in forwarding the money? No one thought to check if there ever was a valid Judgment entered. Donnie told them time and time again the check would be delivered. At some point, one of the investors retained a lawyer and the court file was checked. Donnie's jig was up on the Whitehall lie.

The retribution was swift. There was no more telling the

group the check was in the mail. The clients knew that Donnie lied and that the lie was big. There would be no recovery of their investments. The funny thing is if Donnie could have simply said the bankruptcy terminated the claims and any monetary damages would not be recoverable, the clients would not have been happy but they might not have felt that their own attorney had personally victimized them.

All of the Whitehall investor's anger, venom, and resources turned from fighting Whitehall and their developers to fighting Donnie. For a second time, they had been duped in regard to the purchase of this property. The Whitehall clients were not only angry, they were looking for retribution.

At the same time, the board of the Las Haciendas condominium association decided to get a second opinion on the lawsuit and the slow progress in their case. This was one of the first cases that Donnie filed after he began his own practice. The new litigators informed Las Haciendas the lawsuit filed by Donnie in 1977 was dismissed for want of prosecution because Donnie failed to appear at the hearing. Donnie had not appeared at the court for the trial.

Periodically, something like this happens. You can file a motion to vacate the dismissal within 30 days. Donnie filed the vacate motion on day 31 and it was denied. The review by the new attorneys found there were three dismissals for want of prosecution. Three times Donnie did not show up to court for the case. The lawsuits he filed against certain individuals were not served properly and in some cases were the wrong individuals. Donnie released liability to some of the defendants in the case without the consent of Las Haciendas. At some point, Donnie told the Board he obtained a judgment for $4,024,575. However, the file reflected that the judgment was obtained against the wrong party resulting in the judgment being vacated. The final allegation was one of failing to diligently pursue discovery and obtain depositions, answers to interrogatories, and production of documents. The angry board of directors paid Donnie for work that was not performed over a 10-year period of time. Donnie received notice that the Board would be filing a lawsuit against him for his mishandling of the case.

Joseph, the Whitehall investors, and the board from the Las Hacienda condominium association all commenced legal proceedings against Donnie in late 1986. While Donnie's law partner was happily putting the finishing touches on the new office design, Donnie was trying to do damage control and keep knowledge of the lawsuits from everyone including his partner. Once again, Donnie was coming to the proverbial fork in the road. He was now facing litigation on multiple fronts. He was backed into a corner and had to tell Mom he was in trouble. Mom was appalled but had built up a certain stress tolerance to these issues over the years. After dealing with a multiplicity of Donnie's client problems, she was no longer shocked by what he had done.

Mom summoned me to help her figure a way out of the storm of angry clients. "We need to slow down all of these court proceedings while I figure out what needs to be done," Mom said. She pulled the court files and had all of Donnie's correspondence and pleadings spread out on the dining room table. Donnie sat at the other end of the table with a glass of Tia Maria sitting in front of him. He listened as Mom explained to me what she had been able to figure out from the various lawsuits.

"He told them he entered judgment for more than $1 million dollars," she said, as she pulled a copy of the Order of Judgment from Donnie's file. "One million dollars," she said again. She looked pale as she repeated the amount Donnie promised he would recover for the Whitehall investors.

"Donnie," I asked, "Why would you do this? Where were you going to get the $1 million dollars to pay them? You don't have that type of money. What were you thinking?" Donnie thought about the question before answering.

"They are assholes," was all he was able to come up with as he took a puff from his cigarette and blew a smoke ring. He seemed calm and was remarkably uninvolved in the discussion of how to slow down the noose that was slowly tightening around his neck.

"Does anyone from your firm know about this?" I asked him. I knew Donnie's law partner was not going to be happy Donnie had entered those court orders in the name of their law firm.

"No one knows," he said curtly.

"If I were you," I told him, "I would be more afraid of your partner than of the Whitehall clients."

After a few minutes, he finally asked, "What should I do?"

"Get some help!" I responded. "This isn't normal." It was the only thing I could think of.

Mom was more deliberative. "I need to find a lawyer," she finally said.

"Does he need a criminal attorney?" I asked.

"I need a lawyer for *me*," she replied. "I don't know what to do about him." Mom was finally starting to understand the enormity of this new situation.

The next morning, Donnie checked into the local hospital claiming he was seriously ill. He was admitted for observation. He told the nurse's station he wanted no calls. This effectively cut him off from his clients, his partner, and us. It gave us little time to figure out what to do with the increasing mob of angry clients and business associates waiting to confront him. With Donnie not answering his phone or going to his office, the clients would be looking for someone else to talk to. That person would be Mom or the lawyers at his firm. It meant that someone needed to tell Donnie's partner that the firm was in serious trouble.

Donnie's partner was horrified. Donnie was unreachable, and was left at the office to answer the phone calls from the angry

Whitehall clients. The fact Donnie filed the fraudulent court order in the name of his law firm meant that his partner was jointly responsible for the misrepresentations made by Donnie. Mom continued to run interference while she pondered the next step.

Donnie's partner called Mom and told her that he was dissolving the partnership and suing Donnie for his half of the liabilities, including the increasing number of malpractice claims. The partner's business relationship ceased that day. Donnie never talked directly to his partner again. Any questions were routed through Mom or her attorney.

Donnie's partner never moved into the brand new, professionally designed suite of offices. When the office was complete, Donnie moved in alone. The lease included a concession for one year of rent. Donnie knew that he could move in and would not be responsible for paying any rent for one year. It gave Mom a year to figure out exactly what Donnie had done and what the damages would be. Donnie quietly slipped back into the role of practicing attorney.

Over the next few months, the litigants started lining up for monetary damages from Donnie. At this point in time, he and Mom did not have significant assets, but they did have the townhomes and a couple of pieces of real estate. Mom had now been pushed into a corner. She would lose everything.

In early 1987, Mom spoke the words I never thought I'd hear.

"Lori, I think I need to divorce Donnie. If I don't, I am going to be responsible for his debts."

"Are you really divorcing him or just divorcing him because he is being sued?" I asked, after letting the reality of the situation slowly sink in. "You can't just divorce him to avoid the debts. You have to really *want* to divorce him. To leave him. To get him out of your life."

I knew it was unlikely Mom would really divorce

Donnie and move on with her life. But the pressure from Donnie's actions seemed to have been taking its toll on her.

"I don't want to be married to him. So the divorce would be real," she responded.

"Do you want to be rid of him or do you want to be with him but not be married to him?"

I was trying to find out the truth, which was always difficult when dealing with Donnie and Mom.

"I am thinking it would easier to not be with him if I am divorced," she answered carefully. I wasn't sure exactly what that meant, but there seemed to be an air of truthfulness in her response. It was easier to understand she wanted to divorce Donnie than why she would stay with him.

Ultimately, Mom decided the best course of action would be a divorce and a subsequent bankruptcy filing by Donnie. The filing of the bankruptcy would stop the pending legal cases by effectively wiping out the monetary damages. Although there might still be a risk for the fraud claims, it seemed unlikely the majority of the plaintiffs would continue their cases.

"If you are going to divorce him," I told her, "you better get yourself a good divorce attorney *and* a good bankruptcy attorney."

Mom decided to wait and see what the fallout would be from the various litigations before she decided how to handle her personal liability. In the meantime, she reincorporated Donnie as a professional corporation and he continued to represent condominium associations under a different legal entity. The hope was that the problems would stay with his previous partnerships.

But there was more to come.

In the spring of 1988, Donnie's business troubles and deceptions went public. The article appearing in the May 6, 1988 edition of the *Chicago Sun-Times* was brutal. The headline was "Is Mr. Condo Really Mr. Con?" It stated that:

> *The lawyer known to many Chicagoland condominium associations as "Mr. Condo" apparently has left some prominent clients feeling like they were conned.*
> *Donnie Rudd, one of the state's best-known lawyers in the area of condominium law, is being sued for allegedly misleading would-be condominium owners who hired him to recoup the down payments they lost when the luxurious Whitehall Park condo development in Oak Brook failed in mid-1986.*
>
> *Rudd promised to get their money back and more. He said he could obtain punitive damages of $25 million from developers Milton Zic and Sidney Weniger and First South, a failed Arkansas savings and loan.*

The reporter went on to recount the allegations made by the Whitehall investors. It appeared Donnie was not going to get away from some measure of accountability for this group of problems.

In 1988, Mom got a divorce lawyer and initiated the divorce proceedings against Donnie. The divorce was granted on September 14, 1988. Mom was given the majority of the real estate in release of her claim for alimony and maintenance and his interest in his law firm.

Shortly thereafter, Donnie initiated bankruptcy proceedings. The listing of claims on the bankruptcy petition included the $7 million claim by the Whitehall investors, the claim by his law partners, the Las Hacienda Association and the $25,000 judgment entered by his former client, Joseph. Ultimately, Donnie's debts were discharged in bankruptcy and Donnie was free to rebuild his financial position. The Whitehall clients, Joseph, and the former law partner walked away with no chance of financial recovery from Donnie.

The Bankruptcy proceedings stopped the Whitehall investor's litigation, but it did not stop the Illinois Attorney Registration and Disciplinary Commission (ARDC) from proceeding with the multiple claims filed against Donnie. ARDC is responsible for the ethical practices of attorneys. If your attorney does something unethical, you can file a report with ARDC and they will investigate. They have the power to take away the law license of an attorney who is proven to be involved in unethical practices. Joseph, Whitehall, and Las Hacienda — all of Donnie's misdeeds — came together in one very large ARDC claim. If they could not get a judgment against Donnie, they were going to try and get his license to practice law pulled. These were smart, strong businessmen who had been wronged. Donnie checked himself into the local mental hospital as the ARDC commenced their investigation and asked him to appear to give a statement.

Mom worked ferociously to defend Donnie at the hearings. For the first time, Donnie went to visit a psychiatrist and received an official diagnosis: manic-depressive disorder. He started on medication and was ultimately pronounced temporarily "cured" by his doctors. Donnie's mini medical breakdown was his defense at the ARDC hearing. Much to Mom's delight, the Commission decided to take no action against Donnie. However, they did give him a strong admonition that any future similar misconduct would result in the revocation of his license to practice law.

Astonishingly, Donnie would once again walk away virtually unscathed from the tsunami of destruction he'd created. Like Nero, who continued to play his violin as Rome burned, Donnie continued to practice law, live with Mom, and had sufficient income to live a good life. And although there was hope the divorce would actually stick, it was not surprising that Mom continued to live with Donnie. "Baby steps," was all she would say. Once again, Donnie appeared to have broken free of almost certain ruin. He was financially clear of all claims of wrongdoing. He extricated himself from several lawsuits. The clients he had misrepresented were left without any legal recourse. He was divorced from Mom and free from his law partnerships. The office lease was no longer a liability and Donnie was essentially debt free with a license to practice law. He was free to start again as Mr. Condo.

Contrary to dire predictions, the "Is Mr. Condo Really Mr. Con?" news article in the *Sun-Times* had no significant effect on his ability to attract clients. His charm, promises, and his focus on women board members was a winning combination in the condominium law business. Donnie took up where he had left off with both his clients and his women. Mr. Condo was back in business … at least until another claim arose. The dismissal order of the ARDC case was clear: If Donnie came back with another similar charge, all of the dismissed charges would be reinstated. Donnie would never be able to practice law again. All he had to do was *not* lie to any client, *not* manufacture any court orders, and file *all* of his cases in a timely manner. It should have been easy.

But then, remember, we are talking about Donnie Rudd, the man without a conscience. The man never held accountable for his actions. All we could do was shake our heads and wait for the next round of trouble.

It was only a matter of time.

CHAPTER FOURTEEN
The Girlfriend

Donnie was not a man who thought about consequences. He was impulsive, enjoyed risk taking, and did not seem to fear being held accountable. As soon as the order dismissing the ARDC charges was entered, he stopped seeing the psychiatrist and quit taking his medication. He was willing to portray himself as a mentally troubled man only if it engendered the pity that was required to manipulate the system. Without any further need to manipulate, there was no longer any need to continue to seek help for his "problems." The swiftness of his actions following the ARDC dismissal was a statement regarding his use of the mental health system. It was just a tool to get to where he wanted to go. He beat the system. He was the winner. Donnie was on a roll.

In some ways, the dismissal of the disciplinary charges made him more energetic. He truly felt invincible. He appeared to be above the rules and the law. He was back in the business of practicing law. He slowly began to recover from the publicity and news coverage of the Whitehall disaster, and his recent misdeeds quickly faded into the past.

Mom knew Donnie continued to have affairs throughout the course of her marriage. He was impulsive and made no attempt to be monogamous. He was a serial philanderer and followed a certain pattern with his outside women. Most of Donnie's women were clients. Again, the freedom associated with his lack of moral constraints left few boundaries when it came to looking to satisfy his personal desires. His affairs were not casual liaisons or one-night stands. Donnie delved into affairs with a stream of flattery, love notes, poems, and focus that made women think that the relationships were truly special. He had no difficulty seducing women who found him interesting and different and they were flattered at the attention they received from him. He never hesitated to use lies to add to the allure of his charm. He would forge bank statements to convince women he was wealthy. He would talk about deals that were about to close that would bring him immeasurable wealth. He lied about serving in the military, portraying himself as a war hero and wounded veteran. He would show pictures of a kitten he claimed he was nursing back to health. He would portray himself as a widower without mentioning his subsequent remarriage. There was no hook Donnie would not use to break down the defenses of a target. Every woman Donnie bedded felt she was experiencing true love for the first time in her life. The fact he was married was immaterial to his relationships with these women.

Mom continued to look the other way even though she found increasing evidence of his indiscretions. At first, she found it extremely painful to know he was involved with other women. Eventually, she seemed to accept it as a character flaw that was beyond his control. It became less personal when she dealt with it as a defect. Mom had decided she would stay with Donnie. Nothing seemed to provide any hope that his actions would push her to remove him from our lives.

One of the cases that Donnie undertook was a case involving structural defects at a condominium called Astor Towers. The case would ultimately be argued before the Supreme Court of Illinois. Although the firm would ultimately lose the case, Donnie became friendly with a woman who was also involved in the case. Once again, his business and personal life became intertwined. He began another affair that would once again impact our lives. Initially, Mom treated his relationship as another aberration that would pass. But this girlfriend was emboldened to try and encourage dissolution of Mom's relationship in a move that would allow her to marry Donnie. Although Mom was always devastated when she had to deal directly with one of Donnie's affairs, she also became more adept at handling them.

Unlike many of Donnie's girlfriends who had no idea Donnie was living with Mom, Donnie's newest relationship was fully informed. This woman was the executive director of a statewide nonprofit. She sponsored educational seminars for condominium boards and occasionally worked with Mom. Donnie was an occasional featured speaker for her nonprofit association. Mom recognized the warning signs as Donnie talked frequently about the woman. There were numerous conversations all of which ended with Donnie vehemently denying any involvement with her on a personal basis. Mom held on tighter to Donnie, demanding to know where he was, calling him more frequently, and checking up on him. Donnie lied with ease and continued to see his newest conquest more frequently. But like most affairs, this one was reaching a boiling point.

Emboldened by Donnie's promises to leave Mom, the Girlfriend decided to give him a push in the right direction. Mom was upstairs in her bed sleeping and Donnie was watching television in the living room when the front door opened. The Girlfriend marched upstairs to the bedroom where Mom was asleep. Mom was less than enthusiastic to be woken up by a woman sitting on the edge of her bed talking to her about Donnie. What really angered her was that the woman was all dressed up and wearing makeup. The woman had an unfair advantage coming in all dressed up like this while Mom was in her old frayed nightgown.

"Dee," she said insensitively using Mom's nickname,

"Donnie loves me. You need to let him go." She crossed her legs as she sat on the edge of the bed impatiently tapping her booted foot on the floor. Mom's response was brutal. She told her exactly what it meant to be married to Donnie. The affairs, the lies, and the legal problems. Finally, she became irate, yelling for the girlfriend to leave the bedroom. Both women headed down the stairs yelling and trading profanities. Donnie retreated to the bathroom with his cigarette and his Tia Maria. He locked the door behind him, determined not to get involved with the two women battling in his house. The girlfriend began to pound on the bathroom door demanding Donnie come out and tell everyone the truth about how he felt. There was no answer behind the locked door. Donnie, invariably sitting on the edge of the bathtub with his drink and a cigarette, the chaos and emotions destined to stay with those around him.

Mom was determined to confront Donnie and used a bobby pin to unlock the bathroom door. Donnie threatened to kill himself by drinking a bottle of Windex that was sitting on the back of the toilet. He took the Windex bottle and began unscrewing the top. Mom, meanwhile, had her own threat. She had a bottle of pills, which she was waving at Donnie. As the Mexican standoff escalated, it became less amusing to Glory, who witnessed the whole thing. She began madly dialing the phone, calling me for help. After Glory called, I sat for a few minutes looking at the phone. For the first time, I had no desire to grab my purse and head into the melee. I no longer wanted to participate in the circus. I could not understand what went through Mom's head when one of these incidents occurred. She once told me that she'd lost so much to be with Donnie, that she just couldn't see leaving him. She was reluctant to walk away from her investment in Donnie. This incident with the girlfriend was just another blip.

Now that Donnie had been found out, things would calm

down. There was no doubt in my mind that by next month, the visit to Mom's bedroom would not necessarily be forgotten, but it would not have changed anything in Mom's life. All four of us kids were starting to become less tolerant of Mom's problems. We still loved her, but knew we couldn't change her. It was her life and her mistakes. So we all had a slightly different attitude when we got the call from Glory that there was another problem. No one was quick to get involved.

After initially hesitating, Cindy finally decided to go to the house and see what she could do. She was studying for the CPA and was less than enthusiastic, but still never knew how to say no.

"I am not coming," was my response. "It will pass. If I come over nothing will change. Within a week, everything will be back to normal."

My relatively new husband, Ron, was not so sure. He had not lived through the many Donnie incidents and didn't understand my lack of emotion and refusal to get involved. For Ron, Mom was in trouble and it warranted family involvement.

"It's your *mother*," he said repeatedly. "If you think it is so important, then you go," I responded. I was adamant about not getting involved or going over to the house. So, he went alone.

Cindy got to the house a few minutes before my husband, but they could not find Donnie or Mom. Glory said both had left the house, although all cars were in the parking lot. A search was initiated to find Mom and Donnie. Mom was lying in the bushes on the side of the house. The sleeping pills started to work and she was drifting off. This time it didn't look like walking her around until the sleeping pills wore off was going to correct the situation. Donnie was located in the backyard holding the Windex bottle. It is not clear whether he was drinking the Windex or simply using it as a prop to divert attention from the visit to the house. Based on past experience, neither Glory nor Cindy saw the Windex as a real threat and left him sitting in the backyard by himself.

By this time, my husband had convinced me that this was a real emergency and I needed to come over. Reluctantly, I pulled up to the house just as Cindy, Glory and her boyfriend, Nick, appeared from behind the house, dragging our unconscious mother behind them. I ran into the house and grabbed the keys to Mom's Town Car. I figured it would be big enough to get all of us to the hospital. I flipped them to Nick and directed him to pull the car up so we could get Mom into the back seat. Meanwhile, we carried, dragged, and pulled Mom — who was like dead weight — to the street where we each took an arm or leg and lifted her towards the car.

"Oh, my Lord," I exclaimed as I opened the back door. The car was filled with Mom's dry cleaning, which she had been collecting for quite some time. There was no way we would all be able to fit in.

"I need another car!" I yelled to Nick. He zoomed out in Mom's Town Car and very quickly pulled up in Glory's car. We piled into the vehicle with an unconscious Mom and headed towards the nearest hospital. We brought the pill bottle to the hospital so they would know what she had taken, and after several hours of sitting in the waiting room, a small Indian doctor with a thick foreign accent appeared to give us a status on Mom. She was going to be all right. Her stomach had been pumped and she was now alert. The doctor thought maybe they should keep Mom in the hospital for a few days for a psychiatric evaluation. I think we all agreed it would give us some breathing room. However, Mom was not on board with that plan. She got wind of the doctor's intentions and recited the legal consequences of restraining a patient against their will. Mom could run circles around just about anyone (except Donnie) when you got her going. That doctor didn't even see it coming. Before Mom was finished with him, he retreated from the room looking like he just got the licking of his life.

My husband was still trying to figure out this strange family he married into. He decided to head back to the house to talk to Donnie as we worked to get Mom discharged from the hospital. None of us really thought we would be lucky enough to have the Windex do Donnie in, so we figured he would be waiting for us. Eventually, Ron found Donnie hiding in the bathroom (surprise, surprise). As time went on, he was becoming afraid of us. He knew he could get the better of Mom, but he was definitely not able to get the better of us. He hated our confrontations.

Mom later wrote in her diary about how she already knew about the Girlfriend before her visit. A few months earlier they were having a Valentine's Day party at her office. She arrived at the office early and found a crystal glass vase with a single red rose. A small card was attached to the vase and was addressed to Donnie. The rose for Donnie was from the Girlfriend. Mom always said that was the day she stopped loving Donnie. The woman's bold acts including confronting her in her own bedroom were demoralizing and disgusting. Every word the Girlfriend said and wrote burned at what little was left of Mom's heart. Still, she refused to give Donnie up — even now.

Mom continued to believe Donnie damaged her in so many ways, but she gave up so much to be with him she couldn't back away. First, she had given up her religion and marriage. She traded Donnie for her immortal soul. She reasoned she already made an agreement with the devil and she was going to burn in hell for what she had done. No matter what Donnie did to her, that was the agreement she made and she was going to take her punishment. I could not understand it and neither could my siblings. We didn't make the deal, so why did *we* have to live with the consequences? Mom was brilliant in so many ways, yet she could not see straight when it came to her life with Donnie.

Unfortunately, I was right. By the following month, things had kind of returned to normal. Mom was still angry about the Girlfriend visit, but nothing had really changed. The Windex bottles were back under the bathroom sink. The sleeping pills went back into the medicine cabinet. Life went on.

After years of private practice, Mom surprised us in 1990 by announcing she was closing her law office and taking a temporary job with the federal government as a staff attorney for the Resolution Trust Company. Mom was particularly skilled at real estate transactions and the savings and loan crisis of the early 1990s opened up some opportunities for her. The RTC was part of the FDIC and was created for the purpose of handling the large number of assets owned by the FDIC as bank after bank failed.

Although the job was supposed to be temporary, Mom was named a full-time contract attorney shortly after she was hired. She loved her work and finally found her niche in the unlikely area of government law. Working with affordable housing projects built with loans from failed banks reconciled her desire to help people as well as her need to have a stable job. With the federal government, Mom had health and life insurance benefits for the first time. She finally faced the inevitable fact that Donnie was going to get into trouble again. That realization made it possible for her to start planning realistically for her future. Timing is everything in life. The change came at exactly the right time.

Although Mom loved her small private practice and wide assortment of poor and quirky clients, working in a corporate office gave her some separation from Donnie's business problems. It was harder for her to be involved in the day-to-day operation of his law firm when she had a regular job. The job gave her time each day to concentrate on something other than Donnie. As she got older, things like medical insurance, retirement, and life insurance were becoming increasingly important. Over time, she started to realize she was the breadwinner of the family. It was impossible to talk to Donnie about alternate careers or future plans but she tried to talk to him in terms he could accept.

"What if you became a judge? What would happen to your clients," she would ask him. "What if one of these clients wanted you to work only on their matters? Who would take your existing cases?"

Donnie's condominium association clients were a valuable book of business. He had several hundred associations that consulted with him on a regular basis.

"Lori, why don't you start working with Donnie," she asked me several different times. I knew she was trying to work out the plan to withdraw Donnie when it became necessary, but I couldn't see myself working with him. Living with him was difficult enough. Working with him would put me with the zone of knowledge and danger for all of his cases. I couldn't do that.

Mom's new office was located in Arlington Heights, Illinois. It was really the first time she worked in any kind of structured environment. Surprisingly, she thrived in the new corporate world. She was smart and hardworking and quickly developed a core of good friends who lived normal lives and were a welcome distraction from the craziness of her life with Donnie. Shortly after she started, she was able to recommend her former law partner for a similar job. She was content knowing that her friend, Gordon, was still working with her and that she had not left him to handle their former law practice alone.

Donnie was fascinated by Mom's work with the RTC. The properties and money that flowed through the government agency seemed to excite him. He started doing research on different property deals that were overseen by the RTC and liked to stop by Mom's office while she was at work. It was a period of adjustment for her, but she seemed to love her work.

Mom made another deliberate decision about the time she started working at the RTC. She purchased a disability insurance policy for Donnie. The policy would pay a significant amount if he were unable to practice law as a result of a medical condition. She read the policy very carefully but finally made the commitment to pay the substantial premium. Mom started to accept the inevitable truth about Donnie. He would not be a lawyer forever.

After all these years, Donnie was still a mystery to us. Mom believed he got himself into trouble with clients because of his "mental illness." She wanted to believe he was not in touch with reality when he lied. But mental illness did not explain his perfectly rational reactions when his deceptions began to unravel. He knew immediately when the jig was up. He didn't try to tell you why he did it. He didn't try to rationalize his actions. He didn't cry or become emotional. He simply stared blankly at his accusers or family members as the scramble for the truth began.

Donnie expressed no regret or sorrow when his actions dashed dreams or caused people pain. Much of the time, he was content to turn crisis management over to Mom. Mom was responsible for telling the victim that he was a victim. Or that the check was not in the mail, or that the lawsuit was not won. Once Donnie turned a crisis over, he was no longer involved. He hovered on the edge, listening silently to the nervousness in Mom's voice as she sought advice on what to do next. A slight smile sat on his lips as he smoked and drank, seemingly basking in the glow of the emotions and excitement, which were all about him. *He* did this. The powerful Donnie! All of us were talking about him, trying to figure out what he actually did or did not do. He manipulated us through our concern for Mom and our desire to help her. It made us weak. Vulnerable. Everything that caused us worry, sadness, and anxiety was because of him.

"We should do something about Donnie." Cindy was resolute. Again, we were trying to find answers that never seemed to materialize. Cindy was right, but neither of us knew what to do.

"We could go to the police," she suggested. I had thought the same thing for years, but couldn't prove what I knew. He was like smoke; you see it, but when you put your hand out you can't grab it.

"What would we tell the police?" I asked her. "That we *think* he might have killed his second wife 15 years ago? That we *think* that something is going to happen?"

The conversation was repeated every couple of months. I made lists of everything that happened over the years. Cindy and I talked about Noreen at family birthday parties, holiday gatherings, and family vacations. There was an overwhelming sense that something needed to be done about Donnie. Occasionally, one of us would try and talk to Mom about Donnie. We were fearful that she would be harmed. But in between the crazy lies, the women, the lawsuits, and the angry clients, there were interludes of normalcy. Mom and Donnie sat on their patio and sipped wine. Occasionally, they traveled. Donnie told jokes and entertained us with stories of people he had met. The normal moments seemed to give Mom hope that somehow life with Donnie would be OK. Maybe he won't do it again. Maybe the worst was over.

There was a sense of impending doom as we held our collective breath waiting to see what would happen next and hoped it could be handled. After all, how could we do what the police and the ARDC charged with responsibility for men like Donnie could not do? We are just the family. Just about the time we were giving up, it seemed things were decided for us. Once again, the police became involved in Donnie's life.

CHAPTER FIFTEEN

A Murder in Arlington Heights

Loretta Tabak-Bodtke was one of Donnie's more interesting clients. She was attractive, outspoken, and stubborn. Donnie said she was a model when she was younger. In early 1991, her name started coming up frequently at our house during his after-dinner monologues. Mom told us Donnie was representing Loretta in a business disagreement with her former partner in an interior design company. Loretta actually met Donnie through Mom. Mom had filed the incorporation papers for her design business years before. Donnie and Mom became friendly with Loretta and her husband and eventually Loretta retained Donnie as her attorney when the dispute arose.

In addition to representing Loretta in the business dispute, Donnie also began working with her husband, Robert Bodtke, in a business to market a disposable razor that Robert invented and patented. The patent was issued and stated that the razor was a "relatively inexpensive, disposable and foldable razor" that was compact for efficient storage. At one point, Donnie and Robert opened a small office and obtained an investor for the marketing of the razor, which they believed could be sold to commercial airlines to put in the small packet of complimentary accessories given to international travelers. Donnie repeatedly assured the Bodtkes that he would extract a significant amount of money from Loretta's former business partner, which could be used as capital for the razor company. Loretta invested about $30,000 of her own money in the razor company, confident that she could recoup her money from the proceeds of the lawsuit.

Donnie talked frequently of famous people who might be interested in investing in the razor company. He claimed to know the president of United Airlines and promised Robert that he would make an introduction. But as month after month passed without any introductions or viable business inquiries regarding the razor, Robert started to realize that Donnie was more talk than action. He started pulling back from partnering with Donnie on the razor. By the beginning of 1991, Robert and Donnie were hardly speaking to each other, although Donnie continued to represent Loretta in her business dispute. Loretta and Robert also began arguing about the razor as well as the lawsuit. In late 1990, Robert moved out of the Arlington Heights townhome and began to talk about the possibility of divorce.

Although Loretta continued to allow Donnie to represent her, the friction with Robert was taking its toll. Mom believed Donnie was romantically linked to Loretta. However, there was never any definitive proof of an intimate relationship between them. Loretta had two children. Her oldest child, Stephanie, had a close relationship with her mother. The two would talk frequently about the lawsuit.

In February of 1991, Loretta confided in Stephanie that she had serious concerns that Donnie was not properly representing her in the lawsuit. She was starting to realize that Donnie was lying about the litigation as well as his personal relationship with important business contacts. Although she considered replacing him as her attorney in early spring, Donnie convinced her he was starting to see significant progress in the case.

In March, Donnie told Loretta he had won her case and entered judgment against the business partner. He predicted she would see a large amount of money by the end of the month. He provided her with a copy of a summary judgment in her favor which was stamped by a Cook County judge. Despite her disgust with Donnie, Loretta decided to stay with him for a couple more weeks to see if he could finally execute on his promises to complete the case. But the delays continued as the month progressed and Donnie seemed to be no closer to actually handing Loretta a check.

At one point, he told Loretta he had cancer (there's his "cancer weapon" again) and was going to be starting chemotherapy. These treatments were causing a delay in the execution of the judgment. Donnie told her to be patient and that she would get the large settlement very soon. At the same time Loretta's disillusionment with Donnie reached its peak, she reconciled with Robert, and he moved back into the condominium. Robert was not willing to tolerate Donnie. In fact, he did not even want to be in the same room as Donnie when he would visit Loretta to talk about her case.

Although not aware of any direct misrepresentations or lies, Mom knew the signs of impending trouble, and there was no doubt that something was not right with Donnie and Loretta's relationship. Any time ideas would surface that involved patents or Donnie acting as a middleman, it seemed to bring out the maniacal side of his personality. Over the years, Donnie would become immersed in a particular idea every couple of years. His role was always one of an intermediary. His reward would always be from a commission in a sort of broker relationship. Donnie loved to talk about deals that were almost done that would bring him wealth and fame. The excitement in his voice as he talked about Loretta and the disposable razor were clear warning signs, but it was difficult for Mom to know when to intervene.

During the month of March, Donnie's chatter regarding the Bodtkes was ratcheting up in our house. He was talking about Loretta's case, her business partner, and the razor idea almost every night after dinner. He would pour himself a drink and start his monologue shortly afterwards. His face would light up when he would talk about the razor and whom he was going to bring in as an investor. He would repeat the story over and over again. Mom was becoming increasingly concerned about Donnie's focus on the Bodtkes. She started questioning him about the nature of his relationship with Loretta. There was increased stress about Donnie's representation of the Bodtkes for most of March.

Donnie was feeling pressure both from Loretta and from Mom. We didn't know that Donnie had told Loretta the case against her business partner for the interior decorating company was won or that he provided her with a copy of a court-filed Motion for Summary Judgment and order which granted her a judgment of more than half a million dollars. Even if we did, it would not have mattered. There was no judgment and no check coming from Loretta's former business partner. Again, it was relatively easy for Donnie to stamp the orders but not give the original to the clerk for entry into the official court file. It gave Donnie a court-stamped copy but kept the court file clean. Loretta had a filed stamped court order that was worth nothing. But only Donnie knew that at this point. In fact, he never even filed the lawsuit. Donnie was reverting back to his old tricks that nearly got him disbarred just a short time earlier.

The Bodtke problem was rapidly escalating. Although Loretta probably appreciated the fact Donnie said he entered a Summary Judgment for her with a substantial judgment against the defendant, she wanted to see the money. A half-million dollars was not as easy for Donnie to manufacture as the court order entering judgment and awarding her the money. As March progressed, Loretta became increasingly impatient waiting for her settlement check. She couldn't understand what was holding up the money. Donnie's excuses were starting to wear thin. She had bills to pay and wanted her money. The stress building in the relationship was spilling over into Donnie's personal life. Donnie was starting to drink a little more. He continued to talk about Loretta, but in a less than flattering way. He started talking about a possible connection with "the mafia," supposed associations with criminals, and her abrasive personality. "She is crazy as a loon" was one of the things he often said about Loretta in his after-dinner monologues.

Loretta was a very outspoken individual and was becoming increasingly confrontational about collecting on the judgment. On Wednesday evening, April 3, 1991, Donnie went to Loretta's house to try and calm her down. She was calling his office several times a day demanding to talk to Donnie. Loretta was becoming increasingly belligerent with the receptionist at Donnie's law firm. Donnie assured her the funds would be wired to her bank account the following day. In the meantime, he agreed to advance her $9,300 so that she could pay her bills. He wrote her a personal check for that amount and left the check on her kitchen counter. Although Loretta didn't know it, there were insufficient funds in Donnie's personal account to cover the check. The lies were closing in on him. Once Loretta tried to cash the check, he must have known it would be increasingly difficult to keep her from finding the truth. And Donnie did not have the money to pay the judgment. He was running short of options and time.

In the meantime, Loretta showed the check to her husband. She told him Donnie said the remainder of the judgment funds would be wired to her account the following morning, but she was doubtful she would see the money. She didn't believe Donnie anymore. Her husband looked up the number for the Attorney Registration and Disciplinary Commission and suggested that if the money did not come that she make the call and file a formal complaint. The piece of paper with the number was left on the counter. Loretta also talked to her daughter that evening. Stephanie said Loretta was angry and fed up. If the money did not come the next morning, she was done with Donnie.

Donnie was back at Loretta's house first thing the next morning. Mom thought he was going downtown to his law office, but he stopped at the Arlington Heights townhome before 8:00. It is not clear what he did or said to Loretta that morning, but he left and drove to his downtown law office. Shortly after he left, Loretta made the first of several calls to her bank to see if the promised funds had been received. The bank told her that there was no record of the wire transfer. She would call the bank several times that morning trying to verify whether the funds had been deposited.

In the meantime, Loretta repeatedly called Donnie's downtown law office demanding to talk to him. It was becoming increasingly difficult for Donnie to put her off. She called Stephanie mid-morning and told her that the money had not been wired. She said Donnie was coming over and she was going to have it out with him. Finally, Donnie had his secretary cancel his afternoon appointments telling her that he did not feel well and was going home after lunch. He left his office shortly after lunch but he did not head home. He headed back to Loretta's condo. He was driving his white car with "MR CONDO" license plates prominently displayed. It was a cold, rainy April day, and he was wearing a beret hat and his winter coat, along with his usual snake skin boots. He would arrive at Loretta Bodtke's condo sometime after noon.

Stephanie made one last call to her mom that afternoon. "You are home, so Donnie must not have shown up?" she asked her mom.

Loretta avoided answering the question. Stephanie would later say her mom sounded strange. She asked where Stephanie was.

"I'm at school. Is he there?" Again, Loretta avoided the question.

"OK," Stephanie answered. "You must not be able to talk. I'll call you when I get home."

Loretta hung up without saying goodbye. Stephanie held the phone for a second thinking the conversation was odd. But she shrugged it off and went back to class. She got home around 3:30 and immediately called her mom. There was no answer. She called again and again, her concern increasing as the hours passed.

Thursday, April 4, 1991, seemed like a normal day for the rest of my family. It was a typical gray, rainy, Chicago spring day. Mom was working in Arlington Heights for the Resolution Trust Company, not far from Loretta's condo. I talked to her as I left my downtown office to head back to Schaumburg about 4:30. She told me Donnie left work shortly after lunch because he did not feel well and was at home in bed. This was actually quite unusual for him so she was going to go home a little early to figure out what was going on. She sounded worried. Any break from his normal routine was always an indication of a problem. She said she heard from him about 4:00 and he was at home. She said that Donnie was very talkative and they talked for about 15 minutes, also a very unusual act for Donnie whose phone calls were usually nothing more than, "Yo. I'm home."

"Something is going on," Mom said. "I'm worried."

Loretta (Teri) Tabak Bodtke was found lying in a pool of blood in the kitchen of her upscale Arlington Heights townhome by her husband at approximately 7:30 p.m. on April 4th. She had been shot four times in the head at close range. There was no sign of a struggle or forced entry into the home. A neighbor reported hearing a sound like gunshots at approximately 3:20 p.m. Two other neighbors reporting seeing a white compact car parked in the driveway and reported that a queer looking man with a briefcase entered the home. The neighbors also reported seeing the car leave the townhome around 3:30 pm. It did not take the Arlington Heights police long to trace the car to Donnie Rudd.

Murders in quiet Arlington Heights are not common — especially the extremely violent murder of an attractive woman. The Bodtke murder was the top story on the 10:00 news. By the time the news story aired, the Arlington Heights police had identified Donnie as a person of interest and showed up at his home. Donnie acknowledged to the police he stopped at Loretta's condo earlier in the day to talk about a possible settlement of her case, but adamantly argued that she was alive when he left. He said he had tea with her and sat at her kitchen table. He insisted that he left the townhome around 3:00.

The police asked if they could come in, and Donnie granted them the right to a limited search of his home. However, without a search warrant, Donnie was able to limit the area of the search. Donnie was an avid gun collector and the presence of multiple guns was the first detail noted by the police. But Donnie was congenial and agreed the police could take any gun in the home so it could be checked with the bullets that had lodged in Loretta Bodtke's head.

He helped the police by getting several boxes and checking each gun as it was put into the box to make sure it was not loaded. After piling multiple guns into the boxes, his hands were greasy with the residue from handling multiple firearms. He was wiping his hands clean, when the police asked him whether he would take a gunpowder residue test to prove he had not recently fired a gun. Donnie was no fool. He had written multiple articles on the validity of gunpowder residue tests while in law school.

"I just handled more than 20 guns at your request," he said. "Of course I can't take a gunpowder residue test. I have gunpowder all over my hands at this moment, but not from shooting a gun."

The police collected the guns and left the condo.

Mom called me to report the killing of Donnie's client. She sounded worried but said Donnie appeared to be very cool and collected. I asked her if she knew where Donnie had been earlier that afternoon and if there was any way to trace his steps. "Well, you know he came home early because he didn't feel well," she said.

"You probably should get your phone records so that you know for sure," I told her. "Try and retrace his steps."

I think we knew the questions around the Bodtke murder were just starting. Donnie's representation of Loretta was an obvious concern. Mom talked of her concern that Donnie may have misrepresented the entry of a Summary Judgment. She was also extremely angry to be hearing of Donnie's multiple visits to the Arlington Heights condo over the past few days. It was not usual customary business to do house calls in the legal world. Generally, business was done by telephone or at the attorney's office. Tea at a client's house was definitely not business as usual. I wasn't clear whether Mom's anger was directed at Donnie because she thought he might be involved with Loretta or her concern he had fallen back to his lies about judgments so soon after dismissal of the ARDC complaint and the probationary status of his license.

At this point Mom and I continued to outwardly act as if there was no way Donnie could have committed a brutal murder. But I don't think either of us was sure. Donnie had been talking more and more about this particular client in the weeks leading up to the murder. The filing of a false judgment was also a motive for murder.

"What was happening in her case?" I asked Mom.

"I don't know," she replied.

"Who else would want to murder her?" Mom didn't know the answer to that question, either. All she said was that Donnie said Loretta was not particularly nice.

The situation took an unexpected turn the following evening when I received a frantic phone call from Mom.

"The police are here with a search warrant," she said anxiously. "Can you come over?"

I ran out the door, jumped in the car, and drove the two miles to Mom's condo. The street was filled with flashing blue lights. Mom was standing in the driveway with a police officer. Donnie was nowhere in sight.

"They want to search my car," Mom said as I walked up.

"Let me see the search warrant," I told the officer. I handed him my business card that identified me as a lawyer.

"The search warrant does not cover my mother's car. She is not married to Donnie so the car is not marital property. This search warrant only covers the home and marital property. My mother is not involved in this."

Mom grabbed my arm and pulled me aside.

"I have to tell you something," she whispered. She stood looking nervously at the policeman standing just a few feet away.

"I married Donnie in Las Vegas," she said. "We have been married for more than a year."

"You got married *again* and never told me?" I am once again incredulous. This is the second time Mom had married Donnie and told no one — not even her own children. I talked to her every day. We always talked about Donnie and his problems. I believed she and I were as close as two people could be. But she had gotten married again without telling me.

"Never mind," I told the police officer. I stood outside the house watching the police remove bags of Mom's belongings. A small circle of neighbors had gathered in the cul-de-sac to try and figure out what was happening. The blue lights from the police cars illuminated the facade of the condo.

The search was finally complete, and as the last officer got into his car, we were allowed to re-enter the house. They had oddly taken all of Donnie's left Texan boots, leaving the right boot from each pair sitting forlornly on the shoe shelf. They requested that Donnie identify the clothes he was wearing the day of the murder. Although Donnie purportedly gave them the clothes, he would later tell the detectives that he had given the clothes to his attorney to hold. The police also took all of Mom's checkbooks and blank checks. They said they were looking for a check. They took the contents of the garbage can in their bedroom. Although, we did not know it at that time, the police had recovered remnants of the $9,300 check from the garbage can next to the bed in Donnie's bedroom — a critical piece of evidence in the murder investigation.

Mom was visibly shaken by the police search of the house.

"I think they are going to arrest him," she said. "He was there. How could they not arrest him?"

"But *why* was he there?" I asked her. She just shook her head.

Donnie arrived home shortly thereafter. He sat at the dining room table behind us as we talked. He lit up a cigarette and poured himself a glass of Tia Maria. He did not appear to be listening to our discussion. He blew smoke rings into the air. The light over the dining room table reflected off his glasses so that I couldn't see his eyes. I wondered what he was thinking.

"Donnie," I said. "What was going on with her case? Did you lie to her?"

For the longest time, he didn't answer, choosing instead to continue to blow smoke rings. Finally, he spoke.

"Sometimes I am not sure when I am awake and when I

am dreaming," he said. Nothing more.

But the police searches were not yet over. The next day, Donnie called Mom to tell her that the police were at his Chicago law office with a new search warrant. They spent an hour looking through drawers and documents before they left again with boxes and documents. Donnie called Mom immediately after the police left his office.

"They missed a gun," he said.

Mom turned to me and said, "They missed a gun ... a .22."

Again, I was absolutely stupefied.

"Donnie has a gun at the office? Why would he have a gun at his law office?"

"He keeps a .22 in the file cabinet," Mom offered.

"Call my law partner and ask him what to do," I tell Mom.

John, my law partner, advised me in a matter-of-fact monotone.

"So, tell them they missed a gun," he said.

"Can *you* tell them?" I ask awkwardly. "I'm family and don't want to be involved."

So John made the call to the police to tell them they missed a gun. The police sheepishly showed up back at the office to collect it.

At first, the gun at the law office concerned me, especially after I heard it was a .22, the same caliber that killed Loretta. But the more I thought about it, the surer I was that the gun had nothing to do with the murder. There was no way Donnie would have called and told Mom the police missed a gun if it had anything to do with the murder. He wanted to prove he was cooperating. It was still a game for Donnie.

Donnie was also starting to put together his public story. Although he still often sat silently drinking his Tia Maria, he started adding a few details to the discussion: Loretta's partner was connected with organized crime, he said. She was shot with a .22. That's what organized crime supposedly uses. Loretta had lots of enemies. She was a bitch. Maybe her husband did it. The police would have a lot of people to look at.

"They can't pin this on me," he said smugly.

The press continued to have a field day with stories about the murder. There was a picture in the newspaper of Donnie's car with the "MR CONDO" license plates and a quote from a neighbor about hearing bangs in the afternoon. We waited for the police to come and make the arrest. But days passed with no contact from Arlington Heights.

"Why are they looking for checks?" I asked Mom. We pored over her check register to try and identify missing checks. There was a recent one that appeared to be missing. Mom was adamant it was not related to Donnie.

We retraced Donnie's steps from Loretta's condo to home and we timed the trip in busy afternoon traffic. He could have made it according to our time line, but it would have been close. It was rainy that day; traffic could have slowed him down. All of the facts were borderline. Just like everything Donnie did. We didn't know what to do, and worse, we didn't know what to believe.

The police had not arrested Donnie. But they were following him. It was a couple of weeks after the murder and I was at Cindy's house with Mom and Donnie. Cindy and I looked out the window and saw the plain-looking black sedan sitting half a block down.

It was still a game to Donnie. Donnie was helping John, Cindy's husband, plant a tree in the front yard. Donnie wanted to take a paper bag and toss it in before the tree was planted. He was curious if the police would dig up the tree the following morning. John and Donnie left for the store with the police following them. Donnie made a couple of quick turns to lose them and raced home and hid the car in the garage. He was not intimidated by the accusations. It was almost like he was trying to prove how invincible he really was.

The police were blatantly obvious and obtrusive. They were not trying to hide. They *wanted* Donnie to know they were following him. They were sending a message to him. Glory was sent out to the black sedan with a plate of brownies for the plain-clothes cops. Clearly, Donnie was their target, but I don't think they could quite get their minds around Donnie's motives or what happened. The police played cat and mouse with Donnie over the next couple of weeks. We continued to try and convince ourselves Donnie could not have committed such a terrible crime. But we couldn't quite get there. There was finally an acknowledgment that it was *possible* Donnie shot Loretta in the head with the intent to kill her.

At one point, I got a call from Mom. She was on the tollway with Donnie returning from dinner and believed she was being followed by the police. She wanted me to open my garage door. She was going to come to my house and did not want to park the car on the street. It seemed reasonable, and I opened the garage door as requested. As I was waiting, my mind started to truly comprehend the seriousness of the situation: *If he pulls into the garage and I close the door, are we hiding him? If they arrest Donnie at our house are we subjecting ourselves to a search?* If he is a murderer, I don't want him in our house. My husband Ron was calm. They can search our house. We had nothing to hide. If Donnie killed someone, the police *should* arrest him. We were not hiding him; we were supporting Mom. Minutes later, Mom and Donnie pulled into our garage and we shut the door. But still the police didn't arrest him.

"I want to talk to the police," I told my partner, John. "Rather than letting them sit in front of the house and follow everyone, let's just call and see what they are looking for. Maybe I can find what they want. I collect stuff. I know Donnie. I know how he thinks."

John made the call to the police, alerting them that I would like to come down to the station and talk. The police officer was polite but he didn't pull any punches. The killing was brutal. Loretta was shot in the face and they clearly believed she knew her killer. The chief suspect was Donnie. Donnie was at the townhome. The number for the Attorney Registration Commission was found by her phone.

The check the police were looking for was a check Donnie supposedly gave Loretta as an advancement of her lawsuit settlement. The balance was to be wired to her bank. Loretta called the bank multiple times that morning looking for her wired funds, which never arrived. It was clear Donnie was meeting Loretta at her condo not just to talk about the case, but in response to Loretta's increasingly angry calls when she did not receive the wired funds that had been promised multiple times. Donnie must have known the meeting was going to be confrontational. Donnie clearly had a motive for killing Loretta. After all, one more complaint to the ARDC and Donnie would be stripped of his law license. However, the police didn't seem to have a clear timeline or time of death. Donnie admitted to being at the house, so circumstantial evidence of his presence was largely irrelevant. It was really all about the timing. The police were friendly with my partner, John. They showed him pictures of the murder scene and discussed the details of the crime.

John and I left the police station and got into his car. No one said anything for a few minutes as he negotiated out of the parking lot.

"You know he killed her, right?" John finally said.

I couldn't bring myself to respond. We drove the rest of the way to our office in silence.

In November, Donnie finally received a subpoena to testify before a grand jury convened to hear evidence in the Bodtke murder case the following month. He was nervous, but Mom spent time preparing him for his testimony. She did not tell me she had also received a subpoena to testify.

In January, 1992, Mom appeared before the grand jury investigating Loretta Bodtke's death. One of the partners in my law firm went with her. She studied for her appearance much the same way she studied for her law school exams. She drove the route between Loretta's condo and her house each day. She drove in different weather conditions trying to replicate the rainy April day so she could judge traffic patterns. She reread all of the newspaper articles to make sure she knew the timeframes of all possible witness statements. She reviewed her telephone records to make sure she knew exactly when she talked to Donnie that day. She pored through her checkbook records trying to verify each unrecorded check to try and pinpoint whether Donnie wrote the check to Loretta from her account. The one thing she didn't do was to question Donnie in great detail.

In retrospect, I don't think she wanted to know the truth. She preferred to look through his files to see if she could find support for her position rather than pushing the silent man who watched her frantic preparations as she tried to save him. Mom seldom talked about her court appearance that day, except to say she was able to express herself fully. She waited weeks after the grand jury appearance to see if Donnie would be arrested. Finally, by spring she began to believe that once again, Donnie would not be charged. But no one believed the investigation was over.

Years later, the police would tell me it was Mom's testimony that saved Donnie from an indictment right after the murder. Donnie had difficulty answering questions and asserted his Fifth Amendment rights. Mom, however, went in loaded for bear. She had her telephone records and her timelines down pat. She created a reasonable doubt that it was possible Donnie had not committed this murder … at least enough of a doubt so no arrest warrant was issued. But still no one was sure what to believe.

Did he do it?

It was a question that would haunt our family for years.

Late one night, a couple of weeks after the murder, I was working late in my law office. I picked up a computer CD to copy a document. The files on the CD flashed on my screen. I saw the name Bodtke and I froze for just a minute before I started opening files. The Motion for Summary Judgment and the order entering judgment were there. To me, it was again irrefutable proof that Donnie was lying to Loretta. Just like the Whitehall mess, Donnie had told her he won a half-million dollar lawsuit for her. He had entered a fraudulent judgment. Again, the amount was too large to just pay.

Did he do it?

I went home and cried for the pain this devil caused and for what Mom would go through if he were arrested.

Eventually, my partner John, who was a gun collector, asked what had happened to all of Donnie's guns. I told him I thought the police probably still had them.

"That's a shame," he said. "I wonder if we could get them."

That evening, I asked Donnie if he would give the guns to John. Donnie agreed and assigned his rights to the guns to the custody of John. Later that week, John went to the Arlington Heights police station with the assignment. To my surprise, the police released the guns to him. It was the first time that I really started to believe Donnie would not be arrested. The thought made me a little queasy.

Did he do it?

Loretta Bodtke's murder changed the way we saw Donnie. Loretta was shot in the head and at least once in the face. She was shot at close range by someone who brought a gun to her townhouse, with the intent to kill her. It was the violent, deliberate, angry way that Loretta died that changed us. I could no longer sleep at night. I was afraid of him.

Over the years there were signs Donnie was capable of violence. There was the altercation with Mom on the balcony. The hammer through the TV. Noreen's death. It was obvious death didn't seem to have the same meaning for Donnie as it did for most people. Donnie was becoming increasingly intolerant of those who stood in his way. If he was capable of killing in a violent, brutal manner, it changed everything. It put us in danger. Mom seemed to know her life would need to change. Every police car she passed could be on the way to arrest Donnie. She worried he was unable to control himself with clients. His life was immersed in this web of lies and she didn't know how to extricate him. Next time, she was certain he would not walk away. In fact, it was still not clear whether he would walk away from this one. Mom was always on high alert, looking over her shoulder as she tried to get ahead of the next problem.

Loretta Bodtke's murder at first seemed like it might break Donnie's winning streak of walking away. It seemed like it would be a slam-dunk case for the prosecution. There was so much overwhelming evidence.

Somehow, even with all the evidence, Donnie just walked away.

CHAPTER SIXTEEN

Mom

Looking just at the events occurring from the time Mom met Donnie until the day she died, it would be easy to think she was a cold and calculating woman who cared only about herself, a deliberate home-wrecker, and a terrible mother. Nothing could be further from the truth. She was an incredibly loving, warm-hearted woman who loved nature, animals, and her children. Despite her wrongdoings, she believed in God, prayed each day, and wanted to be a better person. She had seven "prayer" sisters with breast cancer and she devotedly prayed for them each day.

Mom was never successful in private law practice because she could not bear to collect money for the work she did for her odd assortment of poor clients. She was the protector of the weak and the defender of the indigent. She was tender-hearted and full of mercy. That was Mom. She engendered this incredible loyalty from her friends and family that few outsiders understood. Despite it all, we knew and eventually accepted her terrible character flaw ... the unexplainable weakness when it came to Donnie Rudd. Nothing would overcome that flaw. It was as much a part of her as the color of her eyes. Despite Donnie's evil heart, Mom needed him if she was going to wake up each day. So we learned to live with the devil. We ignored the truth because Mom loved him. In our zeal to help Mom find the happiness and love she so desperately sought, we sentenced her to a life with a soulless, loveless husband. Our attitude towards Mom was not a cover-up or look-away from the character flaw. We accepted it because we loved her. We loved her unconditionally.

In July of 1992, Mom came up with a new strategy for dealing with Donnie's growing legal issues. It had been more than a year since Loretta's death and the talk of a pending arrest slowed to a trickle. No one doubted the Arlington Heights police still held Donnie as the prime suspect or person of interest. But for whatever reason, the evidence did not appear strong enough to arrest him. The possibility of arrest followed him everywhere, but he was still free to continue on with his life. Donnie's relationship with his new law firm was showing some signs of strain. The familiar pattern was starting to emerge. Clients complained about Donnie not filing a lawsuit or missing court calls. Although the firm seemed to stand by Donnie during the difficult publicity regarding Loretta's murder, the search of the downtown law office, and the continued questions regarding his role in her death, it was clear the partners were increasingly apprehensive about Donnie's character. Like all of his other law partnerships, Donnie's relationship with this firm was approaching sunset. Mom again started looking for Donnie's next move.

At the same time, Mom's position at the Illinois Resolution Trust Company was becoming precarious with the announcement the office would be shutting down in 1994. As the savings and loan crisis eased, the government would slowly start closing each of its satellite offices, leaving only its main office in Dallas, Texas. Mom looked at her options and made another decision that was totally unexpected. She put in for a transfer request to Dallas. She was a rising star at the RTC and the transfer was quickly granted. She began plans to relocate to a suburb north of Dallas. The decision would force Donnie to make a change in his life as well. After living her entire life in the Chicago area, Mom was willing to leave her friends, family, children, grandchildren, and aging mother to protect Donnie. She knew Donnie's ability to practice law in Illinois had a limited time frame. It was only a matter of time before something he did would cause the ARDC to revoke his license to practice law. Dallas was also a unique opportunity to put distance between Donnie and the ongoing law enforcement investigation of the murder of Loretta. Although he protested at first, slowly Donnie began to support the move. After all, he was from Texas. His brothers lived in Texas as well as some of his children. It seemed like a compromise that would work for Donnie.

Mom made the initial move to Dallas by herself. The federal government would pay for weekend trips to Chicago for approximately 90 days. Every Friday, she would fly home to stay in the townhome with Donnie. In the meantime, Donnie began the process of withdrawing from his current law firm. The decision was made for Donnie to transfer his clients to my law firm. In January, he would join my firm in an "of counsel" relationship. This is a particular kind of legal relationship that held less liability for my firm. It was not a partnership and not an employer/employee relationship. Donnie would have a very loose relationship with our office. I would begin the tedious process of identifying and solving problems and transferring control of files and clients from Donnie to my staff.

My law partner and I worked through the details of the transfer. Donnie would work primarily from Dallas. He would take phone calls, advise us on the status of cases and work with us to make the transfer. The plan called for Donnie to complete the transfer and retire from the law business by the end of 1993. It seemed like a foolproof plan. I worried Donnie would act up before the transfer was complete, but hoped that I could go through the massive amount of paperwork and files before another crisis occurred. But something unexpected happened that would challenge our well thought-out plan.

For once, it had nothing to do with Donnie.

Mom's routine mammogram in December of 1992 during one of her Chicago trips would change the course of our lives. She received a call from her doctor the next day. He found a small spot on the X-ray. He wanted to have the X-rays reviewed by a surgeon. He told her not to worry, but not to delay the review. Mom made arrangements to have me pick up the actual X-ray films from her gynecologist's office. Both of our offices were in downtown Chicago. My job was to bring the actual films to the consulting surgeon's office.

I picked up the X-ray packet right after lunch and walked slowly back to my office holding the folder. The Christmas lights were all aglow on Michigan Avenue. It was two weeks before Christmas. The brown folder that contained pictures of Mom's breasts was in my briefcase. The folder wasn't sealed, so I slid the X-rays out of the packet. Looking at the slides seemed an invasion of her privacy, but I decided to look anyway. The written report used words like "highly suspicious" and "consistent with malignancy." I walked to the window of my office on the 23rd floor overlooking the Michigan Avenue Christmas scene and held the X-ray of my mother's breast up to the window. The small "two-centimeter" oblong smudge looked back at me. Its edges were irregular. The shoppers bustled below me among the Christmas lights. There was no need to wait for further tests. The X-ray was indisputable, even to a layperson. Mom had cancer. We were coming face to face with an evil almost as strong as Donnie. Cancer. Donnie and cancer were going to be formidable opponents over the next few years.

Not surprisingly, Donnie was unfazed by the possibility that Mom might have cancer. However, the fact he was no longer the center of attention caused him considerable consternation. Throughout Mom's illness, Donnie competed with her for that focus. No matter how bad Mom would get, Donnie always tried to be worse. He came to the hospital the day of her biopsy with his arm in a sling. This was the first but not the last time he would use some sort of medical equipment to elicit a response. Ultimately, he would collect a wide array of braces, slings, and even casts that he could wear whenever Mom had a test or procedure. On the day of Mom's biopsy, a crowd of children, friends, and clients crowded into the small waiting room of Chicago's Northwestern Memorial Hospital to await the fate of Mom's results. Donnie was there as well, but did not relish the attention Mom was receiving for what he considered to be a relatively minor medical procedure.

During the actual biopsy, Donnie spent his time soliciting medical advice for an arm problem that developed earlier in the day. He didn't have much to say to us and said little to Mom as they wheeled her into surgery. Later in the recovery room, we crowded in, waiting for the doctor. Still in his surgical hat and shoes, the doctor went directly to Mom and took her hand.

"What we have here is breast cancer. The initial pathology report is positive."

Mom wept silently from her gurney. No one knew quite what to say. The news was earthshaking. I shoved my hands into the pocket of my suit jacket in an effort to hide the trembling. Glory helped Mom get dressed. Cindy sat in the chair silently. We were in utter shock. All of us, that is, except Donnie.

As I leaned down to hug Mom, I could see Donnie standing away from the group. His face was emotionless. He made no attempt to approach her and said nothing to the doctor. It was clear he was processing what this pronouncement would do to his life. Instead, he started talking to the nurse about some of his health problems. I could sense his irritation as we crowded around Mom. All of us walked slowly together to the doctor's office. A crowd of friends and family were supporting Mom as we slowly made our way down Michigan Avenue. Donnie lagged several steps behind, still reluctant to become part of our group.

The doctor avoided most of our questions, including our unspoken question regarding her prognosis. Despite my intent to take notes, I walked from the doctor's office with a blank legal pad. All I could think about was that Mom was sick and living with Donnie in Texas. Nothing else seemed to matter on that afternoon. Cancer. Donnie. What chance would Mom have to beat both? No matter what the doctor said, the odds for survival would be small.

Mom underwent a mastectomy within three days of her diagnosis. As she was wheeled in for her surgery, she handed me an envelope that said, "To be opened only in the event of my death." I opened it as soon as they wheeled her away. I was never good at following directions. The simple note said:

> *"First of all, no funeral, no wake, no flowers. It is my desire to be cremated. If you must do something, have a celebration of my life and let my friends talk about me and why they will remember me. I do not have my financial affairs in order. I want to make sure that you take care of Donnie. Lori, I leave it to you to keep the family together. The others will help, but you will make final decisions on everything."*

I couldn't help but sigh when I read it. After all of the love, and support, and prayers we sent her, it was still Donnie who grabbed her heart and her soul. Taking care of Donnie was a burden that all of us would carry throughout Mom's illness. The doctor was very positive about Mom's prognosis. The cancer was less than two centimeters. The doctor optimistically stated that the survival rate for this type of cancer was very good. But Mom was inconsolable. "I have been given a death sentence," she would say.

Mom's recovery from surgery was hard. The doctor removed 13 lymph nodes from under her arm. She had several tubes inserted into her incision that needed to be cleaned on a daily basis. Donnie would not do it. He refused to look at it let alone help with caring for Mom. I could not bring myself to look at her scar either, but Cindy and Glory took turns helping her drain the incision. Right after Christmas, the surgeon called with good news: No cancer had been found in the lymph nodes. Mom was officially "node negative." This was a good indication that the cancer was caught in time. No errant cancer cells managed to get caught in the filter of the lymph system. I breathed a sigh of relief. The cancer was gone.

The doctors recommended a course of what they call "preventive chemo." This is a very light dose designed to catch any stray cells that may have escaped from the tumor before it was removed. Mom wanted a stronger protocol of treatment but because of her node negative status, she couldn't qualify. Against our advice and pleadings, Mom decided to do her chemo in Texas. She wanted to be able to continue to work and not risk losing her insurance. So a couple of weeks after the surgery, she returned to Dallas to start looking for a house. In February, she purchased a house in Wylie, Texas, just a couple of miles from the South Fork ranch where the TV show *Dallas* was filmed. It seemed to make the move so much more final. Donnie always reminded us a little bit of J.R. Ewing, the show's egocentric, narcissistic protagonist, so I thought it was appropriate he was now a neighbor to the Ewing family.

Mom's first chemo session was scheduled at Baylor University Medical Center in early February. Not willing to leave anything to chance, one of us would be flying to Dallas for each of the chemo sessions, which would be scheduled over a three-month period. Luck would have it that the session was scheduled for the same time as the arrival of the movers with

Mom and Donnie's furniture. Donnie was in a helpful mood and agreed to accompany Mom to her first chemo session at Baylor. Glory stayed at their house in Wylie to direct the movers when they arrived with their belongings. It would be the first and only chemo session Donnie would attend with Mom. Glory waited back at the house for their return. Hours passed. No call. Just when we assumed Mom must have had some sort of fatal heart attack during the procedure, the car pulled into the driveway. It turned out that after the chemo, Donnie insisted he needed to stop at the hospital emergency room to have his sinus infection checked out. Once again, Donnie's actions overshadowed everything else — even chemotherapy.

After her first chemo, Mom became more resolute about her illness. The day after the first chemo, Mom woke up with a request for Glory: "Shave my head." Glory used to be a hairdresser. She was appalled at the thought. Cindy and I received a phone call.

"Mom wants me to shave her head."

We had her put Mom on the phone.

"We don't understand why you would want to do that now," we reasoned with her. "You don't know for sure your hair will fall out."

"My hair *will* fall out," she insisted. "Adriamycin makes your hair fall out. I want to have control over it. I don't want to wake up one morning and find half my hair on the pillow."

So Glory shaved Mom's head. Mom was bald, but only after Glory first gave her a Mohawk cut.

"Next thing you know she'll want us to all shave our heads to show solidarity," I grumbled.

Mom completed her chemo and was pronounced cancer free in June of 1993. Even though we appeared to have won the war on cancer, all of us were still a little shaky. It's the same feeling you have when you just avoid an accident. You brake hard.

Your arms stiffen in front of you in an attempt to brace for an expected impact. Your body reacts to the emergency instinctively. You have no control over the physical effects. Afterwards, when the danger is gone, when the adrenalin stops pumping, fear sets in. Your mind replays the almost-accident over and over — reminding you of how close you came. Your body again reacts physically to the possibility of harm. Only this time it is different. Your hands shake. Your legs feel weak. You find you're a little lightheaded. Finally, you shake off the fear and feel just a little giddy over your close call. Mom's brush with death made us feel just like that.

I called her every morning just to hear her voice. When she was in Chicago, I liked to walk next to her with my hand resting on her shoulder. Touching her was reassuring. I had a vaguely disquieting feeling that I needed to re-examine my own life. Death — even a brush with death — causes one to look more closely at life. Mom was 55 years old. If she hadn't been lucky, could she have died peacefully knowing what she had accomplished during her life? Would she continue to feel the same about staying with Donnie?

Mom's hair started to grow back quickly. Only it was grayer and whiter than before the cancer. I had hoped this new life would mean we had left the cancer nightmare behind. We were alive. And as Mom liked to say, "As long as everyone's alive, we can fix it."

The plan was for Donnie to accelerate his permanent move to Texas. He was turning more and more of his legal cases over to my practice. My law partner and I made tedious progress going through each of his files, fixing problems, handling issues, and cleaning up his current cases. We knew he could not leave permanently until we had completed this process of taking over his clients.

Everyone held their collective breath as we headed towards the big move. Donnie was spending a couple of days a week in Illinois and a couple of days in Texas. Our plan was for Donnie to leave for Texas by the end of the year. The end was in sight. For the first time in a long time, I was starting to believe that everything would be OK.

But we should have known that Donnie would throw up a roadblock just as everyone was starting to breathe a sigh of relief. When you dance with the devil, you're sure to get your toes stepped on.

CHAPTER SEVENTEEN

Duped by the Devil

I am sitting in the far corner of my closet, behind the skirts, so I can be as far as possible from the closet door, which leads to the outside world. The lights are off and I have my arms folded tightly around my knees. I'm still wearing my suit jacket. For a minute, I consider taking it off and putting it over my head to shield me from whatever is happening outside the door. I know that my husband is out there because I can see his shadow under the crack as he paces back and forth in front of the door. I also have an overwhelming urge to hum. I am working as hard as I can to keep my mind from focusing on anything outside of this closet. I don't want to think. I just want to be. I am never leaving the safety of my closet. I hate Donnie. Whenever my thoughts drift toward him, I hum louder.

I hear the door creak open and then close. I realize that I am not alone in the dark of my closet. The skirts push to the side and Cindy crawls in next to me. She has a bottle of wine, two glasses, and a flashlight.

"It could be worse," she says. "You are still alive. Not everyone who deals with Donnie can say the same thing."

So how did I go from being a partner in my own law firm to sitting in the corner of my closet, hiding and humming?

Donnie did it.

I have lived through the breakup of my family, the affairs, the pills, the violence, the anger, the strange deaths, the manipulations, the stories, and the legal wrangling but he has finally done me in. He has gotten the best of me on something that was so simple. Something that I knew so well; a real estate closing. A simple refinancing. I could do those in my sleep.

I have been caught in the web of a Donnie lie and now my reputation as a lawyer is at stake. I am honest and hardworking and do my best to always tell the truth. But my association with Donnie has moved from an incredibly difficult personal situation to an even more complex business problem.

Thinking back, I still can't believe it happened.

George was a respected businessman in Hoffman Estates. He was the chairman of a local business and owned a large commercial real estate business. He was involved in Hoffman Estates politics and probably knew Donnie from local village and school board meetings. I heard Donnie talk about George quite a bit over the years. He always acted as if George was a good friend of his. But then again, Donnie liked to talk about the important people he knew and would frequently talk about possible business deals he was working on with them. A lot of his business deals involved brokering some sort of business deal or putting two people together to earn a commission. When you would listen to Donnie, you always felt like he was just a few days away from becoming rich and hitting the big time.

In late November 1993, Donnie called me at my law office. He asked whether I would be able to attend a refinancing closing on his behalf, which was scheduled for two days later on November 22. He indicated the files were almost complete and all I had to do was to provide an attorney's opinion and update the closing figures. Donnie said that the closing was for his good friend, George.

"It's a chance for you to get to know him," Donnie said. "He could be a good source of business for you in the future."

The next day, the file was sitting on my desk. I slid it open and began reading the details of a transaction called the "Brookside Plaza Partnership." It seemed routine. And even though I was always hesitant to become involved in any transaction initiated by Donnie, this one just seemed straightforward. Besides, the pull of additional business made it more worthwhile than most closings.

I called George and told him I would be attending the closing on behalf of Donnie. He was friendly and agreeable. We talked briefly about the deal, which involved the refinancing of a mortgage loan on a small strip mall that George owned through one of his real estate partnerships. I did my initial review and calculated the final closing figures. An hour or two later, I called George and told him he would need to have $1.6 million to complete the closings. "No problem," he said. "I will see you in the morning." Nothing unusual, nothing to set off warning bells. Typical day, typical closing.

I attended the closing at the office of the seller's attorney. George arrived a little early and asked to talk to me in the hall.

"The wire is late," he said. "I don't have the closing funds in yet. I'm hoping they will be here shortly."

"Routine problem," I told him. "Let's see if we can do a dry closing and as soon as the funds are wired in we will be good to go. You won't even have to come back."

I went back into the closing and worked out the details of the dry closing with the attorney for the bank that was providing funds for the refinancing. We went through the closing documents and completed the routine review of the transaction. I shook hands with George as I got my files together.

"Check on the wire first thing in the morning, and give me a call," I said.

That was it. I gathered my files, put my coat on and stepped out into the cold Chicago wind. I was satisfied that I had done a very good job on a real estate transaction for a fairly important client. I was reasonably certain George would consider me for additional legal business.

The next morning, I touched base with George. Still, no wired funds. In the afternoon the same thing. We agreed to talk first thing the following morning. As soon as I got to my office the next morning, there was a message from George sitting on my chair. *Wire is probably in*, I thought to myself. I got my morning coffee, sat down at my desk and returned the call. George answered after the first ring.

"The wire is still not in," he said.

"This could be a problem," I told him. "If we don't get the funds soon, we may have to break the escrow and redo the closing. Is there anything I can do to try and expedite the funds?"

There was a moment of silence on the other line. Finally, George said, "I don't know if you really can help, but your dad is not answering my calls. He was supposed to have wired the funds yesterday and I can't get hold of him. I know your mom is sick, but I need him to get the $1.6 million into my account."

My heart dropped.

"*Donnie* is wiring you the funds?!" I didn't want to sound incredulous, but I could not believe what I was hearing. "*Donnie* is the one who is supposed to wire you the $1.6 million?" I asked again.

"I know you don't know the details," George said innocently, "but he is cashing in RTC (resolution trust) certificates. If you could see if you could get hold of him, please have him call me. Maybe we still have time to get the funds wired before the close of the day."

"OK," I said very slowly, "Let me try and track down Donnie and find out what is happening."

I sat in my chair holding the phone for several minutes after George hung up. My office was in the front of the building and I had a large window that overlooked the parking lot. I watched a small white car maneuver into a parking place. I watched the traffic flying by on the highway. My mind was alert and numb at the same time.

It was not going to be hard to track Donnie down. He was sitting in the office down the hall. I got up and headed towards his office. Who knows? Maybe I was wrong. Maybe Donnie *was* wiring the $1.6 million. Maybe there was something I didn't know about that will explain all of this. But I think I knew as soon as George started the conversation that the $1.6 million was going to be a problem. The question was how big.

I knew I was totally, absolutely screwed.

Donnie was sitting in his office, his briefcase was open, and he had his yellow pad out on the desk. I stood in the door for a few seconds until he looked up.

"Yo, what's up?" he casually said.

"Donnie, George wants to know what you have done with his $1.6 million."

Donnie looked at me, his eyes blank through his glasses. He waited a minute and finally said, "You better call your mother."

I walked out of his office back down the hall, stopped at my office, picked up my purse and car keys and headed out the door. And that is how I ended up in my closet on the evening of November 24, 1993.

"You know you are going to have to fix this … or at least face it," Cindy said after the second glass of wine. "You would get bored here in this closet."

"I know," I finally said. "I just don't know if I am up to it."

"Well," Cindy says, "fixing can probably wait until tomorrow."

We both started our slow crawl out of the closet.

"Tomorrow works for me, but there is something I need to do tonight," I told her.

Cindy and I drove over to my law office. She stood next to me shivering in the cold, damp Chicago wind as I took a razorblade out of my coat pocket and methodically scraped Donnie's name off my office window. I wished I could just as easily scrape him out of our lives.

The next morning, I called Donnie and told him to leave every piece of paper he had on the George file on my desk. He brought a file and handed it to me without saying a word. I spent the next two hours looking through the mess that was now *my* problem.

The Brookside shopping center was owned by a partnership in which George was a principal. It had been financed with a mortgage with the Republic Savings Bank. In August of 1992, the Resolution Trust Company was appointed the receiver for the Republic Bank. The Resolution Trust Corporation (RTC) was a government-owned asset management company that was responsible for liquidating real estate assets that had been declared insolvent during the savings and loan crisis in the late 1980s. After the RTC took over the loan, George met with Donnie to talk about his options for refinancing the loan now held by the Resolution Trust Company. At that time, Donnie represented that he could negotiate a reduction of the principal balance on the Brookside loan, which would allow George to refinance the balance at a much more favorable interest rate.

Donnie represented that the RTC had mishandled many of the loans it managed. He indicated he "knew someone at the RTC" and could negotiate a transaction in which Brookside would obtain "Receivership Certificates from the RTC in exchange for Brookside's forbearance from filing suit against the RTC for their mismanagement of the loan." The certificates could then be used to pay down the principal balance of the

Brookside loan allowing George to refinance his reduced mortgage at a lower interest rate.

Between December and May, Donnie had worked with George and the attorney for the refinancing bank representing the necessary funds that would be coming to pay down the mortgage. In the meantime, Donnie failed to provide the documents requested by the attorney for refinancing the loan in a timely manner, which resulted in a significant interest rate increase for the refinanced loan.

The closing was initially set for October 12, 1993. Donnie did not show up at that closing although he telephoned the parties and said he was in Texas finishing the documents for the certificates and would be able to deliver all of the required documents. A second closing was set for November 22. Donnie called and indicated he was ill and could not attend. It was this third scheduled closing that Donnie asked me to handle.

The file Donnie handed me contained handwritten letters from Donnie explaining he had a "contact" at the Resolution Trust Company. There were pages of figures that showed how Donnie had come up with the $1.6 million from the sale of these RTC certificates. I cannot say to this date exactly what type of "Receivership Certificates" Donnie was thinking of when he started the transaction. Generally, there was always some kernel of truth in a Donnie fantasy. I knew a bankruptcy Trustee could issue Receivership Certificates that could be sold and the proceeds used to maintain the assets of a bankrupt estate. The asset of the bankrupt's estate would be used as collateral to secure the certificates, which would take priority even over first mortgages. It would seem Donnie had taken this concept of Receiver Certificates and told George he could do something similar. There was never any documentation presented that showed Donnie dealt with anyone at the RTC concerning these certificates, including Mom, who happened to be one of the staff attorneys at the RTC in Plano, Texas.

Interestingly, there was also a commission agreement between George and Donnie. George had agreed to pay Donnie a percentage of what appeared to be the amount of money that would be brought to the table. It was almost as if Donnie thought he could get the certificates wrongfully and then sell them at a profit. Hours later, as I explained the situation to my ever-patient law partner, John, he would look at the commission agreement and say, "He was going to take a piece of whatever he got from the RTC?" For whatever reason, John was never rattled by Donnie shenanigans. It was almost like he found Donnie's action so unbelievable it was almost amusing. It was hard to explain.

"It's not like he was being greedy," I told John. "Think about it. He negotiated this commission agreement when he knew there were no certificates. He knew he was never going to get any money. What sense does that make? It's all part of the fantasy."

"I don't get it," John muttered. However, John did volunteer to be the one to go tell George his $1.6 million dollars was not going to materialize. I think he knew I was more on edge than usual about this Donnie problem.

We needed damage control. I called Donnie and asked him to stop by my office. He shuffled in about an hour later. I wrote a name and address on a piece of paper and handed it to him.

"What is this?" he asked.

"It's the name of the mental health clinic you are going to check yourself into after you leave here. Get some help!"

"Will it help the case?" he asked.

"I hope it will help you. Get on some meds. Figure out what is wrong with you. Just do it," I sigh. I am really not into trying to explain things to Donnie. He has lost his voice in these types of decisions.

To my utter surprise, he did as he was told. Mom, as usual, was devastated by Donnie's behavior. She made the following entry in her journal.

> *"Yesterday, I discovered that Donnie put everything at risk again with his sickness. Father, I know he has this sickness and I don't know what to do about it. It's so easy to ignore the fact of its existence when things are smooth, but I know it's always there. Give me the wisdom to know what to do and don't let his actions hurt anyone. I cannot handle this by myself. I need my job more than ever now. Is this the reason this job has led me to Dallas? Won't Donnie be the same here as he is in Chicago? Lord, my mind is open to your power. Show me what to do and I will do it. Comfort Lori in all this distress. Help her to be calm and to make good decisions. I need your peace – so many things are running in my mind. All the memories of situations I faced in the past because of Donnie's sickness. Should I call his family? They must know about him. I think he has been this way all of his life. Please don't let this hurt the people I love. Forgive me for getting so comfortable with the situation that I let this happen again, I have some of this sickness too. I want to believe him so much even when I know the truth is not in him. I must put this in your hands or it will destroy me. Give me wisdom, and strength today."*

I wish I could say this was end of the George story, but it was not. In December of 1995, my law firm was served with a lawsuit filed by George and his Brookside Plaza Partnership. The lawsuit requested the $1.6 million George never received from the sale of the nonexistent RTC certificates. Eventually, a claim was added saying I should be held liable because I should have known Donnie was crazy. And maybe I should have known. Or maybe I am just as much a victim as George.

I was haunted by Donnie's past and wonder what I could have done to change any of it. I couldn't sleep at night thinking about Noreen, Loretta, Mom, and Donnie's clients. Still, I don't know what I can do. Everyone believes Donnie. A prominent business man believed him. The Attorney Registration and Disciplinary Commission believed him. His women believe him. I was no different, I suppose. I knew he was a liar. If he had tried to sneak something big by me, I would have caught on right away. I have Donnie Radar. He caught me because the transaction was so simple that I let my guard down. I let him win.

I had dealt with some pretty serious stuff with Donnie, but it was hard to accept that Mom continued to stay with Donnie after the George incident. In fact, I had a hard time even being in the same room as Donnie. Although Mom was horrified at my legal troubles, she wanted me to understand Donnie. I am not sure how it happened, but I ended up visiting Donnie's psychiatrist with Mom. I think Mom wanted me to talk to him to try and get over the anger I felt towards both of them. The psychiatrist was friendly and open about Donnie's condition. He talked about manic depression and bipolar disorders. The grandiose stories, the schemes ... they are all indicative of his disorder.

Eventually, my malpractice insurance carrier paid a sum sufficient to allow the dismissal of the case against me. It was the end of the George story, but I think Mom realized she was going to need to expedite Donnie's exit from the practice of law. In fact, it was becoming increasingly apparent he needed to leave the state of Illinois. Loretta's murder and the George fiasco had highlighted the fact that Donnie seemed to be increasingly losing his grip on the little bit of reality that remained in his world.

Everyone knew there would be no more lying low, bankruptcy filings, or mental health respites to save Donnie's career.

All of the reprieves were gone, the excuses were all used up, and the explanations were over. Donnie Rudd was not coming back as Mr. Condo or even as a practicing Illinois attorney. This phoenix would not rise from the ashes again. The miracle resurrections were over, along with Donnie's legal career.

Mom's focus turned towards averting financial ruin and jail.

"It's time to get him out of Dodge," Mom told me. "He can't stay here. Texas is bigger. He doesn't know many people in Texas. I'm moving him to Texas permanently, right now."

It sounded good, but it wasn't as easy as just packing a bag and driving south. Second chances are hard to find in a world that runs on email, electronic background checks, website searches, and interstate communications. Donnie's involvement in the Bodtke investigation had made him something of an Internet sensation as his name brought up newspaper articles, pictures of his car with the Mr. Condo license plate, and theories as to whether or not he was a murderer. There were loose ends Mom had to figure out in order to have a clean break with the state of Illinois. The various investigations that were ongoing regarding Donnie's activities had the potential to open the door to more possible criminal actions. Controlling what Donnie said was impossible. Therefore, Mom had to control access to Donnie.

The ongoing investigation by the Illinois (ARDC) Attorney Registration Commission posed the biggest immediate threat. The assigned investigator wanted to talk to Donnie. Donnie used his only "get out of jail free" card when the Commission dismissed many of the complaints based on his representation that his medical condition was stabilized. Donnie would need to take the Fifth Amendment if he was forced to appear before the ARDC Board. Mom started strategizing about legal options for keeping the investigators from talking to Donnie. Because she had given up the idea that Donnie's law license could be saved, she believed she could leverage the license to avoid the requested testimony. She started the arduous process of meeting with various attorneys on behalf of Donnie to make sure that she had all of the consequences of such a decision considered.

While Mom seemed almost relieved to give up protecting the law license, I was not so sure the worst was over. I was willing to bet there were more clients waiting for a windfall check promised by Donnie. I was not as sure as Mom that Texas would be far enough away to protect Donnie from the growing mob of angry clients, although the distance might discourage the actual filing of some lawsuits. On occasion, an irate client would show up at Mom's townhouse inquiring about a check or asking if Donnie filed his lawsuit. It was impossible to explain to these clients why they were not going to get the promised money. It made no sense to us, even though we had been through it many times. The client's initial reaction was almost always the same; Donnie must have stolen the money. Surely, he is a thief. There was no other logical explanation for Donnie's repeated assurances regarding the wire transferring of money.

Donnie was detached from the details of his defense. He showed no apparent emotions regarding the looming loss of his license to practice law. Once the loss was inevitable, he seemed to step easily into the next phase of his life, scarcely pausing to wonder how he would fill the void left by the departure of the famous Mr. Condo personality. He was not particularly interested in the details of how Mom intended to disentangle him from the mess, but was amenable to following her directions.

The next step was to actually have the medical community put a stamp on Donnie's precarious mental state. Donnie needed to be deemed incompetent to practice law by a mental health professional before he was required to testify regarding the pending ARDC complaints. Not surprisingly, this was a relatively easy task. Mom wanted to make sure the determination was ironclad. She went to two different psychiatrists, one in Illinois, and one in Texas. After numerous doctor appointments in which Mom recounted the numerous stories about Donnie including Noreen, Loretta, and George, Donnie's unstable mental condition was officially confirmed with several psychiatric opinions. The official diagnosis was maniac depressive disorder.

Donnie was completely unfazed by the issuance of professional opinions regarding his mental health. He had only agreed to go through this process as part of a strategy to avoid responsibility for his legal issues. Therefore, he looked at the opinions as evidence of his success in convincing the psychiatrists he had a problem. At one point, he inquired as to whether a diagnosis of cancer wouldn't be a more effective illness than maniac depression. In his world, the diagnosis didn't mean he had a problem. Donnie viewed it as proof that he was smarter than the doctors examining him. At times, he was actually almost gleeful that the plan for releasing him from the vise of his problems seemed to be falling into place. The juggling job now became Mom's responsibility. She had to face each of the clients and tell them Donnie was no longer representing them, the wire transfer was never going to happen, and no one was going to get rich.

It was during this time that the depth of his misrepresentations began to emerge. A typical letter would be like what she received from a client named Richard on March 20, 1994. Richard was furious that Donnie had not completed a patent application for his son. In the March letter, Richard stated:

> *"Indeed, a friendship should have added to the ethical imperative that is operative in any attorney/client relationship. I must remind you that to 'toy' with the future of my son in that fashion seems remarkably cold, unprofes-*

sional, and unfriendly. In actuality, it seems devious and bizarre at best. The possibility of other motives, as well, is raised by your lack of cooperation."

Mom had no ability to explain Donnie's actions to friends and clients. No matter what she said, there was no excuse or reasonable explanation for Donnie's behavior. It was just what Donnie did.

After several months of doctor appointments and discussions regarding the appropriate strategy, Mom filed a petition for guardianship in the Texas courts and was able to have herself appointed as Donnie's legal guardian on grounds of his mental incapacity. The legal guardianship papers allowed her to step in between Donnie and anyone who needed to talk to him. She could respond to letters on his behalf, return his calls, and make decisions. It helped her exercise some control over his actions, although there was never any way to totally know what Donnie was doing while he was at work. The next step was to shut down the investigation at the Attorney Registration Commission. She started by petitioning the Supreme Court of Illinois to transfer Donnie to an inactive lawyer status because of his mental disability. The Attorney Registration Commission opposed her petition and to her surprise, the request was denied. The Arlington Heights police had been in contact with the commission regarding the Bodtke case and George had also filed a complaint.

Instead of simply allowing Donnie to move to inactive status, the Commission appeared to want to proceed with a finding and formally disbar him. This would prevent him from forever practicing law. More importantly, it would give them an opportunity to question Donnie. The ARDC filed a Motion for a Mental Examination of Donnie as part of their opposition of Mom's petition to move Donnie's name to inactive status. Mom responded in her own inimitable way:

> *"As you know from the medical reports you have, Donnie has been examined by four physicians, two in the state of Illinois and two in the state of Texas ... All of these physicians have confirmed the diagnosis of manic depressive disease which is a recognized mental illness pursuant to the DMS.*
>
> *"... The Texas Court says he is not competent but the Illinois court refuses to transfer him to inactive status. The Commissioner refuses to accept a petition for a voluntary name strike signed by both us ... If Donnie is incompetent, my signature as his Guardian should be sufficient to present the name strike. If he is competent, his signature should be sufficient to present the name strike. If we both sign, we have covered all the bases both with the Texas court and the Illinois court."*

Mom was clearly maneuvering the ARDC into a corner. She was winning in the procedural game of cat and mouse as she continued to fight the fight of her life to once again protect Donnie. Mom ended her petition by stating:

> *"It appears there is nothing to be gained by submitting him to another mental examination here in the State of Illinois. In fact, after I have finally obtained control of Donnie and his situation through the order entered by the Texas court, you are asking me to make that order subject to attack in the event your physician in the State of Illinois were to disagree with the reports of his physician and the findings of the Texas Court."*

The ARDC disciplinary report issued on September 23, 1994 was damaging and brutal. The first three counts all involved litigation in which Donnie told clients he had filed litigation and won substantial amounts of money for them when, in fact, he never did. The summary found Donnie guilty of engaging in conduct involving dishonesty, fraud, deceit, or misrepresentation and violation of the Code of Professional Responsibility. The fourth count was the case involving Loretta Tabak Bodtke. As to his representation of Loretta, Donnie asserted his rights to plead the Fifth Amendment and not answer any allegations in this matter. The ARDC gathered information in support of the allegations of misconduct involving the case and will preserve the evidence if Donnie decides to reinstate his license. Donnie was allowed to strike his name from the Illinois role of licensed attorneys.

Somehow, this was a victory for Donnie. He removed his name from the state of Illinois licensed lawyers on his own terms. He did not have to respond to any questions related to Loretta Bodtke and her murder. There was no formal disbarment and no in-depth investigation that might have increased Donnie's risk of being arrested. Once again, Donnie would walk away from all vestiges of responsibility for his actions and was virtually unscathed.

CHAPTER EIGHTEEN

Do You Believe in Heaven?

All of us thought Donnie would lie low after the series of disasters starting with Loretta Bodtke's murder and ending with the closing of the disciplinary investigation. The Illinois problems were a distant memory as he settled into his new home in Wylie, Texas, just north of Dallas. He had a new life there. If Donnie stayed home in Wylie, there might be peace in Mom's household and peace in Illinois. Sometimes, we felt sorry for Mom and what she went through as a result of her relationship with Donnie. But it was undeniable she was very complicit in many of the things that happened in her life.

Despite the lawsuits, the bankruptcies, the murder investigation, and his inability to practice law in Illinois, despite his misrepresentations regarding his ties to the Resolution Trust Company, despite the lawsuit related to Whitehall, a Resolution Trust-owned property, a remarkable thing happened. In 1995, Donnie got a job at the Resolution Trust Company in Plano, Texas.

While it was true he was never convicted of a crime and had been released from most of his claims and judgments in his various bankruptcy filings, he was still under investigation for murder and could no longer practice law in Illinois. Nevertheless, as 1995 progressed, Donnie once again rose from the ashes of almost certain catastrophe and resurfaced as a fraud investigator for the federal government. Once again, Donnie was back on top. During one trip to Dallas, he began talking about his work.

"I am involved in investigating the Whitewater scandal with Bill Clinton," he proudly announced. "I almost have enough information to indict Bill Clinton." I sat in a patio chair with my eyes closed listening to him talk. I found myself asking him questions and discussing the issues of his case.

"*Damn!*" I said to myself as I headed upstairs to my room. "*He can still pull me in!*"

I know everything about him. I know he is crazy. I know he is not working on the Whitewater investigation. Yet I still get sucked into the conversation. It gives me an additional understanding of Donnie's many victims. He has a way of making you believe what he is saying. Although I refused to talk about the Whitewater investigation again, Donnie continued to be obsessed with the idea that he was somehow involved in the complex investigation.

During Glory's next trip to Texas, he pulled her aside as she was leaving for the airport and handed her a prepaid phone card and a slip of paper. The paper had a name and a phone number on it. He had written a statement on the paper about the Whitewater case.

"When you get home," he dramatically told Glory, "take this phone card and go to a phone booth. Call this man. He is a reporter for the *New York Times* and read him this statement. That will be enough for them to know where to look about Whitewater."

Glory took the card and the piece of paper and headed back home. She showed the paper to her husband, Chris.

"You aren't calling," Chris declared. "I don't know if they will lock you up for being crazy or if the black helicopters will show up, but you are *not* calling anyone about Hillary or

Bill Clinton!"

Unfortunately, Mom was not as lucky as Donnie. Despite her doctor's reassurance that her chances of seeing a return of her breast cancer were less than 1 percent, on May 5, 1995, our mother was diagnosed with an aggressive recurrence of breast cancer, which had now wrapped itself around her mesenteric artery. For all practical purposes, it was the death sentence Mom always feared. The only question was whether Donnie or cancer would get her first.

The news of Mom's cancer returning caught the four of us unprepared. Each of us has a story as to what we were doing, where we were going, and what we were thinking when we learned the news. I guess it was never really gone. Mom was right. Those cancer cells were lurking in her body all along, waiting for a moment when we let our guard down and turned away, unprepared for the attack.

Again, I think of Donnie. Maybe God gave Donnie to us so that we could deal with Mom's cancer. Donnie had made us strong. Stalking us through the years and striking when least expected. Sometimes I felt like we had been in a war for years — a war that started in junior high and followed us into adulthood. A war that never ends.

Mom's viewpoint was fatalistic. She always maintained the cancer would kill her. She didn't really want to talk much about it now. Her only reference to her inner turmoil was a single question she asked Cindy.

"Do you believe in Heaven?" she mulled. "I just can't imagine we are all here by coincidence."

For Donnie, it was time to start planning his life without Mom. He was counting on the proceeds from Mom's life insurance to fund his life after her death. Sensing Donnie's interest in her estate, Mom decided not to give him any information. Donnie persistently dogged her about insurance the month following the discovery that her cancer had returned.

May of 1995 was particularly brutal for Mom and for us. As she struggled with her own mortality, Donnie's lack of feeling was especially difficult for her. Over the years, her overwhelming fear of being alone contributed to her decision to stay with Donnie. As cancer ravaged her body, she started to realize that *despite* her marriage to Donnie, she was going to end her life alone. For the first time, Cindy and I began to realize that Mom was dying and we would have to deal with Donnie. No more buffer from Mom.

"The police are here," Mom whispered. I could barely hear her voice over the phone. I was preparing for a case that I was supposed to present the following morning when I received the frantic call.

"What do you mean the police are there?" I asked her. "At your *house*? Do they have a search warrant?"

"No," she answered. "They are here — at my office. In the lobby. They want to talk to me."

There were only a few reasons that the police would be at the Resolution Trust Company in Dallas, Texas. It had to be something to do with Donnie. I closed my eyes and waited for the familiar feelings associated with a Donnie crisis to begin to sweep over me. The rapid heartbeat, sweaty palms and urge to flee were so familiar.

"Do you think I should talk to them?" Mom was still whispering, probably to keep the conversation private from her co-workers. It was hard for me to give her advice. I didn't even know for sure why the police were there. Was it Noreen? Loretta Bodtke? A former client? There were an increasing number of reasons the police would want to talk to Mom about Donnie. After a brief conversation, Mom decided to talk to her visitors. Information always seemed to help her feel in control.

I waited impatiently next to the phone for the next hour

for Mom to call and tell me what they wanted. Finally, the phone rang.

"It wasn't the Arlington Heights police," she said. "It was the postal inspectors."

"Why would the postal inspectors want to talk to you?" I was puzzled.

"I think it's because they are trying to prove he crossed state lines with one of his schemes," she answered. "They heard I was dying," she continued in a matter-of-fact tone. "They said if I want to give them a deathbed confession of what Donnie has told me, they would be available."

Now it started to make sense. Word of Mom's terminal illness had apparently rekindled the Loretta Bodtke investigation. Over the next couple of months, various law enforcement officials would visit both her and me, hoping Mom's impending death would unearth a Donnie confession. They never understood that we were fighting the same battle. The battle to try and figure out the truth.

However, shortly after the visit, talk about the murder, the Arlington Heights police, and the postal inspectors stopped in our family. We were caught in the vortex of death that was pulling Mom away from us. For the first time, cancer had begun to look more dangerous than Donnie even though as Mom's condition worsened, Donnie's behavior kept pace.

On May 23, 1995, less than two weeks after her release from the hospital, Donnie wrote Mom the following email.

> *"I mentioned last week that I needed to know which credit card to use this morning for my RK. Since you have not spoken to me since then, I assume you will let me know of your preference in the next three hours. If not, I will do the best I can without your help or assistance."*

Donnie sent a second email on May 24.

> *"For whatever reason, you will no longer talk to me except when screaming or when making unfounded charges. This has left me with some important decisions to make on my own. I will be having surgery, probably next week and will not be able to work for several weeks. Therefore, I intended to quit work at the RTC within the next week. This has the additional benefit of you not being able to use the job to threaten me. If I should be doing anything with the insurance or anything else, please let me know. I expect to be submitting my resignation letter this morning."*

Mom was inconsolable about the return of the cancer. The situation with Donnie was deteriorating by the day. We sometimes wondered how she was able to get up each day and go to work. The strength she showed in her work was the antithesis of the weakness she showed in dealing with Donnie.

On July 6, she wrote in her diary:

> *"It has been almost two months since I found the cancer is back and I have been thinking about writing in this journal for a long time. This has been a very painful time in my life. Most of the time I feel as though I had a shard of glass in my heart. I keep having the same internal dialogue with myself. 'Why are you so upset? Everyone's going to die. Even without cancer, death will come for you some day.' I don't understand why I can live with the knowledge that death will come someday, but I can't accept the fact that it will come soon and it will not be quick or pleasant. There is so much emotional pain here, my heart must be bleeding. I know I will be remembered — I think I made a difference."*

At the same time she was anguishing with the thoughts of her demise, Donnie continued to pound at her about the life insurance, the medical insurance, and her last will and testament. He showed no compassion for the pain she was feeling and provided no support in her time of need. It was almost as if he simply stopping trying to put on his "normal" face and let all of the crazy, chaotic, meanness come out. And all of it was directed towards our dying mother.

On July 21, he wrote her an email, which really revealed the madness that was engulfing him.

> *"I talked to doctor today. Ulna nerve is all but gone. If there is any more injury to it, it will be finished. In 2-3 years, at current rate it will have deteriorated to nothing. Nothing can be done to improve it. Alternatives are to do nothing and let it go downhill with no insurance to cover it or to have part of arm taken off by end of year and replaced. If arm is replaced before nerve is completely dead than use of device can be almost like real arm. Cost of arm is approximately $160,000 and will be paid by insurance; it looks like in full amount. However, if I wait 2 years, I obviously will not have any type of insurance and it will be a problem. They can take arm off just above elbow and I can be home in 2-3 days. Could have new arm on in about 3 weeks. If I am going to do it I need to get started so new arm can be made. You have all the insurance etc. which you refuse to discuss. Is there anything wrong with my thinking? Shouldn't I get it done by year end while I still have insurance?"*

"So he says he is getting his arm cut off?" I was trying to process the email that Mom showed me. "Is he having a problem with his arm?" Mom shrugged. None of us could be sure what was causing Donnie to lose control during this period. Maybe he realized his time with her was coming to an end and he didn't care if she saw him for what he was. I think there was also an element of fear in Donnie's eyes. Mom had run interference for him for years. She provided him with a regular source of income and medical insurance. He was about to lose his protector and he wasn't handling the situation very well. He was looking past her to make sure his needs would be met.

So as his wife lay dying, in typical Donnie fashion, he sought and found another woman to take her place. To replace Mom, he needed to find a professional woman who could provide for basic needs. He began a relationship with a woman who was attending medical school in Houston. Ironically, she planned to be a psychiatrist. Mom's dying took longer than expected, so Donnie found himself living two lives (something he was no stranger to). One in Dallas with Mom, and one in Houston with a woman who was going to find out she was involved with one of the most interesting psychiatric studies she would ever come across in her medical studies.

Mom's attitude changed after it was clear she was going to die. It became harder for Donnie to manipulate her emotions. For years, Mom had been like a puppet on a string for Donnie. He knew what to say to cause her anxiety. He knew how to get to her. But cancer was changing that. For the first time, Donnie saw his control over Mom slipping. Cancer had become the true evil in her life. Donnie was becoming inconsequential. He was less relevant than he had been for 20 years and he did not like it. Not one bit. She talked about this change and about his ensuing actions again in her journal entry of August 3:

> *"Donnie gets so happy when he can tell me something I should worry about. He doesn't understand that when they told me the cancer was back I stopped caring about*

98% of what I used to worry about. I don't care about the house. Let him blow it up or burn it down. I don't care about the furniture. He can put his cigarette out on the furniture until there isn't any furniture left and we can sit on the floor. I don't care if he ruins the pool. The only thing I care about is my kids and my poor little animals. And maybe my job a little bit. He can't hurt me by destroying my things because I don't care about things. Well, after he got through ranting and giving another one of his irrational monologues about how terrible his life is and it's all my fault and some morning he's going to run into the barricades on central expressway and then I'll be happy. I am so tired I could sleep for 14 hours and still be tired when I got up. It is hard to breathe because I am so tired."

I was adamant it was stress that caused the cancer to return — an indirect consequence of living with Donnie. But not all of my family agreed. Some thought Donnie played a much more direct role in her cancer return and ultimate demise. Mom's form of cancer was particular sensitive to hormones. Glory recalls one of the first things the doctors told Mom after her initial diagnosis was to "never take any hormone replacement therapy and to always be cognizant of anything that might increase the hormones in her body." Such a mistake could accelerate the growth of cancer and greatly increase the odds of its return. Glory remembers Donnie being particularly interested in this advice and asking several questions about estrogen. As a chemical engineer, it would seem normal he would be interested in a chemical reaction of this type. But as Mom always said, "there is no such thing as a coincidence" when it came to Donnie.

Shortly after the birth of her daughter, Sam, Glory flew to Texas to visit with Mom during one of Mom's chemo treatments. Sam was still nursing. Mom would lie on her bed next to Sam, just watching her. During one of these "resting sessions," Sam threw up a little on the bed. Mom dabbed at it with the blanket but was too tired to get up. Later than afternoon, Donnie noticed the small stain in the middle of the bed where Mom and Sam were laying. He didn't say anything at first. But later on that evening, he dumped a bucket of water on Mom's side of the bed. When she went to slip into bed that night, she found she could not sleep on her side, forcing her to sleep on the couch. It was emotional and physical torture for Mom.

These sporadic incidents were difficult, but Glory had a bigger problem after one visit. Shortly after arriving home from her visit with Mom, she noticed that her baby, Sam, had developed a rather large lump in her breast. Everyone always worried about breast cancer, but the thought of a baby with breast cancer seemed impossible. Glory took Sam to her pediatrician to alleviate her fears. The lump turned out to be the result of excess estrogen in Sam's system, presumably because Glory had excess estrogen and was still nursing. We discussed whether Glory could have gotten unexpected doses of estrogen during her visit to Texas but we could not come up with anything concrete. We had no clear proof of that. However, we decided not to drink anything that was open while at Mom's house.

A short time later, Glory dragged an old computer out of Mom's closet to use while she was in Dallas. The computer had been Donnie's personal computer. Once it was up and running, she noted the bookmarking of article after article about estrogen and its effects on breast cancer. There were also sites where hormone replacement vitamins and drugs could be purchased. She asked Mom whether she had been doing any research on the causes of her cancer. Mom had not. It was reasonable to assume that for whatever reason, Donnie had been researching hormones and breast cancer.

Glory searched the house for any evidence of hormone replacement drugs but could not find any. Although the computer bookmarks were troubling, we really couldn't document anything specific. Was it cancer, chemo, stress, or Donnie? Everything was becoming jumbled and we could no longer figure it out. But that was usually the case with Donnie.

The next few months continued to be stressful, and everything continued to get worse. For the first time, we were on the wrong end of the odds. The 1 percent chance of reoccurrence was a distant memory. It gave new meaning to the word relevant. When *you* are the 1 percent, odds mean nothing. It is only the 99 percent who talk about odds.

According to *Dr. Susan Love's Breast Book,* after discovery that cancer has spread, the average life span is a pretty dismal. Fourteen months. Even Susan Love really can't find much to write about this part of cancer. I figured by the time someone was looking for that chapter, they had pretty much given up on finding a cure or looking for choices. They were just buying time.

Meanwhile, Mom was losing weight fast. I couldn't tell if the cancer was making her thin or the depression. She was adamant that she would not do chemo again. She joined the Hemlock Society and bought books like *Final Exit,* the controversial self-destruction book that became a treatise for this movement of people who believed in the right to end life on their own terms. Mom told me she had a suicide plan. She said her former law partner, Gordon, was going to help her. I bought my own copy of *Final Exit* and read about half the book before I decided I would not finish it and threw it into the fireplace.

Donnie, on the other hand, had already started making the adjustment to the life he would have after Mom died.

"I'm going to go live with my parents after you die," he announced at breakfast one morning. The statement, naturally, hurt her feelings.

"He's planning his life without me," she cried. "I'm making plans about how to die and he is planning his life after me. He's not even grieving about the things we won't get to do together."

Despite her morose feelings over Donnie's lack of sympathy, she was also — incredible as it sounds — figuring out ways to take care of him after she died. She decided to purchase an additional life insurance policy. She already had a significant policy through her employment at the Resolution Trust Company.

"You have cancer; you will never be able to get that type of policy," I told her. "I am sure there is a requirement for a short medical exam."

Mom was bald, breast-less and the skin was hanging off of her. She wouldn't fool anyone, I told her. But she had a plan. She decided to buy an accidental death life insurance policy. She bought a realistic looking wig, put her makeup on, and transformed herself into a woman who was not dying an imminent death anytime soon. The exam went as planned, and she was now the proud owner of an accidental death insurance policy in which Donnie was named as the beneficiary. The only problem with that policy was that she had to die by accident instead of cancer. Donnie was the only one who had thought the accidental insurance policy through. We certainly didn't. Mom was swimming in the pool when Donnie "slipped" as he was walking with the hedge clippers, which were still plugged in. The clippers dropped into the pool but did nothing more than short out. So much for that idea. Then Mom claimed Donnie was trying to poison her by feeding her hormones to accelerate her cancer. Donnie denied it.

"I think she is trying to kill herself so I can get her life insurance," he said, feigning ignorance.

I didn't know what to believe. At one point, Mom told her oncologist she thought Donnie was putting something in her Gatorade. Donnie sat silently in the same treatment room as the doctor listened to this and gazed incredulously at each of us. He called me into another room.

"Do *you* know what is going on?" he asks. I shook my head no. The doctor continued by shaking his own head and responding, "Well, neither of them are intent on her recovery, that's for sure."

It certainly seemed like *someone* was trying to hasten Mom's death, but it wasn't clear if it was her or Donnie. So we did what we always did; we kept moving forward … and Mom continued to get worse.

She left a note sitting on the kitchen table in the Dallas house that read:

> *"Don't evaluate the success or failure of my life by Donnie. Donnie was an accident, an aberration, a boulder that rolled down the hill and hit me on the head. The worst mistake of my life was believing he cared about me. In my little naïve world that's what people did — they cared about you, they said they cared about you and then they took care of you for the rest of my life. What I went through to be with Donnie damaged me in so many ways. First I had to give up my religion, which has been a part of my life since I was six years old. I traded Donnie for my immortal soul. I made some agreement with myself that if I could have Donnie, I would spend eternity burning in hell. I wonder if there is a God whether he will hold me to that promise. Bad bargain. I bargained with the devil for my soul and Donnie's out getting married to Noreen."*

The entire situation escalated to a crescendo in August.

Jack, Cindy, Glory, and I engaged in one of our more spirited debates over mom's treatment. Glory seemed to feel Mom might not be as bad as we thought. Jack wasn't sure we should do anything but let things play out. Cindy was undecided and not sure we should get involved. She didn't want Mom to use her strength battling us. And I took the position that Mom needed professional help. We were all fearful that she was alone with Donnie in this condition. "I'm not sure who is dragging who down in Dallas," Cindy finally concluded. "Maybe we can bring Mom home."

Later that night, after a particularly cruel conversation with Donnie, Mom called us. She had checked into a hotel. She brought no clothes with her and had only her newest prized possession … the damned *Final Exit* book. Donnie was nowhere to be found.

Cindy and I plotted on how to get Mom back to the hospital. Cindy caught a plane to Dallas and was able to convince Mom that she might be dehydrated and needed to get checked out. At the hospital, the intern concurred that Mom was likely clinically depressed. He ordered an IV to fully hydrate her and sat down to discuss the situation with us. Mom was one tough cookie when she decided to be. She was angry at the discussion regarding her mental state. The intern told her he was going to recommend she be admitted for three days for a full psychological workup.

"I hope you have a good lawyer," Mom told the hapless intern. She quoted the Mental Health Act and went through all of her rights.

"Do you know I am a lawyer?" she taunted. "You'll be sorry if you admit me. *No one* makes decisions for me — at least, not yet!"

The intern was quite intimidated. Besides, when she was angry, Mom did not look all that depressed. The nurse came into check the IV.

"I watch *E.R.*," Mom informed the nurse. "On *E.R.* everyone moves fast. How come everyone here moves so slowly?"

The nurse just looked at her.

"I want this IV out now!" Mom demanded as she became more and more combative.

"I'll be back in 10 minutes," the nurse told Mom.

Mom timed it, and after exactly 10 minutes, she'd had enough. She removed the IV herself. Blood shot out of her arm and sprayed the ceiling before she was able to totally disconnect the tubes. The examining room was mayhem. There was blood everywhere, but Mom was calmly getting dressed. The intern, knowing he'd met his match, meekly signed her discharge papers (surely thinking "Good riddance!" the entire time), and Cindy and Mom headed for home.

"You can't take her home!" I told Cindy on the phone. "What if Donnie is there? It might be dangerous."

"Lori," Cindy said slowly and deliberatively. "At this point, if Donnie kills her, he might be doing us and her a favor." Everyone was tired of the constant battles.

There was no more discussion and Mom was taken home. We would take our chances with Donnie.

CHAPTER NINETEEN

Running With the Devil

In the middle of craziness, there were occasional normal moments. Those were delightful … but short-lived. My husband Ron and I flew to Dallas to spend a few days with Mom. We sat by the pool and talked. We'd go to dinner. Ron would rub her feet at night. We'd drink coffee and talk about Carleton Road and wonder what happened to our neighbors. I was sad when Ron had to leave. I still had a few days before my shift would end.

Before Ron had to catch his plane, the three of us went for a swim. The weather was beautiful. I pulled out my video camera to catch Mom, her bald head gleaming in the sun, floating in the pool. She caught sight of me and waved.

"Look!" she yelled. "No hair!" She waited a second and added, "No boobs … and no gallbladder … but still kicking!"

She looked at the camera and smiled. I panned over to Ron, who was floating next to her. Suddenly, through the viewfinder I could see her smile quickly dissolve. She moved slowly to the edge of the pool. She pulled herself up the ladder and stepped onto the pool deck. Then I saw her fall. My camera fell out of my hands as I yelled to Ron. She was on her hands and knees, obviously in pain. Water dripped from her head onto the pool deck.

As I reached down to help her, I caught sight of Donnie's reflection in the sliding glass door. He was standing to the side watching the entire scene unfold. He made no move to help. He said nothing. He simply watched as Mom struggled to her feet, both knees now fully skinned and bleeding. The image of Donnie watching all of this unfold and not moving a muscle to help his ailing wife chilled me to the bone. I realized that I was very afraid of Donnie. The balance of power had shifted. Donnie was back in control.

The next morning, Mom woke up and felt better. She wanted to go to work. I had no idea why. It was absolutely mind-boggling to think I had flown all this way, taken time off from my job, so that I could drive her to work. But it was not worth arguing about. Mom was very shaky. She was five days post-chemo. It really started kicking in at this point. She bottomed out on Day 12. The next week would be all downhill. At this point, I knew that her white blood cell count was dropping. The chemo was killing the cancerous cells, but it was also killing the good cells. Her mouth sores were starting. Whenever she'd sweat, a slightly sweet chemical small emanated from her.

Regardless, she was putting on a brave front this day. She had a pretty, flowered dress on. She was wearing her red wig and her "purpose" glasses. She had a briefcase full of papers. We stopped and got coffee at the corner store for the drive to work. The walk from the parking garage to her office was not easy. Her wig was slightly askew and she had a bead of perspiration on her upper lip. She looked straight ahead as she walked and I could tell she was concentrating on the task of getting safely to her desk chair. We finally reached the elevator, and as the door opened, several people greeted her. From the back of the elevator, a man greeted Mom with a peculiar question.

"How is Donnie feeling these days?"

"Pretty good," Mom answered.

"When does he start his chemo?" the man asked.

The question rattled us both. Mom looked at me. I raised

my eyebrows to see how she would handle this.

"No one is sure about that," she said masterfully. She was careful to not lie, but also not to give Donnie away. Incredibly, she continued to act as Donnie's protector.

As we stepped out of the elevator I burst into laughter. Donnie was *still* trying to compete! He was telling people *he* was going through chemo (have we lost track yet of how many times Donnie has feigned cancer?). Here's my mom, bravely working through an aggressive round of chemo, and he was telling people *he* was ill.

Mom's office was small and disorganized. I sat in the chair across from her desk and watched her work for about an hour. I had my video camera and videotaped her sitting at her desk. The phone rang and she answered boldly: "Dianne Marks." Such a routine thing. Answering the phone at work. I had heard her say that a thousand times, but I was happy to now have it on videotape. I could only hear one side of the conversation.

"I'm feeling kind of puny today," she said. It was more than she had let on to me.

"I'm skinny though — aren't I skinny?" I realized she was talking to me.

"You have cancer, Mom," I retorted. But Mom was back on the phone.

"I ate a banana today," she continued telling the caller, obviously proud of her eating accomplishments. "Oh … and Donnie has a girlfriend," she blurted. "He couldn't even wait until I was cremated."

With that, I slammed the magazine down and left the small office. I found it harder and harder to breathe as I stood in the elevator waiting to get to the first floor. Outside, I turned into the small alley next to the building and leaned against the wall.

"Mom," I said aloud, "Donnie *always* has a girlfriend!

Why would your cancer slow him down?"

I might have been talking to myself, but there was urgency to this one-sided conversation.

"He didn't support you when you went to law school, when you had to file bankruptcy, and he is *not* going to support you when you're dying!"

I know this. Mom knows this. Cindy knows this. We *all* know this. This is how the Hart family handles the truth in the face of all of the lies. This is how we learned to fight the battle. In this crazy, chaotic Donnie world, we try not to show emotion and keep moving forward. Outwardly, we are cool and collected while talking of infidelity, murder, death, cancer, police and investigations as easily as we talk about our vacation, children and jobs. Preparing lists to deal with a Donnie crises that are kept on the refrigerator next to our grocery lists. Praying for peace but hooked on the adrenaline rush that accompanies any mention of Donnie. This is our life. It seems that it has always been our life.

This story should be about an amazing woman who is slowly dying. But it's not; it's about Donnie. It's always about Donnie. Donnie is all we talk about. He's all we think about. He's the subject of every conversation, every phone call, every document. It has always been about Donnie. Even terminal cancer can't seem to draw us away from him.

The worse Mom got, the worse Donnie got. We were in his life now almost all of the time. It gave him a lot less room to control the drama. Donnie's antics — his cries for attention — also started to grow more and more bizarre. As Mom's cancer worsened, we entered a phase very similar to those early "Donnie Years." Only this phase focused on food and automobiles.

The initial round of the Food Wars was fired while Glory and our 90-year-old grandmother were visiting the Wylie house. Bananas were an important part of Grandma's breakfast routine.

She needed bananas with her cereal. Each evening, Glory would drive to the local grocery store and made sure Grandma had fresh bananas for breakfast. On one particular morning, Grandma woke up and found that there were no bananas in the house. She searched the cabinets, the car, but no bananas. Glory joined the search.

"Donnie threw your bananas away," Glory confidently told Grandma, while Donnie was sitting just a few feet away.

"Why would he throw my bananas away?" Grandma asked innocently, not being able to comprehend a childish act like that. "Why would he throw away a perfectly good bunch of bananas?"

"Donnie," Glory said casually, "why would you throw away a perfectly good bunch of bananas?"

Donnie looked up from his newspaper but did not answer.

"What would he do with *my* bananas?" Grandma asked, still believing the bananas could be found.

"Maybe you left them at the store," Donnie finally said without looking up.

Not ready to yield, Glory's dogged determination took her to the curb where a black garbage bag awaited its weekly pickup. She ripped open the side and pulled out what she was certain was in there the whole time; the lost banana bunch.

"Look grandma," Glory proudly announced as she walked back in the kitchen with her prize held high. "I found your bananas!"

Donnie immediately got up and headed up the stairs. He hated when he got caught, and in his typical Donnie way, when the heat got turned up too high, he always retreated. Whether it was to a bathroom, a sauna, a closed bedroom, or any other place of solitude, Donnie always disappeared instead of facing the music.

The Food Wars plagued the house all that week. Someone at the Dallas RTC made Mom a strawberry pie and sent it home with Donnie. The coworker called Mom and told her that the pie was on its way to her house. As soon as Donnie walked in the house, Mom and Grandma were asking about the pie. Donnie feigned complete ignorance regarding the pie. However, after he was challenged with the evidence, he finally disclosed that the pie was in the trunk. But the Strawberry Pie Saga was not yet over. Glory walked into the kitchen later that night to find Donnie standing in front of the refrigerator. He slammed the door shut as Glory walked in. As he brushed by her, she saw that his hand was covered with whipped cream. She opened the fridge and found that the strawberry pie was smashed in its pretty, decorative plate in the fridge. Glory set the pie on the table deliberately. She cut the smashed pastry into pieces and served Grandma a piece. Donnie moped all evening that his attempt at sabotage had not worked. But by the next morning, the remainder of the pie was nowhere to be found.

If Donnie liked messing with food, it was nothing compared to how he liked messing with cars. Glory needed to use the car to pick someone up at the airport in the morning. The car wouldn't start. She immediately knew why. She was visibly upset but we were all determined not to let Donnie win. The Wylie phone book was pulled out and within 15 minutes, a mechanic from Mr. Rescue was on his way to save the day. The young mechanic with a pronounced Texas drawl found the problem almost immediately.

"Ma'am, it seems your distributor cap has been disconnected. I'll have you movin' in a jiffy," he said cheerfully.

The following morning, Glory awoke to find the car disabled again. Again, the young mechanic from Mr. Rescue was called to get her on the road. And again, he cheerfully announced the distributor cap had been disconnected. After yet a *third* trip out, the repairman deviated from his typical response. He took off his baseball cap and wiped the sweat off his brow.

"Lady," he began carefully, "I hope you don't mind me asking — and I don't mean to be disrespectful — but is someone f*****g with you?"

If only he knew. *If only he knew.*

Our trips to Dallas were becoming more and more frequent. As Mom's cancer progressed, she was having a harder and harder time dealing with Donnie and his shenanigans. Cindy worked for United Airlines and was our de facto travel agent. She was responsible for getting one of us to Dallas every time a crisis developed or Mom needed help with her treatment.

Cindy knew it was her turn by the sound of Mom's voice that morning. As she hung up the phone, Cindy suddenly felt she could not even swallow. The lump in her throat kept growing as tears welled up in her eyes. It was so difficult to hear Mom in such an uncontrollable state. Donnie was so out of control that Mom had called the police the night before.

From Mom's diary:

> *"All I want is some peace so I can die and things just keep getting worse. Donnie is so out of control. It's like we've reversed positions and he is the one dying of cancer and I have to take care of him. Sunday night, he just went completely nuts. First, he came into the front room where I was sitting with a glass of wine and some pills which he took while I watched. There were about 8 pills and he said they were blood pressure pills. Then he kept going into the bathroom and I could hear pills rattling around. He said he had saved up 600 blood pressure pills and he was going to kill himself. Well, I reminded him that blood pressure pills were not very toxic and I didn't think he'd be able to take 600 of them before he'd start barfing them back up. So he decided to wrap plastic cleaning bags around his head and asphyxiate*

himself. Of course, cleaning bags are air permeable so I don't think he was in any danger but it was disconcerting to watch him with the plastic bags so after the 4th time I pulled the bag off his head, I called 911. Silly me to think that just because this crazy man was taking pills and wrapping plastic bags around his head that the 911 responders would think he was a danger to himself and take him in for a psych evaluation. They just checked him over and said "Now little lady, if you have any more problems just call and we'll come right back." Of course before they cleared the driveway he was running around in his underwear cutting all the telephone lines so I couldn't call anyone. You know, I never was good at dealing with this nutsy stuff but I don't think I can take it anymore. I think he's trying to drive me into some mental breakdown so he can control my assets. It isn't going to work. I'm not having any mental breakdown over him. And I am much too smart to let him win. But I'm weak now and he's trying to take advantage of that. I have to stay strong to protect my kids. Although he didn't say anything about it after 911 left, by yesterday, he had concocted this story that the police stole his wallet and his money and his credit cards and beat him up."

Cindy called me, completely pissed off. After all Mom did for him, how could he do this to her? If the phone in the house didn't work, what if something happened to her? How would she get help? We were certainly not depending on Donnie to help her. He was just waiting for her to die. We felt helpless when we weren't there. Cindy was worried about her both physically and emotionally. She agreed to fly down there the next day and find a way to get things back under control.

After much discussion, we pulled together a small package of documentation showing the history of Donnie Rudd. Cindy was going to go visit the police who came to the house and explain a little history so that if they ever made a visit in the future they would know who was telling the truth and who was really crazy. Next, Cindy would visit the guard at the front of the subdivision to see if he would check on Mom and make sure her phone was working. If we couldn't get a hold of her, perhaps he could go over and check on her. We needed an ally in Dallas who was close when we weren't able to be there.

Cindy spent a few days in Dallas settling Mom down. She made her way to the police station and even though her documentation was plentiful and thorough, she was not convinced the police knew what to think. The files were real, but why would anyone live with someone like that, especially if they were dying of cancer? The guard was a little more sympathetic. He would check on Mom and follow up when we needed.

In the meantime — and to no one's surprise — Donnie was totally out of control. He was now hiding Mom's pills. He drank himself to sleep at night. He'd disappear on business trips to Houston on a regular basis. We all knew it was to see his newest girlfriend. When it was my turn to go to Dallas, I arrived to find pandemonium. Mom was weeping on the couch. A woman had called the previous evening in the middle of the night for Donnie. He simply took the call in the other room without acknowledging anything to Mom. It had once again thrown her into a tailspin. It was another nail in her coffin. But Donnie, as always, was working on an explanation. A typical Donnie explanation.

Donnie walked in the door with a large bag in tow. His beret cap was perched jauntily on the side of his head and he was smoking a pipe. He unwrapped his package with great fanfare. It was a caller ID phone.

"What is that for?" I asked warily.

"It's to find out who is making these crank phone calls in the middle of the night," he answered innocently.

I couldn't stand it. He would have been better off just not saying anything at all. His pattern with women was unmistakable. I was ready to explode. I took his girlfriend's name, her phone number, and her address out of the side pocket of my purse.

"Take it back," I said calmly. "Don't waste your money on the caller ID. We all know who called."

I handed him the piece of paper.

"I'm smarter than you," I taunted. "I'm not playing today. Mom is dying and I am done with your games!"

Dumbfounded, Donnie just looked at me and walked out of the room (as Donnie always does). He might still try to get the best of me, but on this day I was determined to win. We didn't do direct confrontation often, but it was effective. A few minutes later the phone in the kitchen rang. As I reached to answer it, it stopped. The phone in the bedroom rang. Then the phone in the office rang. He was trying to drive me crazy. I picked up the phone to find it had no dial tone.

"Donnie, you have five minutes to turn these phones back on," I yelled. If you don't, I will march down to the guardhouse and have the guard call the police department. I can assure you they will pay attention because we have a cancer patient in the house."

I sat down and closed my eyes. When I thought five minutes had lapsed, I picked up the phone and breathed a sigh of relief. The dial tone was back. But I no longer felt safe in the house. I had never really been afraid of Donnie, but for the first time, I could feel his anger focused on me.

Mom sat silently in the chair. She had a blanket wrapped around her and her hands were folded in her lap.

"Mom," I whispered, "I'm afraid."

She looked at me silently.

"I think we should leave," I continued. "I know you don't want to, and neither do I, but I am afraid."

She was too tired to fight and nodded her head. I placed a few things in her briefcase and glanced nervously at Donnie's bedroom door. I don't know if he knew we were leaving. I called Cindy on the portable phone and whispered that we were leaving. I held Mom's arm and helped her into the car. I saw the light go out in the hallway of the house as I started to back out of the driveway. I still had Cindy on the portable phone, which finally went dead as we sped away down the street.

At first, I was ecstatic we were out of the house. However, Mom was very, very sick. I was driving around Dallas with a terminal cancer patient and no place to spend the night. I finally pulled into a La Quinta Inn, which was right off the expressway. I checked us into the room closest to the front desk. Once we were settled in, I called Cindy, Glory, and Jack to update them on what had happened.

After I finished the story and we dissected every possible option, I finally hung up. Mom crept into her bed. As I tried to sleep, I heard scratching at the door. I was afraid to look. I heard something tapping at the window. I was dreaming of Donnie and car accidents, murder, guns and lawsuits. Mom was up every hour and appeared to be getting progressively weaker. It was almost 5:00 a.m. and I was sitting on the floor outside the bathroom pleading for the sun to come up. I wanted this night to end so desperately.

Finally, at the first break of dawn, I breathed a sigh of relief. I had already decided I would take Mom directly to her oncologist. But first, I needed coffee. I put my coat on as I started out the door to see if there was any coffee in the hotel lobby. As I closed the door, I heard Mom whisper from the bed, "Check the car tires." I nodded, but felt that we were safe. In the lobby,

I poured my coffee and checked in with Cindy and Glory from the lobby phone. I could talk more honestly away from Mom. As I headed back to the room, I passed Mom's little blue Honda parked by the lobby door.

"S**t!"

Both front tires were flat. The bastard found us. I couldn't even think clearly anymore. Maybe I was just paranoid. Did I really hear someone last night? Was this just a weird coincidence? Again, I heard Mom's voice relaying her favorite saying: "There is no such thing as a coincidence when it comes to Donnie."

So, it was 7:00 a.m., Mom was dying in the La Quinta Inn, and I was sitting on a rock next to my disabled car on this bright Texas morning. I threw my coffee against the side of the hotel. If I wanted Mom to be at the doctor when it opened at 9:00, I had my work cut out for me. I headed upstairs to call Mr. Rescue to fix my car.

The funny thing was, after I got the tires changed and we raced to the oncologist, finished a round of hydrating IV's, and picked up more morphine pills, Mom wanted to go home. She missed her house, her dogs, her bed, her catalogs, and her pool. So, reluctantly, I headed back toward Wylie. Past the La Quinta Inn. Past Mr. Rescue. Back to the pretty brick house with the crepe myrtles blooming in front of the big bay window.

Back to the house where my stepfather was waiting for us. We started again. Over and over we replayed the same scene. There really is no escape from the house in Wylie. No matter what Donnie did, Mom still wanted to be home. And we were going to have to find a work around.

Unlike Mom, we would like to leave Texas behind. We were tired of flat tires, Food Wars, chemo treatments, and Donnie's drinking. So we started to plan how we could bring Mom back to Chicago without Donnie's consent or knowledge. Getting her away from him would be difficult. We agreed we would not tell Donnie. Somehow, we were going to sneak Mom and a few of her important things out of Wylie without Donnie being included in the details. Mom was cooperative, but understandably reluctant to leave her home. She knew that when she left, she would never return. Donnie was at the house only sporadically. He spent a great deal of time in Houston, presumably with his girlfriend. But he gave us little information on his calendar so we had to work around not knowing when he would be gone.

The first thing we had to do was plan what we could take. There would be no moving trucks, no real packing, and no real time to go through everything in the house. Everyone had an idea of what should be given priority in the move. Cindy wanted to take Mom's model car collection for her son. Family pictures were also a priority for all of us. The Christmas ornaments in the attic that hung on the tree since we were little were a must. Mom was concerned that her legal files were safe. She wanted to make sure her clients were protected after she died.

Personally, I wanted to find anything that would tie Donnie to Loretta Bodtke's murder. Cindy and I were responsible for all the logistics of the first week of our undercover move. Cindy received a discount at FedEx, so they would play a large role in helping us get this move done. We spent hours looking through boxes of papers, trying to pull personal letters, emails, files — anything that seemed important. We looked through file after file for anything with Loretta Bodtke's name but found nothing. We packed anything that looked important into boxes and dropped them out the second floor window so that we wouldn't have to go up and down the stairs. The boxes were loaded into Cindy's rental car and she periodically ran to FedEx to ship them back to Chicago.

The weekend went quickly and Donnie returned before significant progress was made. As soon as he walked in, all hint of packing had to stop. Glory and Jack also flew down to spend the next few days trying to pack up additional items. And finally, Cindy would make the last trip. She had three days to pack whatever was left. When she left, Mom would leave with her. We knew the plan was dangerous and I was really frightened at what Donnie might do if he found out.

Cindy hopped on a plane and made her way to Texas for the final time. She was also carrying a secret with her that she has not shared with anyone, including her husband. We might be losing Mom, but her spirit would live on. Cindy was pregnant. Normally, the birth of a child is such a happy event. But what Cindy was doing was dangerous and the stakes were higher because of her pregnancy. This is why she was particularly apprehensive about the plan to move Mom. Cindy didn't tell us because we would not have sent her on the last trip. She knew it.

Unlike previous trips, Cindy was going to rent a car instead of driving Mom's car. The cars were an important part of the escape plan. It would not be easy to take Mom's car with us, so the plan was to hide it. But this meant Cindy needed to have alternate transportation to get out of the house. It also meant Donnie would have to flatten the tires on at least two cars if he wanted to slow her down during her last two days at the house.

When Cindy arrived, Mom was lying on the couch under the hand-knitted afghan her mother made for her years ago. She was pale and a mere shadow of her former self. Donnie walked out of the kitchen in his pajama bottoms and a T-shirt as Cindy let herself in. He had on bedroom slippers that made him shuffle a little when he walked. He had his usual Tia Maria in hand and was well on his way to being quite drunk. But today, there was something startlingly new. Despite the fact she was bracing for the unknown, Cindy is still shocked: Donnie is bald. Bald as a billiard ball.

When he left the room to refill his drink, Cindy looked quizzically at Mom. Mom hardly looked up from the magazine she was reading.

"It's difficult for Donnie," she said in an unemotional drone. "He has told everyone at work he has cancer. So he had to shave his head."

Donnie was having difficulty with the attention Mom was getting because of her illness. So he did what he did best — redirected all the attention back to him. Who could beat this story? Poor Donnie and his wife were dying of cancer together.

Cindy headed upstairs to the guest room to get ready for bed. She carefully followed the routine we discussed. She had pepper spray with her, which she kept under her pillow. We talked about getting a gun, but since none of us knew how to use it we settled for pepper spray. "The last thing I need is a shootout at the Wylie house," Cindy said when she elected the pepper spray. She carefully positioned a chair in front of the bedroom door. If Donnie tried to enter the room, she would have some advance warning. Just before turning out the lights, she called me.

"Make sure the window is unlocked in case of fire," I told her. One of our fears was that Donnie might start the house aflame and we would be unable to escape from the upstairs bedrooms. If Donnie were going to try and kill Mom for the accidental life insurance, time was running out. Although Cindy had no life insurance, she figured Donnie would think she was expendable, so we took the necessary precautions. Sleep at the Wylie house was difficult. Each noise was suspect. *Has Mom taken a turn for the worse? Is the cancer winning? Or has Donnie decided to do something that will hurt us?* Nighttime was not our friend.

The next morning, Cindy watched Donnie leave for work. Overnight, he had transformed into a cripple. Unlike the previous evening, Donnie was showing difficulty walking as he made his way to his car. He had a cane and limped to the driver's door; a true method actor if ever there was one. Knowing that time was limited, Cindy sprang into action. Today was Mom's day to select the clothes that would be shipped.

The first thing Cindy did was to check the tires. As usual, both of Mom's car tires were flat. No surprise there. Also, the garage door opener was no longer functioning, making it difficult to get the car out of the garage. Luckily we had hidden extra cans of inflatable air in the garage rafters. Mr. Rescue was getting expensive! Cindy was able to inflate the tires quickly. A couple of phone calls to her husband and she was able to also reset the garage door opener. She had only lost about 45 minutes from our tight schedule.

The serious task of packing was now underway. But Mom was not interested in packing her clothes. She wanted to start with more legal files, which were up in the attic. The house had six crawl spaces, and it was about 100 degrees in Dallas on that day. The attic was about 130 degrees by mid-morning. Cindy climbed into the attic where Mom had an additional 75 banker boxes of legal files stored. Which one did she want? All of them, of course!

Cindy brought each one down and Mom looked through it and made a determination. Some were mailed back to the clients, some were thrown away, and some were readied for shipping back to Chicago. There was no way possible to carry and go through *all* the boxes. So the decision was made to simply ship all of them. Cindy had to laboriously carry each box down the rickety wooden ladder from the attic and down the main stairs where she packed both cars. When both cars were packed, she took the first car to FedEx and shipped the boxes. She then returned to the house and had to do the same thing with the second car. It took almost two of the three days to ship the legal boxes. And they still had not gotten to Mom's clothes and personal belongings.

Each night, as soon as Donnie's car pulled into the driveway, all evidence of packing and shipping had to be hidden. Donnie walked into the house each evening to find Cindy and mom sitting contently in front of the TV. He hardly noticed Cindy was drenched in sweat, her face beat-red, and her breathing labored. Cindy realized quickly that she'd never finish in time. She needed reinforcements. She needed someone to help Mom focus on the small stuff while she got the rest of the boxes out. Cindy was reporting in from the pay phone at a small shopping center down the road. We were afraid the phones were bugged so we were careful to only talk about neutral things whenever Cindy called me from Mom's house phone. We decided that Cindy's return would be delayed by a day and Mom's best friend, Pauline, would be sent to Texas the following morning to try and help with the difficult task of packing the remaining things.

Somehow, Donnie had gotten wind of the move, but we decided not to stop. He watched from the kitchen as final preparations were made. He was drinking heavily and made no attempt to show control. He poured vodka directly into a shot glass and drank it quickly. "You're not taking her car," he finally said to Cindy. Mom was adamant that she was not leaving without the Honda del Sol. Cindy was throwing everything that she could fit into the Honda. Pauline got into her rental car and drove away as Cindy ran interference with Donnie. Mom was putting on her sweater. She had her *Final Exit* book tucked firmly under her arm.

Donnie went over to the kitchen sink and began throwing up, so Cindy used this as an opportunity to usher Mom to her car. As they pulled down the driveway for the last time, he chased the car down the street yelling for his garage door opener (a pretty incredible feat for a man who was walking gingerly with a cane just the day before). Cindy opened the window and threw the opener onto the grass. She looked in the rear view mirror for one last view of Mom's house. The crepe myrtles were still in full bloom. Donnie stood at the end of the driveway in his pajama bottoms holding the garage door opener, watching the car speed away. We were leaving Dallas behind. We were leaving Donnie behind.

Mom was still worried about her car. Donnie had an extra key and she believed that anywhere we left it, he would get the car. But we had a plan. They drove the little blue Honda to a cow pasture, which belonged to a friend of Dad's. Dad had left a tarp for us, and Cindy covered up the car and left it in the field. Pauline, Cindy, and Mom finally make it to the Dallas airport and safely to Chicago. As the wheels touched the runway, Donnie called me at home. He wanted to know where we had left Mom's car at the Dallas airport. "The airport parking police called," he said. "The car is illegally parked and they are going to tow it." He would be happy to go pick it up if we just let him know where it was. I simply hung up. There was no longer any reason to humor Donnie. There was no longer a reason to listen to his lies. For the first time in years, there was hope that we had left Donnie behind. The miles between Chicago and Dallas made me feel safer. Now it was just Mom, us, and cancer. It would be easier to fight one evil at a time.

CHAPTER TWENTY

Mom's Final Chapter

It doesn't help to logically know somebody is going to die. It's always still a shock. People close to us couldn't understand how our family was so unprepared for Mom's death. To us, the end came quickly. In reality, it played itself out over several years. Death didn't sneak up; it announced it was coming a hundred times before it actually knocked at the door. But the cancer battle is about changing your own perceptions of how bad things can get. As sick as Mom was the night she died, we thought it could get worse. That was the way it always worked. I was always afraid she was going to die — that night, next week, next month, before Christmas. But she never did. She simply got worse.

Some people say they want to know when they are going to die. That way they could handle their affairs, say their goodbyes, resolve differences, take a vacation, maybe stop working, and complete their "bucket list." But the simple truth is most people don't stop living their normal life. To do so is an acknowledgement you are really on your way out. Only people who are really dying stop working, run their credit cards to the limit and see the world. Work, routine, and housework — no matter how little satisfaction we may get out of these mundane tasks — often define our lives.

It was Saturday, June 8, and in the midst of despair over Mom's progression towards death, Donnie was coming to Chicago to visit Mom. Despite her precarious position, she seemed happy he was making the trip. I couldn't help but think it would help her validate the love she clearly still felt for him if he bothered to spend time at her deathbed. One of her arguments for staying in the marriage was that she would have someone when she got old or sick. It was clearly not working out for her that way with Donnie.

I was apprehensive about the visit because I knew Donnie had an ulterior motive; he always did. He sensed the end was near and needed to be part of whatever was happening. I picked him up at O'Hare Airport. It had only been a couple of months since we left Texas, but Donnie seemed like a stranger when he exited the airport. It might be because the last time Cindy saw him, he was vomiting in the sink with the bottle of Tia Maria open on the table. On this day, he almost looked jaunty with his beret hat and a new suit. He had not told us how long he would stay, but I noted he had no suitcase as he got into my car, just his leather briefcase. He was not staying long.

"Yo," he said as he closed the car door. Like nothing had happened. Like Mom was not dying. Like he was not crazy. Like this was just a typical business trip to Chicago. Neither one of us said a word for the rest of the drive. I thought he might ask how Mom was doing or how long she had left. It would seem the polite thing to do even if he really didn't care. But there were no pleasantries or civilized questions on this particular day. Donnie only played the role of concerned husband when he saw benefit to himself. He was aware that I knew he didn't care, so he made no effort. I was not a big enough audience.

Mom did her best to get herself together for the visit. She put on her red wig. I could see that she had shakily applied lipstick and eye shadow to her pale face. She was arranged on the couch with a blanket over her knees, which would allow her to hide her shaking hands. She had a hopeful expression on her face as Donnie entered the room. Donnie gave her a quick, impersonal kiss on her head and pulled up a chair across from her. I headed to the kitchen to make coffee and Donnie leaned close to talk to her. As the smell of coffee filled the kitchen, I looked out into the backyard and remembered how beautiful this world was despite Donnie. For a few minutes I lingered there, watching the sunlight glint off the bird feeder. The thought of making small talk with Donnie was almost too much for me.

But there was no small talk happening in the tiny living room. Donnie was now sitting next to Mom. His briefcase was open on the floor next to him. He was showing her papers, a car title, and a quitclaim deed for the house (a legal instrument by which the owner of a piece of real estate transfers ownership to another person. The owner "quits," or terminates any right to the property). Mom looked at me. Her hands were out from under the blanket and were shaking. Anger filled my heart and the room. Mom wanted so much for him to love her. Just a single kind word from him. She had stuck with him all these years and handled all of his misdeeds. All the while, she feared he would leave her alone. And now she was sick, dying, and alone. Donnie had moved on. To him, she was already gone. Just paperwork to wrap up.

"No paperwork today," I exclaimed, my voice surprisingly steady. Donnie looked at me and at Mom who shook her head. He put the papers back into the briefcase. Everyone sat silently for a few minutes, the coffee cooling in the cups I had placed on the table. Finally, Donnie stood up and looked at his watch.

"I am going to try and catch the noon flight," he announced to no one's surprise. His visit lasted less than an hour. It would be the last time he would see Mom alive. They had been married almost 25 years. Even worse, I had to drive him back to the airport. Still, I felt a slight ping as he disappeared into the airport. Without Donnie, we were alone with Mom's illness. No distractions. No bad guys. Just us, Mom, and the cancer.

I visualized Mom's death many times during the years she was sick. I wanted it to be peaceful and meaningful. Music would play. The four of us would stand around her bed and hold hands. We would tell her how much she was loved as she slowly slipped away. Mom would have no fears as she left this world surrounded by the people who loved her most. But death isn't like that. You can't plan death. Cancer isn't like that either. It's vulgar. Horrible. Everything is black. The family is numb, shocked. The patient is uncomprehending. It's darkness and rain. It's watching the morphine drip faster and faster. It's lonely. The doctors desert you because their job is with the living. The nurses avoid you because they don't want to answer your questions. The outside world ceases to exist. It's a subtle change in the way you view such simple things as vital signs. There's the realization that these vitals are moving a loved one towards death and not life. It's the contradiction of wishing for the end, but still hoping that maybe this is not going to happen. We were almost at the end of Mom's journey. Donnie was gone and we were left to wait with Mom for her inevitable death. We had lost the cancer battle.

It was June 15, 1996. Mom's birthday. I always celebrated my birthday with her since my birthday was the day before. "I was a teenage Mom for an hour-and-a-half," she always said. I woke up at 4:00 a.m. and couldn't get back to sleep. Trying to sleep was more tiring than getting up, so I headed for the hospital. It was still dark outside. I stopped at Dominick's 24-hour grocery store and bought the biggest floral arrangement I could find. Purple lilies. They smelled beautiful. They reminded me of Mom's "White Shoulders" perfume.

Jack had spent the night at the hospital and was sleeping in the chair next to Mom's bed. I bent down to kiss her on the forehead and her eyes opened. She sat straight up in the bed. Her eyes were open and she seemed startled. As clear as a bell, with no hint of fog or morphine, she exclaimed, "Lori, I'm going to die and my affairs are a mess! What am I going to do?"

Jack's eyes opened as he looked unbelievingly at Mom talking about her affairs and her estate. We had assumed that we would never really have a chance to talk to her again. I tried to reassure her that we will take care of everything, but she was beside herself. "I haven't left anything to Terisa," she said. "She'll think I don't love her!" I told her not to worry, that we would think of something. But she was determined. It was as if the cloud had lifted and she knew that she had only a short time before the fog settled again on the last few hours of her life. She demanded a piece of paper and pencil.

"I am going to amend my trust," she said. She tried to write, but her pencil went in circles. The cloud may have passed from her brain, but she no longer had the ability to write. Cancer had taken even that from her. She was frustrated and crying, but still determined. I took the pencil and paper from her hand.

"Just dictate," I told her.

"I, Dianne Marks, comma," she began, and continued to dictate an amendment to her trust. She wanted to make sure that her little blue Honda went to my step sister Terisa. Mom tried to sign her name on the amendment that I had written, but again, she wrote in circles. Cancer in the brain left her unable to write. It would be her last wish and we needed to work this out.

"Where is your car title?" I asked her. She said it was in the glove compartment of the car, which was parked in the hospital garage. I sent Jack down to get the title. When he returned, I held her hand and guided it to sign her name at the bottom with a nurse as a witness. Next, I called Cindy. She was sleeping. "There is someone who wants to talk to you," I told her. I handed the phone to Mom. "I love you, Cindy," she said. Cindy was sobbing but we had a short time for Mom to say her goodbyes. I began dialing the phone, searching for people who were close to her. We made each call and she told each of them that she loved them.

Last, I called Donnie. Although I hated that he was included in the ceremony of death, he was part of Mom's life. "How are the kitties," Mom asked. Her voice was loud and cheery. "I'm feeling a little low but not too bad," she said. She was listening and frowning. I could tell she didn't like what she was hearing. I gently took the phone from her hand, Donnie didn't know it, but it was the last time he would ever talk to her. I hung up the phone without saying goodbye to him. But Mom's right hand was still by her ear as if she was holding the phone. She continued to talk, and at first I thought she was talking to me. But she was still "talking" to Donnie on the phantom phone.

"Leave my children alone," she said. "I always took care of you. Please. Don't do anything to them." She was pleading and bargaining with Donnie. She was having the conversation she meant to have with him before she got too sick. I tried to move her hand away from her ear and she slapped me away and said, "Don't trust him!" She tried to sit up and swung her legs over the side of the bed. I pushed the button calling for the nurse as I tried to keep her in her bed. "You don't know him," she continued. "He is crazy."

The cloud had returned and was slipping gently over her brain. We were losing her. Losing her to cancer and morphine. Although the reality is that we lost her years ago to Donnie. Her eyes closed and her body relaxed.

"You don't know him," she continued. "He is crazy."

"I smell smoke," she muttered seconds later. Glory tried to tell her it was from her cigarette. "Am I going to hell?" she asked. "Am I going to burn for what I have done?" We tried to calm her, but to no avail. She droned on about smoke, hell, burning, and Donnie. Finally, Mom reached over and grabbed Glory's arm.

"I'm afraid," she said simply.

I asked the nurse how we would know Mom was close to death. She said that bodily functions would start shutting down. There was usually a decrease in urine output. Vital signs would slow. It would almost be as if someone were slowly turning off each light.

By June 21, Mom was close to death. Each labored breath from her was tortured. Her eyes were wide. Cindy tried to hold her down. I began counting seconds between breaths. Almost a minute passed before she sucked another mouthful of air. I held my own breath in between her breaths. Sympathy dying. *It's a little like birth*, I think to myself. *The way you count the time between contractions. Maybe there's some circular theory to life.* But there were no happy endings here. A nurse stopped me in the hall to tell me how sorry she was that Mom was suffering. She handed me a newspaper article which I slipped into my purse. Weeks later, I would pull it out and read the short article about why nurses couldn't participate in the euthanasia of a dying patient.

Glory and Jack examined the morphine pump. The unsaid thought was that maybe we could find a way to end this faster. The pump seemed burglar proof. Mom was mumbling. Again, she talked of fire and fear. Jack held her hand. I told her it was OK to go. It was OK to leave. We would be safe. Our family was strong.

Finally, Jack said it. "She's afraid of going to hell. She thinks she made a bargain with the devil when she married Donnie." I don't know what difference it makes, but I know this is the truth. Jack picked up his Bible and began reading a passage about forgiveness. Slowly, Mom became less combative. She was still. Each breath was still loud. She looked directly at Jack and was listening to what he was saying. His voice was soothing as he continued to read and reassure her that her life with Donnie had not sentenced her to eternal damnation. My heart was hurting and my throat was swelling. Grief permeated me. Time had stopped.

On June 21, 1996, Mom died surrounded by her friends and family. Her husband (if we believed Donnie) of more than 25 years was not at the hospital. He was not in the state of Illinois. He was back in Houston, staying with his girlfriend while his wife died.

CHAPTER TWENTY-ONE
The Funeral

The morning after Mom died, Glory, Cindy, Jack, and I met to discuss funeral arrangements. No one was really sure whether Mom was married to Donnie but it seemed appropriate for us to take charge. Our funeral meeting was held at Dave & Buster's. Nothing about our family had been routine and we wanted to follow that tradition. Dave & Buster's is really an adult Chuck E. Cheese's. It is filled with video games, pool tables, arcade games, and virtual reality items. We ordered every appetizer on the menu and hit the video games. Jack sat at a game that looked like a tank. He cheerfully played war games while Cindy, Glory, and I bowled endless games. Occasionally, we would break and jot down ideas for the celebration of Mom's life. Funeral arrangements would be finalized at a meeting with a pastor at Mom's church. I asked Dad if he would go with us to meet with the Pastor. Donnie had been absent for weeks and it seemed more appropriate that Dad help us with plans for saying goodbye to Mom. After all, he had been trying to do that for 30 years.

Each of us had ideas about the service. Glory wanted to hear "Ave Maria." Mom liked that song. The minister was young and very nice. He wanted us to tell him about Mom. We talked all at once, excitedly interrupting each other. We recounted the story about Mom getting rear-ended on her way to a chemo session. She said she got hit so hard her wig fell off. She thought the other driver would think she was decapitated. We told him about Mom's catalog obsession, her fights with the doctor, and her assortment of friends, relatives, and business associates who cared so much about her. We even talked about Donnie and her major character flaw when it came to him. We told him about Mom's endless quest to find peace for herself and keep Donnie out of jail.

The minister told us the church would provide music. "Is there anything else the church can do for you?" he asked. Startled, we let that question settle for a minute.

"Can we have a hundred white doves?" Glory asked. "Mom always said if you don't ask, you won't get," she whispered to me. The minister thought for a minute and countered with "How about a hundred white balloons?" We sealed the deal.

Back at my house, the four of us sat cross-legged on the ground in my backyard. I had Mom's small jewelry box she gave me before she died. I opened the top and we looked at Mom's prized possessions. I took out a panda charm.

"Mom wanted you to have this," I said, handing the charm to Cindy. The heart-shaped locket went to my daughter, Abby. There was a solidarity pin we set aside for Mom's Polish friend, Jacek. A four-leaf clover pin was for her best friend, Pauline. I chose her skin cream, Cellex, which was still in the box. Mom swore by it. She would only put it on one hand, though. That way she could show you the difference and prove it worked. I wondered about families that fight over a loved one's possessions. It is hard to understand, but the four of us always worked best together under challenging circumstances. This was was one of those times.

That night I dreamed of Mom. There was a pond. I could see trees and grasses in the water. She was standing in water up to her waist. She was reaching for me. She had no hair. I wanted to go to her, but I was afraid. If she touches me, I, too, will die.

My need for her touch is too much. I put my head on her shoulder. I could feel her. I could smell her. She put her arms around me and I awoke with a start. I sat on the floor in my hallway and wondered if Mom was at peace. Then I realized my mind was drifting to thinking about Donnie and wondering if he would be at the funeral. Donnie was redirecting attention again.

Donnie said he wasn't going to come to the memorial service unless we paid for his plane ticket. We argued about whether Mom would have wanted him there, but eventually we unanimously voted not to buy the ticket. The memorial service was for us, not Mom. We didn't want him there. The funeral day dawned bright and clear. I couldn't talk on the way to the church. The large poster board with Mom's pictures was at the front of the chapel. People hugged and murmured sympathies. Some said ridiculous things like, "I hope she died in peace." I wanted to say she died the same way she lived: Like a warrior; struggling, scheming, angry, defiant, and fearless.

I slipped in next to Cindy and Glory wearing their sunglasses and sitting in the first row. Cindy nudged me and I looked up to see the pathetic sight of Donnie limping pitifully into the chapel on his crutches. No one was surprised he showed up. Donnie would *never* miss the chance to be the center of attention. There was no way would he let Mom, even in death, steal the spotlight from him. Glory started to giggle as he made his way slowly down the aisle. I couldn't help but smile. My stepsister, Terisa, shrugged and went to sit next to him. The sun was streaming in through the window. I could see the birds flying around the pond outside. It was beautiful. The music started and I closed my eyes, all the while holding my crumpled eulogy in my hand.

Afterwards, we gathered on the steps of the church. The pastor brought out the hundred white balloons. We gave each grandchild a handful of balloons. On the count of three, the balloons were released. Every eye gazed skyward as the balloons gently floated upwards towards heaven.

I was one of the last to leave the church. I loaded the picture board with all of the photos into the car and drove back to my house. The funeral luncheon would be held there. As I approached the subdivision, I saw that traffic had stopped along the entranceway. I wondered why traffic was so heavy on a weekend. As I inched along, I realized it was friends and family waiting to make the turn into my street that was causing the backup. There was no parking for blocks. People spilled out onto the patio, drinking, laughing, and reminiscing about Mom.

Donnie sat on the edge of the couch with a plate of appetizers balanced on his knee. A single tear trickled down his cheek as he told the crowd of sympathizers he did not know how he could live without Mom. I watched him silently as he talked about the pain of watching her die from cancer. He saw me watching him, but never looked my way and hardly acknowledged my presence. To this day, it still amazes me that he could talk of Mom's illness in front of me. He did nothing to help her the last six months of her life. He wasn't there when she died. He made her life hell right up to the end. Did he hasten her death? The questions haunt us. But here he was. The man was in *my* house sitting on *my* couch making small talk. He acted as if nothing happened and that he was not part of the incredible pain and suffering Mom endured until she took her last breath. He talked and smiled as if we were strangers who didn't know the truth. As the visitors began to dwindle, he stood up and limped out of the house, using the crutches to help him walk to his car. Cindy pulled the curtains back from my window and watched him open the trunk of his rental car and throw the crutches in the back. Without any hint of a limp, he opened the door to the driver's side and got in. He never looked at the house or the window where we watched.

"He'll be back," Cindy said. "We will never be rid of him."

* * * * * * * * * * * *

It is a beautiful Texas afternoon. Donnie slowly rows the small boat towards the middle of Lake Lavonne. Mom always said she wanted to be cremated and have her ashes scattered over the beautiful lake so near her Wylie home. Donnie stands up in the boat and lets Mom's ashes blow across the surface of the crystal waters. He closes his eyes as his wife of 25 years becomes part of the nature she loved. He weeps quietly as he slowly makes his way to shore.

But that's not what happened. That is the story Donnie tells his friends regarding the disposition of Mom's ashes. But it is absolutely not the way we said our final goodbye to Mom.

It is true that Mom always said she wanted her ashes spread on Lake Lavonne. She said it so often Donnie probably figured we had done it. Typical Donnie. He chooses a kernel of truth to build a mountain of a story on. It makes the story more believable.

In fact, Jack had a plane ticket to fly to Dallas with the ashes the day after the funeral to complete Mom's wishes. The four of us were sitting in my living room talking about the ashes after everyone left the funeral reception. Mom's beloved law partner, Gordon, was sitting with us. Gordon listened for a while and finally said, "I hate to say this, but your mom told me right before she died that she changed her mind about Lake Lavonne. She wanted to be buried somewhere more exotic."

"Great," Glory said. "Did she give you a clue?"

"I can fly to Hawaii instead of Dallas," Jack interjected hopefully. We argued back and forth about what she meant when she said "exotic." Different? Unexpected? Grandma suggested we bury her with her father. In a cemetery? The thought horrified us. I'm not sure who suggested we place her ashes in the lake beside Willow Creek Community Church, but the more we talked, the more appropriate it seemed. The only problem was that everyone was scheduled to leave the following morning. It would need to be done that evening. Someone was sent to retrieve Mom's ashes while the rest of us made phone calls to a few of Mom's closest friends. The final funeral act would be to place Mom's ashes in the lake at midnight.

Shortly before midnight, the ad hoc funeral procession headed for the church. The moon was bright and the summer breeze blew my hair as I walked to the lake. I could hear the frogs croaking as we all gathered on a small bridge near the church. Glory had brought a small cooler and we passed around beer and wine coolers, not even thinking about whether we should be doing that on church property! We sat in a circle around the box that contained Mom's ashes. One by one, we tossed a shared memory towards the box. Instead of flowers, we showered her with love and memories. When we had finished, Jack lifted the box and slowly poured her ashes into the still waters of the pond. The tears ran down our faces as we walked back to our cars.

"Grandma told me she was going to die," my daughter, Abby said innocently. "She said she didn't want to, but she was going to die anyway. She told me not to be sad. If I missed her, I could look up at the sky and find the brightest star. That would be her looking down at me."

Looking at Abby's earnest face, I knew my mother's heart would live on through her grandchildren. She was finally at peace. However, Donnie had not quite left our lives.

The day after Mom's funeral, Donnie headed back to Dallas. But he had unexpected company as he boarded the plane. Donnie's youngest daughter, Terisa, and Dad were also heading to Texas that same morning. Donnie was sitting at the gate when they arrived at the airport. Even worse, Donnie was seated in the row immediately ahead of them. It wasn't exactly the somber flight home from his ex-wife's funeral that my father expected. Donnie chose to ignore the people from his past who sat directly behind him on the two-hour flight. Terisa exited the plane first and Donnie was waiting for her.

"You have to help me find where they hid the car," he said. "They have no right to take it."

Terisa looked at her father and carefully said, "Dad, Dianne gave *me* the Honda. I thought I would sell it and split the money with my brother to pay off some of our school loans. She really wanted *us* to have the car."

Donnie looked at her, and for the first time, Terisa saw Donnie in full-rage mode.

"That is not your car!" he shouted. "It's mine!" He then unleashed a string of profanity at her in the waiting area of the airport. Terisa was stunned and visibly shaken by his coldness. "You'll be sorry," he yelled as he walked away, leaving her sobbing. "It's *my* car!"

Terisa was only three when Donnie left Louann. She always tried to understand her dad, but Donnie's contact with his children over the past 20 years was mostly the result of my Mom's interest in their lives. With Mom gone, any hope that Terisa had of establishing a relationship with Donnie ended that day after the funeral in the Dallas airport. Terisa kept the small blue Honda, not because she needed it, but because Mom wanted her to have it. As for Donnie, he showed no emotion as Terisa stood with tears running down her cheeks. Terisa was done with Donnie, but Donnie couldn't let go of the car.

Several weeks later, Terisa received a letter from Donnie that read:

> *"If you don't return the car immediately, the sheriff will arrest you and put you in jail for theft. You will also have*

to pay more than $13,000 of back taxes."

In December, Terisa heard from Donnie for the first time since the car fiasco. She had just purchased a new house and was in the process of moving in when the phone rang. Caller ID was still relatively new, but Terisa was on the cutting edge, so she had it. The number clearly said that the call was from Plano, Texas.

"Yo," Donnie said, as she answered the phone. "I'm in Paris and thought I would check up on you."

Terisa checked the caller ID to make sure that it said Plano and not Paris. She knew Donnie was not in Paris. The conversation was brief, mostly about her new home. *That was weird*, Terisa thought after she hung up. It wasn't like Donnie to call just to talk. She did not hear from Donnie again that year.

In January of 1997, Terisa filed her income tax return as usual. She did not make much money as a designer, and her tax return was relatively simple to complete. She was shocked to receive a letter from the IRS several weeks later stating that she failed to report all of her income. Specifically, they alleged she failed to report $13,500 of income, which was reported to the IRS on Form 1099. It took several calls to get a copy of the 1099 referred to in the letter. There were actually two; one from Donnie and one purportedly from Dianne Marks. He had not forgotten the Honda. In his mind, Terisa took $13,500 from him. It was not about Mom's last wishes. It was not about his daughter. Donnie wanted the car and figured out a way to get his message to Terisa by sending out a fraudulent 1099. The December phone call was not a check-in, but a checking out of Terisa's new address.

I counseled Terisa to call the IRS and try to explain that the 1099 did not reflect income paid to *her* but a property dispute with her father. At first, the IRS officer seemed incredulous. I sent copies to Terisa of the guardianship papers, Mom's death certificate, and court documents regarding Donnie's mental state. After documentation, multiple letters and phone calls, Terisa's income tax return stood as originally filed. Donnie had not won this round; a small victory for the "normal" side of the family. Terisa did not see it as a victory. She realized it would be impossible to have a relationship with her father. She sat down and wrote him an email telling him how angry she was that he would do this to her.

"I always stood by and tried to see over your problems," she said, pouring out her heart. To her surprise, he answered.

"I am mentally ill," he countered. "When I don't take my medicine, bad things happen."

It was probably as close to an apology or explanation anybody would ever get from Donnie.

CHAPTER TWENTY-TWO

Wives, Lies, and Insurance Policies

How do you describe grief? At one time, I would have described it as an emotion — a thought, maybe even a feeling. But grief is physical. Your throat closes and it becomes difficult to breath. It crawls up your arms making them tingle like they are falling asleep. Grief presses on your head until you feel as if you are walking stooped over. It is a constant dull ache in your stomach that turns into a stabbing pain without warning.

Grief swallows you until there is nothing left but sorrow. I am amazed at how much I cried. I cried every day when I got into my car. I cried because the car phone wouldn't ring and Mom wouldn't be on the other line. I cried when I pulled onto my street knowing her little blue car wouldn't be in my driveway. I could no longer tell whether I was crying because she suffered or because of my loss. I cried when I had to make decisions because she wassn't there to help me. I cried after I made a decision because she was not there to hear what was decided. I was afraid to live my life knowing that I no longer had a safety net that would catch me. I am alone. I am an adult. My life is my own. The umbilical cord that bound me to Mom was gone. I missed her. I needed her. No one understood. I dreamed of her at night. The dreams were real. I could smell her White Shoulders perfume. I could feel her warmth and didn't want to wake up. I wandered at the narrow edge between reality and the world of dreams. If Mom was alive in my dreams, maybe that was the reality where I wanted to be. Everywhere I looked, I saw her. She bought me the salt and pepper shakers that sat on my kitchen table. She bought me the water globes that lined my China cabinet, even the T-shirt I wore when I slept. She bought the towels I used when I got out of the shower. The phone beside my bed was her present to me the previos Christmas. The paper-weight collection in the hallway at Cindy's house was Mom's.

I try and think of happy times, Christmases, birthdays, vacations — but superimposed on every memory is a snapshot of her in the hospital, dying and in pain. None of us can get past her death. But even through our grief, Donnie is present. Our beautiful, kind, loving Mother is gone and Donnie is still here. It is almost too much to bear. I struggle with the idea of eternity. The fact that I will never talk to her again is beyond comprehension. I keep a picture of her, laying on her couch, talking on her phone in the visor of my car. I pull my visor down and gaze at the picture of her when I am at a red light. But despite the grief, there is no respite from Donnie. Although he is no longer connected to us through Mom, he stills finds way to wrestle attention to himself as we grieve. Always the center of attention, he robs us of the chance to focus only on our loss. Although not directly in our lives, he continues to wreak havoc with our emotions.

Donnie had already made significant changes to his life by the time he mailed in the 1099 to punish Terisa. Mom was gone and it was time for him to make a more permanent arrangement with his girlfriend. After the funeral, he moved to Houston. His girlfriend was graduating from the University of Texas Medical School and we presumed she had no idea Donnie's wife was dying while they dated. Donnie liked to say that he was a long-time widower. Noreen gave him the right to use that title. She had no real way of knowing Donnie actually had two dead wives. Even though she was in school to become a psychologist, the ever changing life of Donnie Rudd made it difficult to find the truth.

The interesting thing about sociopaths is how easy it is for them to move away from relationships. Donnie had no soul that would let him grieve for Mom. He was ready to begin again even before we sprinkled Mom's ashes on the Lake. Donnie went almost directly from his wife's funeral to be with this new woman. A striking similarity to his move into our house after Noreen's death. An uncanny ability to move on and not look back. It wasn't that we didn't try to warn the girlfriend.

Cindy's husband, John, was blunt. "We need to call her, it's not her fault. She needs to be warned." So John made the difficult call to the girlfriend. Not surprisingly, she didn't believe the crazy story of Donnie's past. The truth about Donnie was outrageous, but we did try. It made me feel a little better we warned her when I heard heard about their divorce.

The months following Mom's death were very difficult for our family. Not only because we had lost her, but because there was no longer a buffer between Donnie and us. Especially when it started becoming clear that he was not going to financially benefit from her death.

Right after the final cancer diagnosis, Donnie convinced Mom to undertake an extensive estate plan review. He hired a local attorney who worked to draw up both wills and trusts for each of them. All of this would be logical for most married couples facing a potentially lethal disease. But Donnie always had an ulterior motive. The majority of real estate assets were held in Mom's name because of the various lawsuits and the 1988 bankruptcy. These were considered to be non-marital property in most states. There really was not a significant amount of jointly held cash. However, the years at the Resolution Trust Company had resulted in a hefty 401(k) as well as close to a million dollars of life insurance. In view of the precarious legal state of their marriage, Donnie needed to be sure that Mom's affairs were in order. However, Mom had second thoughts about what would happen when she was gone.

Mom filled out the change of beneficiary form for her life insurance naming the joint trust as the beneficiary as directed by the attorney. However, she did not turn the form in.

"I'm not doing it," she told me. "I'm not putting his name on the life insurance. He'll be using my money to live with his next girlfriend. Do what you think is right," she whispered to me one night as Donnie sat in the next room. "He's not getting anything from me."

There never was any doubt there would be a confrontation when Donnie discovered he was not the beneficiary of the million dollar life insurance policy. The only question was how it would play out. Because the trust was never funded with the life insurance, her estate was worth essentially nothing. Mom instead directed the beneficiaries of her life insurance to be her four children. Cindy, Glory, Jack and I became the equal beneficiaries of the Resolution Trust life insurance — approximately one million dollars. My sisters, my brother, and I honored each of the monetary bequests she made in her will to her friends. We wrote checks for close to $60,000, gifting proceeds from the life insurance policy to make sure Mom's last wishes were fulfilled. Donnie transferred the Wylie home into his name by signing Mom's name to a quit claim deed. We chose not to contest the transfer, but we knew that wouldn't make it easier when it came to the life insurance proceeds.

Mom's will named her longtime law partner and friend, Gordon Zikic, as her executor. Gordon was a wonderful man who loved Mom and understood our family. He lived through the Donnie years and knew exactly what he would be dealing with when it came to Donnie. It was probably the reason Mom chose him to wrap up her affairs.

Gordon was the first to hear from Donnie after the funeral. On August 15, Gordon received the following email from Donnie:

> *The papers that Dianne signed transferring the beneficiary of the FDIC insurance policies to you as trustee need to be filed with the FDIC. I cannot do it as I am not the executor. If this is not done, my proceeds from the trust will be lost, and I will hold you personally responsible. Your lack of activity on getting me documentation has the potential of creating a loss to an FDIC insured institution, a violation of the ethics of the FDIC. The matter will be transferred to the Office of Inspector General today if I do not hear from you. The law firm of Marks and Zikic handled Sandpiper for several years. If you do not straighten it out, you can defend a lawsuit in Texas. Since you have not responded to me, a prospective guardian filed disciplinary charges against you yesterday. There are certain things you have to do under Texas law even if the estate has no assets. This will be my last communication to you. I am going to testify against you at the grand jury and you will have to deal with the attorneys from now on. Gordon, you are going to lose your license, your job and go to jail, all because you did not have the courtesy to write or call me.*

The gloves were off. Donnie wanted his insurance policy just like he wanted the little blue Honda. Gordon was a little pale as he showed me the letter.

"Be strong." I told him. "Good will triumph over evil. Don't be scared."

A week later, I got my own letter from Donnie. I had

to admit it was easier to tell someone else to be strong. Donnie terrified me. The letter was brief and to the point.

Lori,

This will be the last letter I write. I have had no response to my letter to you. I have written Gordon more than a dozen times with no response to date.

I need all of my family files, financial and otherwise. They were jointly owned files and when your mother died, they became mine. If any of you need copies, make them and return the files to me. I cannot operate and deal with the problems here without the files. You said you were sending the information on Sandpiper, but I have received nothing, By the way, I did not sign the mortgage on Sandpiper, your mother signed my name on it. When your mother and I were planning the estates, we agreed that the trust would pay me a minimum of $100,000 to pay the mortgage on the house. That is in the trust. She signed the papers to have the insurance payable to Gordon as trustee. I have written Gordon that these papers need to be filed with the FDIC but he has never responded. The insurance is trust fund money. To the extent, through neglect of the executor to file the papers or otherwise, the money gets disbursed elsewhere, it will be a major problem. I am not going to do anything on the lawsuit from the real estate closing you handled. First I was never legally served. Second, with what is happening in the estate, I am judgment proof in Texas. Any joint judgment would be paid by the insurance company if there is one. More importantly, the letter from the insurance company states that the policy will be re-

scinded if there is a material misrepresentation that affects the risk and that the firm answered negative when asked if it represented any financial institutions. During the entire time that I was employed, I represented several financial institutions. Should I inform the insurance company of this? I still do not have my computer. Your letter stated that the credit cards I am paying on was for computer items. It appears I am being asked to pay for the computer while someone else has it. I will not say anything more about it. I have talked to my brother who is currently head of licensing agencies for the national CPA's. If Cindy wants to exchange her CPA license for the computer that is her choice, but I will not be the one who deals with it any more.

I need the $100,000 that was promised to me and is stated in the trust. It would be better for each of you to sacrifice a little to do what is right rather than us all spend a lot of money in Texas.

- Donnie

Donnie managed to threaten Mom, me, my law firm, and Cindy in a couple of paragraphs. For a minute, I wanted to blink. Donnie was using the case from the real estate closing (where he claimed he was transferring more than a $1 million dollars of RTC certificates) as a pretense to blackmail me into sending him money. If I sent a check for $100,000, maybe he would leave us alone. It was Gordon's turn to remind *me* to be strong. But my anger at Donnie began to redirect my grief.

I received a second letter from Texas on September 5, 1996. The envelope showed the name "Richard Driver" and was addressed to me at my home. I knew from the minute I saw the envelope it had to do with Donnie. Mr. Driver wrote that "Donnie was incapacitated and I will be handling his affairs pending court. It appears that the only way to clear title to the properties would be to open an estate in Texas and since the claims against the estate would exceed the value of the properties, there appears to be no value in the property." Donnie really wanted the estate filed in Texas. He would have easy access to the court file, while we would have to fly to Texas to ensure that there were no forged court orders or court documents

My first thought was to call Mr. Driver. However, while the letter had an address, it had no phone number. *What kind of a guardian fails to put a phone number on a guardian-related correspondence?* I asked myself. I sat back with the letter in my lap thinking about what the letters from Donnie and Driver might mean in terms of future litigation. This was blackmail. No two ways about it. I looked again at Richard Driver's name. Richard Driver – Donnie Rudd. RD – DR. Richard Driver was not real. He was Donnie Rudd gambling that I was afraid of him. Gordon read the letter and agreed with me that Richard Driver was not acting as an officer of the court. He suggested I simply ignore the letter.

A few nights later, Gordon was back at my house. He had his own Richard Driver letter in his hand. Mr. Driver (a.k.a. Donnie Rudd) sent a letter to the Attorney Registration and Disciplinary Commission (ARDC) that Gordon was stealing from Mom's estate and not representing her interests. Gordon was not quite as calm about his Driver letter as he was about mine. Like me, he took his position as an attorney and his reputation very seriously.

"Let me handle it," I told him. "You handle the estate, I'll handle this. That way we can each do what we do best."

The next morning, I called the ARDC and asked to talk to the attorney who previously worked on the many complaints against Donnie. At first he was confused as to who I was and what Richard Driver had to do with Donnie Rudd. Eventually, he understood that I believed Richard Driver was a code name for Donnie Rudd. I am not sure what happened at the ARDC, but Gordon received a letter closing the inquiry a couple of weeks later.

There was some hope we would have a brief interlude of peace as we moved into October of 1996. I did not receive any more letters from the "guardian," Mr. Driver. But Mr. Driver made me start to wonder what had happened to Donnie and his guardianship. At the time of her death, Mom was Donnie's legal guardian. I decided reaching out might cause him to redirect his attention to me again. But in October, I heard that Donnie was seeking to terminate his guardianship in Texas. Dad said Donnie was trying to get one of his nephews to vouch for him at a hearing, which would dismiss the guardianship. Apparently, after Mom's death, a temporary guardian had been appointed for Donnie. I couldn't help but wonder if this new guardian had any idea of the history, the claims of murder, the misrepresentations, and the lies that had instituted the guardianship in the first place.

I struggled with wanting to call the guardian and not wanting to have anything to do with Donnie. "Call him," Cindy urged. "It's about the truth." In the end, I decided to do what I felt in my heart was the *right* thing to do.

I called the courthouse in Collin County, Texas, first. The clerk was very helpful and told me that a John Wishnew was Donnie's guardian. Mr. Wishnew was an attorney with a practice in Plano, Texas. Plano was the next town over to where Donnie and Mom had lived in Wylie. She also told me that Mr. Wishnew had just appeared at a hearing with Donnie three days ago.

I sat for a few minutes looking at the phone number I had written on my yellow legal pad. It was an hour earlier in Texas, but I figured his office was probably open. A woman answered the phone after the third ring. But she did not sound like a receptionist. She was sobbing and almost incoherent.

"I'm sorry; I must have the wrong number," I said. "I was calling the office of John Wishnew."

"No," she answered. "I am so sorry. This *is* his office. We just learned that Mr. Wishnew was killed last night in an accident."

There is no such thing as a coincidence when it comes to Donnie Rudd.

I did not know what happened to poor Mr. Wishnew. But there always seemed to be drama when it came to Donnie.

A short time later, we heard Donnie was selling the Wylie house. He systematically was scrubbing the 20 years he spent with Mom from his life. The furniture was sold. No one knew what he had done with any of her clothes or her personal items that were left in the house. The four of us notified him when we donated her wigs and glasses to a local charity but received no response. Despite the craziness of the past few years, the house still held fond memories for us. Mom loved that house and it reminded us of her. The backyard was beautiful, with a pool, spa, and a three-tier fountain. It was professionally landscaped with beautiful lilac bushes that scented the air when you sat by the pool in the afternoon. The Dallas sun would heat up the backyard as we floated in the pool. Cindy would say she could close her eyes and hear Mom telling her to use more sunscreen. We worried about Mom's little dog, Dinky, and her clothes and childhood photos that were left behind in the mad dash to leave Dallas. Our new reality meant that we needed to let go of these things. Only the memories would stay with us.

For a long time, Cindy and I tracked Donnie's business ventures. There was a sense that by holding on to Donnie's life, we were holding onto Mom. Because he was no longer licensed to practice law, Donnie could no longer practice the profession that had given him such access to people and places. However, the Illinois licensing issue did not stop him from representing himself as an attorney in Texas. More specifically, he decided that being a retired patent attorney with a penchant for humanitarian causes would be a good transition from his previous life. Donnie was transforming himself. He was creating a new Donnie Rudd that didn't have to deal with things like a lawyer's code of ethics or the attorney registration and disciplinary processes. To us his new business sounded dangerously similar to the businesses that had gotten him into so much trouble in the state of Illinois.

Around 2002, Donnie started referring to himself as Dr. Donnie Rudd on some of his social media posts. His online biography stated he had a Ph.D. in bio-science and a Doctor of Science degree in bio-engineering. Donnie held none of these degrees at the time of Mom's death. I can't say for sure that he did not get these degrees, but it seemed highly unlikely. His science background, coupled with his previous law practice, allowed him to assume the role of an inventor and scientist.

As the months turned into years, my family started to collectively exhale with the realization Donnie appeared to be gone. The whirling, chaotic kaleidoscope of life with Donnie was slowing down. At first, no one noticed. A Christmas family gathering where no one told a Donnie story. Wistful stories of Mom with no mention of Donnie. Occasionally, an Internet story on Donnie would catch our attention, but the personal connection to what was happening in Donnie's life started to slowly fade. Photograph albums filled with pictures of Mom and Donnie gathered dust on a shelf in my basement next to Mom's green purse. Boxes of Donnie documents were moved to the basement. The familiar feeling of adrenaline-fueled excited conversations about Donnie came less and less. I was no longer fearful of police, thunderstorms, lawsuits, and flat tires and no longer found myself looking over my shoulder. The dream of

Mom standing in Willow Creek Lake interrupted my sleep only occasionally. Except for an occasional story through our family, our life with Donnie Rudd was winding down. We were leaving Donnie behind though I couldn't help wondering if the truth would ever come out. A troubled peace settled over our family.

Contrary to Cindy's prediction at Mom's funeral that we would never be rid of Donnie, we never saw him again.

CHAPTER TWENTY-THREE

A Blast from the Past

For almost 15 years, the strange peace of life without Mom and Donnie became a new normal, creating a delicate balance between the past and the present in the lives of the Hart family. In November, 2012, an email would retrigger a tsunami of memories of our past life with Donnie. The message from an old friend said he was sending me an interesting news story. He called it a "blast from the past."

I clicked the link in the email and a familiar face flashed across my computer screen. I paused the screen and sat for a few minutes looking at the face of an aging Donnie Rudd. Without having even looked at the full content yet, I forwarded the email immediately to Cindy, who was vacationing in Mexico at the time. The link took me to a Fox News story, done by a local Chicago affiliate, about the famous "scientist" under suspicion for a murder that occurred more than 20 years ago. A scientist? Really?

A thousand miles away, my sister clicked the link I had sent her and watched the same newscast. From the ashes of our past, Donnie had reentered our lives. He was back. I couldn't help but shiver at the thought.

The murdered woman profiled in the television news story was Loretta "Teri" Tabak Bodtke. It was the unsolved crime that baffled investigators and family members of the slain woman for years. The prime suspect in the case from the very beginning was reiterated as Donnie Rudd. The TV news story described Donnie as a prominent Texas stem cell scientist and a former well-known Chicago attorney. It also referred to Donnie's website, which said he worked with NASA and was named one of NASA's most outstanding inventors. While it was true Donnie practiced law in Illinois, it failed to mention the removal of his name from the Attorney Registry. I was also reasonably certain he was not a legitimate stem cell researcher and he had not invented anything for NASA.

Over the years, Donnie's numerous websites and Facebook claims had grown increasingly bizarre with claims similar to the stem cell research and NASA work. Occasionally, one of us would start talking about Donnie and eventually end up checking out his Facebook page. Cindy was usually the designated Facebook "creeper." I had an irrational fear that he would know I looked at his site and somehow find me. Everyone crowded around the screen waiting to see what new adventure Donnie concocted. No one wanted to actually be his Facebook "friend." Our stepsister, Terisa, noted that the attractive women who did "friend" him were his only real inventions. She actually found pictures of the models he pasted into his Facebook as his "friends." It was the ultimate narcissistic act, akin to flirting with himself.

One interesting Donnie website that Glory found several years ago advertised that he could mail packages and letters for people from his Houston post office box. It was a drop box for people who wanted something mailed without letting the recipient know who or where it was mailed from. "He's the drop box for the Unibombers of the world," Glory reported after finding the strange site.

Sometimes you could tell from his Facebook messages on his newsfeed that he seemed to be getting into trouble. Someone would inquire about a check or ask why he was not returning a phone call. Donnie would respond with cryptic answers like the "SEC is investigating the issue." These messages would make my heart pound hard and my hands sweat, but a click of the *off* button on the computer solved that problem. It wasn't like that when we lived with Donnie. There was no turn-off switch for real life.

But the Fox News story warmed up this very cold case when it appeared on the local news during the Thanksgiving Holidays in 2012. Loretta's daughter, Stephanie Tabak, never gave up on her quest to bring her mother's killer to justice. She was unequivocal about who she believed shot her mother: Donnie Rudd.

"Every fact that I've looked at and everything in my gut tells me he's the one who did it," Tabak said in the Fox interview story. "The week before the murder, she [Loretta] just had it with him and she said, 'This is it. I'm not going to take any more excuses from him.' And she said if there's one more excuse, she was going to file a complaint with the Attorney Registration and Disciplinary Commission."

The news story reopened old discussions in our family. Cindy suggested we call Stephanie and see if we could provide information concerning Donnie. All of us feel a kind of kinship with the woman still grieving for her mother after all these years. But our family walked this road many times in the past, all without success. Did we have anything new to tell? The question was bantered back and forth as the discussion continued regarding our involvement in the reopening of the cold case.

Stephanie made it clear that she was pushing for a review of her mother's case and an immediate arrest of Donnie Rudd. She got at least part of her wish. The TV coverage had an impact on the Arlington Heights Police Department who investigated the murder almost 20 years ago. Although the file had been periodically reviewed, a new group of Arlington Heights detectives was assigned to investigate Donnie Rudd and determine whether there was sufficient evidence to charge him with Loretta Bodtke's murder so long after the fact.

It is not clear why the police seem more optimistic about proving Donnie's guilt today than they were 20 years ago. Certainly, no smoking gun has been found. But there have been recent changes in the Illinois hearsay laws after the trial of Drew Peterson that would make it easier to present evidence in cases such as this. It is possible some of the evidence collected almost 20 years ago could now be utilized under the new laws to increase the chances of a conviction. And maybe, for the first time, a group of police officers committed to doing everything possible to find whoever killed Loretta Bodtke were in charge of the case.

So, the Bodtke files were pulled out of police storage and an Arlington Heights detective by the name of Richard Sperando was assigned to relook at the cold case involving Loretta Bodtke's violent death. Sperando was a rising star on the police force. In 2010, he was awarded the "Crime Stopper of the Year Award." The award is presented each year to a member of the police department who has made a recognizable contribution to the community's crime fighting efforts. Sperando headed an initiative that resulted in the shutdown of a northwest suburban Illinois cocaine ring. And he was focused on reviewing the allegations against Donnie. He was puzzled as he looked through all of the case notes. Although all evidence points to Donnie, there were still things that made no sense.

After the broadcast of the story, the first to hear from the Arlington Heights police was my Dad. At the time, he was living with Louann in a small ranch house in Burleson, Texas. By the end of Thanksgiving break, there was a message waiting for Louann on her home answering machine. An Arlington Heights police officer, Detective Rich Sperando, wanted to talk to Louann about her "first husband, Donnie." He asked that she return the call as soon as possible. Before they returned the call, Dad called Cindy to talk about the case. Once again, Donnie dominated the conversation in our family as the news of the new police investigation traveled to the four states that each of us called home. A very spirited family discussion ensued over the first couple of days regarding the downside of engaging Donnie in any way. Overall, our position for years has been to avoid Donnie and discussion of Donnie acts. But the more we talk, the harder it is to stay detached. Louann and Dad had lived in Texas for more than 30 years. Most of their knowledge of Donnie's behavior is from what they heard from us. But the excitement the call generated was undeniable. It is our love/hate relationship with Donnie drama that draws us back whenever his name is mentioned. The years have really not changed us, after all. No one wants to admit it openly, but we know we are integrally involved in providing information about Donnie. Once again, he hijacks our energy, thoughts, and lives and becomes the main topic of conversation.

Louann returned Detective Sperando's call the week after Thanksgiving. As Louann talked about Donnie on her call with the police, my father listened on the other line. Dad frequently broke in to talk about Donnie and Mom. But the excitement of the call caused him to occasionally refer to Mom as "his wife," which she has not been for quite some time. Sperando found the conversation puzzling. Dad's interjections confused the police until they realized Dad's first wife was Dianne Rudd, my mom. Donnie's first wife was now married to Donnie's second wife's first husband. It was probably a moment of clarity for Sperando that there would be nothing usual about this case. It was about this time they started to understand the need to get inside Donnie's head and his life to really understand what transpired at the Bodtke's condo that rainy spring afternoon.

A couple of weeks later, the Arlington Heights police visited Jack in Pittsburgh. Jack was in the Navy, stationed on a nuclear submarine in the Atlantic Ocean for many of the years Donnie spun dangerously out of control. Like Louann, most of his information was gleaned third-hand from other family members. But he did live with Mom and Donnie around the time of the Bodtke murder.

"I called them," Jack finally said. "I called the police hotline number. I think Donnie murdered Mom."

"Jack!" I answered angrily, "Mom died from cancer. You were there."

Jack was adamant.

"She was node-negative, Lori. She had a mastectomy. The doctors said she had less than a 1 percent chance of dying from the cancer. But she died. Donnie murdered her. He gave her something to make the cancer get worse."

Initially, Jack's opinion was infuriating. I was angry that Jack was trying to solve a question that was no longer solvable. He was revisiting the issues we struggled with for years and were trying to leave behind.

"We did what she wanted — we always did what she wanted," he continued. "Donnie was a murderer and I think he killed Mom. We should have done something about it."

Still, I was not ready to think about whether Mom's death might be attributable to Donnie. Jack also believed he had a clue for the detectives.

"I saw a cane gun in the rafters of the Sutherland [one of the Barrington Square townhomes] basement," he told me. "I think it was a .22 caliber. That was what killed the Bodtke woman."

I was still confused. Somehow talking to the police made me feel like I was being disloyal to Mom. She worked so hard to protect Donnie for so many years. A brief conversation with my law partner reminded me of the past chaos of Donnie.

"My brother thinks that Donnie had a cane gun that killed Loretta," I told him.

"The cane gun was not the murder weapon," he answered immediately.

"How can you be sure?" I was a little aggravated at his confidence.

"I have the cane gun," he answered simply. "The police gave it to me. You should remember that."

I closed my eyes and forced myself to think back to 1992. The police confiscated all of the guns at our house. Some of them Donnie turned over and some were taken with a search warrant. When the grand jury didn't indict Donnie, the police seemed to lose interest in the case. Sometime later that year, all of the guns were released to my partner with Donnie's consent. Mom wouldn't let the guns come back into the house. The cane gun was not the murder weapon. It reminded me how difficult it would be to solve a murder so many years after the fact.

Later that night, I pulled out the small red notebook Mom used as a journal in the last years of her life. The journal stayed safely in my bottom drawer where I hid it after her funeral. The passage of time did nothing to mute my emotional response to seeing Mom's small, clear handwriting on each page. It was — and still is — excruciatingly painful to read.

Tears rolled down my cheeks and dropped onto the journal pages. It's not that the pain emanating from each journal page is new. After all, we were there. We lived it. We walked this path with Mom for years. But on this day, there was a clarity in the words that was difficult to see during her life. During the 20 years since her death, the clouds obscuring the truth about Donnie were slowly dissipating. For the first time, the stark, revealing picture of Donnie and his relationship with our family was emerging. There was no more hiding from what happened. This was not a love story. This was about a family that was repeatedly victimized by an evil man who had no love in his heart and no conscience in his soul. A man who never expressed regret for the pain he caused, the lies he told, or the crimes he committed. A man who came into our lives and blew our normal, all-American family to smithereens. As difficult as it would be to explain what happened and to relive those years, we needed to help the police understand Donnie Rudd.

The Arlington Heights police had methodically talked to each member of our family since the Fox news story aired at Thanksgiving. After talking to Dad in Burleson and Jack in Pittsburgh, Detective Sperando flew to Katie, Texas, to talk to Glory. She spent a couple of hours trying to explain our family tree and recounting stories of life with Donnie. The police were particularly interested in Donnie's extensive gun collection. Glory told them about the time she accidentally shot Donnie's small pen gun back when she was in high school. The police seemed interested in the exact location of the errant accidental gunshot. Both Glory and Jack agreed the police were focused and interested in all aspects of Donnie's life. Surprisingly, the questions being asked pertained not only to Loretta but to Donnie's second wife, Noreen. Noreen, like Loretta, died at a young age. Noreen's accident faded into the background after Loretta was murdered. During the investigation, the police were focusing on the deaths of both women.

Shortly before Christmas, I received a call from Detective Sperando asking whether Cindy and I would be willing to talk to him about Donnie. Although the call was expected, it was still difficult to think of immersing ourselves in Donnie's life again. The meeting was set for Chicago over the Christmas holiday. I was not ready to have Donnie drama come to my home in Atlanta. For years, Atlanta had been a "Donnie free" zone. But a Chicago meeting seemed to be palatable, especially if Cindy was there.

The meeting with the police was heavy on my mind as I wrapped cheerful Christmas presents and prepared for the long ride up north. I crawled up to the attic space to find one last suitcase for the trip. As I started to close the attic door, I caught a glimpse of the boxes stacked against the back wall almost hidden behind a long, silver furnace vent pipe. The wall of memories. Slowly, I opened the door and squeezed around the vent to sit on the floor next to the boxes. The attic was filled with boxes of Mom's belongings. I also had my "shoe box" of Donnie stories, which had grown to a file box filled with reminders of many of the more frightening Donnie incidents. Among other things, the box contained my pictures of Noreen and Donnie, the letter Mom wrote the day after Noreen's death, and newspaper articles regarding Noreen's death. There are also countless legal documents, deposition transcripts, emails between Mom and Donnie, and piles of files and documents collected over the past 40 years. I had several boxes of pictures, transcripts, letters, and memories. I was not sure what I should take to my meeting with the police.

Mom's green leather purse sat in the front of the shelves that held the boxes containing the memories of her life. I had not opened it since the day she died when I took it home from the hospital. I sat cross-legged in front of the purse in the chilly attic thinking about the last time I held the purse.

Gingerly, I peeked inside. The expended tissue used to wipe the sweat off of Mom's upper lip as she struggled to breath still sat in the corner of the front compartment. Her RTC work badge with her picture was in front. A folded paper napkin with a name and a phone number was also tucked in the pocket. At first, I didn't recognize the name, but then I remembered. It was the name and phone number of one of Mom's suicide sitters at Rush Presbyterian Hospital in Chicago. No one ever really understood why the hospital thought Mom needed a suicide sitter during her last hours. All she needed to do at that point was to refuse medical treatment. Despite all of her talk, Mom wanted to live. But she actually liked having someone sit with her, so no one argued. I closed the purse and looked at the boxes lining the shelves. I was not ready to look through the tangible documentation of my memories, but I felt like I was finally ready to talk to the Arlington Heights police. I left the boxes and memories in the attic and closed the door.

Cindy and I were silent as we drove to Arlington Heights for our first meeting with the police.

"What should we tell them?" she asked.

"We answer the questions," I replied. "We are not the police, we are not investigators. We are two 50-something-year-old women answering questions about a long-ago family member. We never were very good at playing Nancy Drew. There is no way we can solve the case."

We drove in silence for a few more minutes.

"It's an interesting story," Cindy countered.

"No one will believe us." I answered.

I was not sure when Cindy became the strongest of my siblings. There was a time when I was the leader. At some point, I abdicated the position and left town hoping that I was also leaving my complicated life behind. But here I was. Back in Chicago. With Cindy. Sitting outside of a police station. Following Donnie's trail. For a minute, it was a 14-year-old Cindy in her pixie glasses and plaid pants sitting next to me waiting for me to decide what I was going to do. It was a reminder that you can't run away from yourself.

The Arlington Heights police station is a modern-looking building that is located in the middle of a suburban downtown area. Cindy pulled into a parking space about a block away from the building. It was a couple of days past Christmas and the street was still decorated with wreaths and lights. Neither of us was talking. It was as if we were both waiting to be told what to do next. I was holding my Dunkin' Donuts coffee cup tightly in both hands as I stared out the front window at the police station. My mom's worn brown briefcase was on the floor between my legs. It's made of leather and has her initials — DLM — burned in the side. I had spent hours trying to decide what to take for this interview, but had only her briefcase and her journal. Every few minutes I reached down and touched the spirals of the notebook. I hadn't decided to share the journal with anyone, but had the idea that this was Mom's story in many ways. She should have been the one who talked to the police and not us.

"I am not sure why we are doing this," I finally said. "I can't even figure out where to start."

Cindy was more certain. "Just start at the beginning," she said. "If we start at the beginning it will make sense."

Cindy's accounting background makes her think of the story as a timeline. In fact, she spent hours making timelines before today to make sure that I didn't miss any of the more interesting points of life with Donnie. Cindy had also worked as a fraud investigator for many years. This gave her the ability to fact check all my memories and provide documentation of the truth. I don't think as linear as Cindy. I tend to remember the spectacular blow-ups that characterized life with Donnie. My timeline was based on the magnitude of the problem rather than the year it took place. I almost always start with Noreen's death while Cindy likes to start with Carleton Road.

Detective Sperando was very professional, and quite likable. He led us to a small office so we didn't feel like this was really a police interview. There was no two-way mirror and he leaned against the wall and started talking. He had been joined by another police officer. Detective Sperando talked about Loretta's daughter, Stephanie, who comes to the police station each year on the anniversary of her mother's death with a freshly-baked cake and reminds the detectives that the killer is still out there.

"I don't know if you will believe us," I finally said. "It is such a crazy story." Detective Sperando and his fellow detective looked at each other.

"We went to Wylie, Texas, to talk to people who knew your mom and Donnie," he said. "Someone followed us while we were there. When we got back, some unusual things happened."

The other detective spoke up next.

"I got calls on my personal cell phone from a real estate broker in Wylie regarding a home he thought I might like to see. But I never expressed any interest in buying a home," he said.

"And someone mailed me a Christmas card from a club in Wylie, but we were never at a club," Sperando said while looking at his partner. "So, we would not find anything you say about Donnie Rudd to be surprising."

I still couldn't figure out where to start. I reached into Mom's briefcase and felt her journal. I need to feel grounded.

"Start at the beginning. Start at Carleton Road," Cindy urged me.

She was right. That was when this story started. When we were children. Before Donnie. With block parties at Carleton Road, Girl Scout campouts, school fun fairs, and sleepovers that careened crazily into the madness of life with Donnie. The affair, divorce, eight kids, lies, Flagstaff, Barrington Square, the complex relationship between the Rudd and Hart families, the women, the violence, guns, funerals, the manipulations, allegations, emails, lawsuits and depositions. Cindy chimed in to add details I had forgotten. The detectives listened attentively, appearing to be transfixed by the story of our life, only occasionally interjecting a question.

The detectives seemed puzzled by the fact we lived in two separate houses as children. Murder and violence was part of their world, and the parts of our story that included those elements didn't seem to evoke as much of a response as what we considered the more "mundane" parts of our lives — the details we had come to accept as "normal," but were probably anything but. I don't think they could wrap their heads around the idea of a mother who would live next door to her children and reconcile it with the children who loved her so much.

As we got up to leave, the detective asked one final question.

"Do you think Donnie murdered Noreen and Loretta?"

Always the question. It is easier to focus on the facts of life with Donnie than the conclusions that are drawn from that life. It is hard to reconcile the brutality of Loretta's murder with Donnie's always-present cowardice. I can see him hiding in the bathroom to avoid a confrontation with his girlfriend. Checking himself into the hospital rather than facing his law partner after a work crisis. But the violence had always been real as well. I quickly recall the hammer through the TV and the hole in the water heater. I wondered why he didn't kill me. I question again if he hastened Mom's death. I knew the answer to the detective's question, but it was difficult to actually articulate.

"Yes ..." I said slowly. "I believe he did it."

Maybe saying it out loud would help with closure. The frantic pace of my life can pause if I am no longer afraid the past will catch up with me. This new group of detectives may be the best hope of getting to the truth of what happened to Noreen and Loretta.

"Was this really our family?" Cindy asked as we leaned against the car outside the Arlington Heights police station. Talking about life with Donnie had left us both a little shell-shocked. Talking about one Donnie incident is not the same as hearing the whole story. The past had come rushing forward bringing all of the chaos, indecision, and disbelief of life with our stepfather.

"I really want to know the truth," Cindy said, before I

could answer her previous question. "The truth about Donnie."

"You're the fraud investigator," I responded. "How would we find the truth?"

"I can't believe that the craziness stopped just because Mom died. There have to have been other things that have happened since he left our lives," Cindy responded.

It was an interesting thought: The Donnie years continuing on without us.

"The police will never be able to figure out what to do. It has been almost 40 years since Noreen died," Cindy added. She was not optimistic this was a solvable mystery. Donnie had a motive and was at Loretta's murder scene. Still, he had not been arrested. It does not bode well for success with the police investigation. But the desire to know was being rekindled by the new police actions. Much like the cold case reopened by the Arlington Heights police department, Cindy and I were reopening our own childhood mystery.

During the meeting, I told Detective Sperando he could come to my house in Georgia and look through my attic files. I wasn't sure it would give any real answers, but it might clarify life with Donnie. Cindy agreed to fly back to Atlanta and help me organize everything. I know there are some things she had never seen. This would give us time to talk about what clues might have been missed and review everything that might be turned over to the police.

Cindy arrived in Atlanta a couple of days later and we began the arduous task of looking through boxes of documents prior to the arrival of the Arlington Heights police. As I searched one of Mom's boxes, I grabbed a file filled with medical records and articles on breast cancer and saw the edge of an email sticking out. It was dated Monday, July 31, 1995. It was from Donnie's RTC email address to my Mom's RTC email address.

Love you. I'm going to leave early and see if I can get my stuff. Sounds like AH police may be there. Where did you say you put the gun that was used? It wasn't mine and cannot be tied to me so let's give it to them. I have absolutely nothing to worry about regarding guns.

Mom's response email came less than five minutes later. It was also on her government RTC email.

Love you too. But I don't know what gun you are talking about.

There was stunned silence as Cindy and I looked at the two emails. At one time or another over the past 15 years, each of us thought that Mom might know more about the facts of Loretta's murder than she ever let on. It never crossed our minds that she might know with certainty what happened that rainy afternoon so many years ago. Although she may have had no direct knowledge or involvement, could Mom be complicit in hiding the weapon that he used? It was a monumental revelation to even consider Mom capable of actually covering up Donnie's horrible crimes. Why would Mom save this email? Had this been a threat by Donnie? Was he trying to blackmail Mom by intimating she was involved in the murder? Could she have helped him hide the gun? But here it was — more than 20 years after it was sent, still in the file where Mom placed it, and living in my Georgia attic for so many years. Maybe she meant for someone to find it and turn it over to the police. Or maybe she just forgot she had it as the cancer overcame her.

I could feel the wave of a familiar emotion sweeping over me. Protect Mom. Instead, I picked up my phone and snapped a picture of the two emails. A minute later it was on its way to the

Arlington Heights Police Department. "I don't want to change my mind about this one," I grimly told Cindy. Mom was gone and it would be up to the police to interpret these strange emails. Cindy and I sat at my dining room table until the sound of chirping birds alerted us that dawn was approaching. The Donnie files and pictures were now neatly organized and tabbed, spilling over the edge of the table and lining the walls. There was something about putting all of the physical remnants of the Hart family's life into order that was letting us think a little more clearly about the past. It was a complicated view.

There were files with the names of the crises that left marks on our lives. Noreen Kumeta. Loretta Bodtke. George. Joseph. Whitehall. Vita Mae. It seemed strange to see each of these files lined up against my dining room wall. These were the people who intersected our lives through Donnie. The people hurt by our stepfather. It was even harder to read the notes and letters written by Mom. She had been gone so many years. There was such pain evident in her words. There is always pain in the people surrounding Donnie Rudd.

Cindy held up a picture of a smiling Noreen and Donnie dancing at their wedding. I looked at the picture of the pretty young blond girl and wondered if she had any idea of the kind of man she was marrying. I was amazed that the wedding had such an air of formality. How could he keep the wedding a secret when he was living at our house? It was so strange that members of his family attended the celebration knowing he had not left my mother.

"What are the chances that we would see our way through the craziness?" I ponder that question as I look at a picture of Mom and Donnie at a District 54 school board event. There was a whole file of newspaper articles about Mom and Donnie's time in the community limelight. I could see Mom's name badge in the picture and recall that she was still Dianne Hart at that time.

The picture must have been taken as she was deciding whether to follow Donnie or stay with our family.

"What's the end of the Donnie story?" I asked Cindy. "If it is not accountability in the legal system, what is left?" Cindy shook her head as she dove into one of the last boxes of pictures.

Finally, we were ready. The boxes were organized. Cindy's timeline was neatly sitting on the table, and the Arlington Heights Police were on their way. For the first time in 40 years, there was a semblance of order to our early life. The madness was meticulously documented, organized, and filed. Among the contents of the boxes was the subpoena that Donnie gave Mom when he tried to prove he was not engaged, numerous letters from Vita Mae to Louann talking about Donnie's early bouts of "cancer," emails and love letters from Donnie to Mom, the letter Mom wrote the night Noreen was killed, and the Sun-Times news article about "Mr. Con."

Detective Sperando and another Arlington Heights police officer arrived at my Georgia home on a chilly afternoon. After spending several hours poring over documents, the detective asked if he could take the documents with him and bring them back the next day. It was hard letting them go, but we eventually agreed, trusting that they'd be in good hands.

"All right," I told Cindy. "The police have everything that we have now. What don't we have?" Cindy was thoughtful for a moment. "I would like to know exactly what happened with his wife," she finally says.

"Which wife?" I wanted to make sure that I had it right.

"Wife Number Four," she answered. "The one he married right after Mom died."

We had heard occasional stories about Wife Number Four from our stepsisters, Donnie's family, and through Dad and Louann who still saw some of the Rudd side of the family.

"So let's start with Wife Number Four." I said. For the

first time in a long time, I felt I had a purpose. It reminded me of when we were young and struggling to figure out a Donnie problem. Cindy and I were on the case. We were on a Donnie mission.

CHAPTER TWENTY-FOUR

Wives Number Four and Five

Twenty-five years after he met Mom, and less than four months after she died, Donnie married his Houston girlfriend on November 4, 1996. We are now sure about the date because Cindy pulled the marriage certificate. Donnie was 54 years old and Wife Number Four was nine years younger at 43. Cindy was able to obtain the divorce file from the Texas court. Slowly, we were piecing together pieces of Donnie's life after Mom. Although we never met Donnie's new wife, the divorce file for Donnie's fourth wife was remarkably familiar.

Wife Number Four knew very little about the man she would marry. The newly invented Donnie was a smart, attentive, retired attorney from Chicago; a philanthropist involved in charitable work; and a war hero who kept his Congressional Medal of Honor in an expensive framed box (fake), mounted in the living room. He had three Purple Hearts from injuries suffered during the Vietnam War. He still had shrapnel in his head from his heroic war years. Just like the stories that would enthrall me when I was in high school, Donnie still talked about his years with the CIA, his undercover operations, and the medals he earned. In fact, he was fond of telling people during this time period that some of the events in the movie *Rambo* were based on one of his CIA operations. It was a story that would eventually find its way to his profile on Match.com. It was not surprising that Wife Number Four did not believe us when we tried to warn her about Donnie. Our story was so incredulous that it sounded ridiculous even to me.

The new Donnie was also a widower — a role he really enjoyed. He neglected to tell his new girlfriend that Mom was not quite dead when they started dating — a mere technicality in Donnie's world. Donnie claimed he was independently wealthy and owned a petroleum company called Rudd Petroleum. Naturally, he did not mention his bankruptcy or that his "wealth" was primarily what he received from Mom's 401k plan and the sale of the Wylie house. He doctored bank statements to indicate he had more than $6 million in the bank, which he would show visitors. He claimed Wife Number Four's engagement ring was worth $126,000, which fit in with his claim to being independently wealthy. I smiled thinking of all the cubic zirconia rings in Donnie's past. However, it was inevitable that this very smart wife would eventually find out the truth about her new husband.

Donnie's new mother-in-law was well known in Dallas. She belonged to a large Dallas church, which Donnie would occasionally attend. About the time Donnie married Wife Number Four, the church was involved in fundraising to replace the rose window located in the atrium. Rose windows are large, circular windows that are found in churches of the Gothic architectural style. They are quite opulent and — as one could imagine — very expensive. At one church meeting, Donnie was resolute about the fundraising. "Let's do it," he said. "I'll donate the balance of what is needed to begin the renovation." He pledged close to a million dollars towards the replacement of the rose window. For a brief time, Donnie's generous pledge made him a beloved member of the church. Everyone was ecstatic the window would be replaced as a result of the generous gift. The church immediately began moving towards replacing the pricey stained glass window.

Of course, there was only one problem. Donnie did not have a million dollars to donate to the church for the project any more than he had a million dollars to pay the Whitehall investors years earlier. He was essentially broke. Donnie used a variety of excuses to initially delay releasing the check to the church. But with each delay, pressure mounted. Slowly, he was being backed into a corner. As some point, he knew he was not going to be able to write the promised check, but, as in countless times before, he was still incapable of admitting the check would never materialize.

Wife Number Four came home from work one day and found Donnie lying unconscious on the floor. An empty bottle of pills was nearby. Donnie was rushed to the hospital emergency room. Donnie's brother was also called to the hospital. As part of the diagnostic workup, the emergency room doctor suggested Donnie have an MRI on his head to make sure he had not suffered a stroke or a head injury when he fell. Wife Number Four was adamant that the MRI could not be performed because of the shrapnel in his head from the war. Since an MRI is a magnetic form of X-ray, it might cause the shrapnel to move, she explained. Donnie's brother gave her a puzzled look.

"Donnie was never in any war," he offered casually.

There was a long, silent pause as she slowly queued up her next question.

"Is Donnie in the CIA?" she sheepishly asked.

There was complete silence in the room. It was at about this time that Wife Number Four probably figured out that the movie *Rambo* was not based on Donnie's life either.

A short time later, a box of Donnie's files was found in the trunk of his car. The documents included information on the Bodtke murder, his problems with the ARDC, and various lawsuits. The truth. Donnie Rudd was clearly not the wealthy retired philanthropist as claimed. Also among the documents found in the car truck was a life insurance policy on the life of Wife Number Four. Unlike Mom, Wife Number Four recognized her mistake and took action to rectify the situation very quickly. She initiated proceedings to have the marriage annulled, based on fraud.

Wife Number Four's divorce filing surprised us. The truth is, we all lost sight of what was normal. A normal woman would not stay with a man who always lied, hurt people, and who could not be trusted. It was Mom who was weak. She stood by Donnie through thick and thin. She never had the strength to say "Enough!" Donnie's brother was quite matter-of-fact as he recounted his conversations with Wife Number Four as the truth began to unfold. He said it reminded him of many conversations he had with Mom after Noreen died.

There was plenty of support for Wife Number Four's Petition for Annulment, but Donnie was not inclined to give up easily. In early August, she found Donnie following her. He was wearing a disguise; a mustache and a wig. He was driving a car she'd never seen before. It belonged to his new girlfriend. Wife Number Four clearly did not want to be the third dead wife of Donnie Rudd. She knew that immediate action was required. On August 24, 1999, she filed a protective order to keep Donnie away from her. She was going through with an annulment of the marriage.

By early 2000, the annulment was finalized and Donnie was no longer married to Wife Number Four. But Donnie was not one to let a wife go without having another one waiting in the wings. He already had a track record of lining up his next wife. Before the ink was dry on the court order annulling this Rudd marriage, another Houston woman was moving up the list of candidates for the title of the new Mrs. Rudd. This woman was about to become Wife Number Five.

Donnie met Wife Number Five on Match.com while he was still married to Number Four. He told her he had been married twice, was very wealthy, and had retired from the practice of his law. His profile on Match.com was eerily similar to the stories he had been telling for more than 30 years. It spoke of how the movie *Rambo* was based on some of his assignments during the war. It boasted about the important people he knew and the businesses he owned. Donnie also starting referring to himself as a "doctor." A Ph.D. degree was added to his resume as well as a degree in biomedical engineering. Donnie proposed to Wife Number Five the day following the finalization of his divorce from Wife Number Four. On February 1, 2000, Donnie remarried. His record of never going more than six months without a wife remained intact even in the face of five marriages.

Wife Number Five fit the pattern of Donnie's romantic interests. Although not independently wealthy herself, she was the trustee of a large estate for the benefit of her disabled son. Her son was severely injured in a motorcycle accident when he was much younger, leaving him a quadriplegic. As a quadriplegic, Wife Number Five acted as the trustee of funds received from his accident. Donnie talked a lot about the son's estate to the few friends and family that still had contact with him. With his legal background, he felt he would be the most appropriate trustee of the estate after his marriage. A quadriplegic son also was a good addition to the profile he was building to pull people in: A wife killed in a car accident, a wife who died from cancer, and a quadriplegic son injured in a motorcycle accident. He would use these three tragic events to redirect attention from his actions in various business interviews and settings. Donnie was recreating himself yet again. However, his new identify required him to have some wealth. The proceeds from the sale of the Wylie house and Mom's 401(k) account were probably dwindling by the time he married in 2000. He began to look for a way to continue to fund the lifestyle that he needed to maintain his new profile.

For years, Donnie tried to find a way to increase the amount of inheritance he might receive in the event of his father's death. Although Eddie and Vita Mae lived a relatively simple life, Donnie was fond of saying that his parents had saved a substantial amount of funds. He would talk of negotiable bonds that Eddie would keep at his small house in Marble Falls. Even when he lived at our house, Donnie would talk to his father about increasing the amount of life insurance he carried on his life. Eddie was stubborn and not interested in increasing his worth for those who would survive him. He refused Donnie's financial advice on numerous occasions, much to Donnie's chagrin. Unsuccessful in convincing Eddie, Donnie turned to his aging mother with the suggestion that she take out additional insurance on Eddie's life without telling him. Although Eddie's memory was failing and Vita Mae wanted to trust her son, she finally wrote and said she wanted to forget about the idea of additional insurance. In the letter to Donnie, she said:

> *"Daddy was talking with a visitor the other day and he is very opposed to any supplemental insurance. There is no way he could not learn about it if I signed up and then he will think I am slipping around doing things he doesn't want. I appreciated what you are doing and it is probably a wise thing, but I think I had better not do it."*

First Eddie and now Vita Mae quashed a possible avenue for Donnie's replenishment of his funds.

After Vita Mae died in 1998, Donnie again turned to the idea of ensuring he would receive a significant inheritance when Eddie passed. After his marriage to Wife Number Five, Donnie turned to the small Marble Falls house where his aging father still resided. At 91, Eddie lived by himself. But his advanced age was taking its toll. Alzheimer's was progressively disabling Eddie. Marble Falls was not far from where Donnie's twin brother lived. Over the years, Donnie's brothers, Ronnie and John, had stepped up to help Eddie and hoped he would be able to live independently in his house for as long as possible.

Donnie visited his father in Marble Falls shortly after he married Wife Number Five. Eddie's increasing senility made Donnie realize it was time for action. He packed up Eddie, stripped the house of many items and withdrew funds from his dad's bank accounts. Donnie took his father from the small house he lived in his whole life and brought him to live at his home in Sugar Land without the knowledge or consent of his brothers. Both Ronnie and John were furious with Donnie when they discovered he had taken their dad and emptied his bank accounts. Ronnie visited his dad and considered taking legal action against Donnie. However, Eddie took a turn for the worse.

Six days before his death, Eddie executed a new will — conveniently drafted by Donnie — giving his Marble Falls home and other assets directly to Donnie. Donnie appointed himself as the executor of the will and named his new wife as the contingent executor. The will appeared to be witnessed by hospice workers. Eddie died on a Sunday, and by Monday morning, Donnie had buried his father. There was a service at the graveside with no other attendees present besides Donnie and his wife. On Tuesday morning, Donnie called his brothers and left the shocking message on their answering machines that Eddie had died and was buried.

The Rudd brothers decided to honor their father and celebrate his life by having their own service at the cemetery the following week. The entire family, including some of Donnie's children attended the service.

Donnie began working on the probate for his father's estate to transfer his dad's assets so that he could sell them and get the money. He hired an attorney in Sugar Land to open the estate. Donnie told the attorney he was in contact with his brothers and they didn't need any notice of service or details of the will. Donnie was the executor and he would handle everything himself. After nearly three months of listening to Donnie, the attorney withdrew as legal representative for the estate, citing irreconcilable differences with Donnie.

Ronnie called and tried to convince Donnie what he had done was wrong. Donnie told Ronnie he would divide the estate equally as his dad wished and did not want litigation involving the estate. Donnie, however, had no intention of sharing the estate with his brothers. His brothers received nothing after their father's estate was settled. Donnie's brothers never challenged the will. They felt that if Donnie thought money was worth losing his relationship with his family, he could keep the money. Both of Donnie's brothers were financially secure. From that day forward, they were officially estranged from Donnie Rudd. While Donnie may have received a small windfall from his father's death, he still needed to find another source of income.

Right around the time Donnie married Wife Number Five, his promotion of his "biomedical" skills started to pay off when he became friendly with the owners of a Houston-based company called Regenetech. Donnie took a job at Regenetech around 2002. His resume stated he was the chief scientist and served as a corporate secretary for the company. In just a few short years, Donnie morphed from a disgraced attorney to a stem cell researcher engaged in innovative cancer research. New releases posted on Donnie's website claimed that he had more than 30 patent pending applications on the use of stem cells for regeneration of human tissue. His "inventions" covered regeneration of the heart, pancreas, liver, and other organs.

Donnie also claimed to have found a treatment for sickle cell disease. By carefully tracking the articles and announcements regarding his success, it also became clear that Donnie had become quite proficient at building an online resume to support his claims of research findings and awards. However, the more Cindy and I pushed to find the source of his success, the more the Internet branding moved in circles. However, the owners of Regenetech seemed to believe Donnie's knowledge of intellectual property law would bring them a huge return on the investment of capital that had been made into the company. The salary from Regenetech allowed Donnie to purchase a new house and supported his claim that he was a very wealthy man.

In January 2005, a published article stated "Regenetech Announces HIV Breakthrough." According to the article, Dr. Donnie Rudd's work with adult stem cells had led to the ability to isolate molecules to prevent HIV transmission. It went on to state this "new discovery was made by Dr. Rudd." Donnie was publicly making claims that he could cure sickle cell anemia and HIV.

As the years passed, Donnie's resume continued to "expand" as he claimed to have discovered cures for a number of diseases, filed patents for numerous inventions and undertook medical research and testing related to a number of diseases. Donnie seemed to be unstoppable. However, reality has a way of eventually breaking through all of the deception of someone like Donnie. It just takes a while for someone to start realizing that things are not adding up. Donnie was going to have a difficult time passing himself off as a nationally known medical researcher for any extended period of time.

It took a little while, but Regenetech would soon realize that Donnie may not be everything his resume said he was. In 2008, the truth began to resurface as a lawsuit was filed against Donnie Rudd and several individuals who orchestrated a coup to overthrow the board of Regenetech. The lawsuit was filed by the

CFO and CEO of Regenetech when they realized they had been ousted from their positions on the board. The allegations specifically stated that the attempt to overthrow the company was organized and driven by Donnie Rudd. The lawsuit went on to claim Donnie falsified the shareholders' signatures to obtain the votes needed to remove the board, which amounted to fraud. There was fraudulent financial information given to shareholders to coerce them into signing the approval for the overthrow.

Donnie's life with Wife Number Five was quite good up to this point. Donnie continued to talk about the millions of dollars that he had saved from his first career and assured his wife that life would be good. However, the truth was Donnie was struggling with the lack of available cash. He had used up the money he received from Mom and had little to show from his time with Wife Number Four. As things started to collapse with Regenetech, Donnie again found himself in a significant financial situation. Wife Number Five started to doubt the stories of wealth and privilege that Donnie had talked about for several years.

When a Notice of Foreclosure was filed for their home, Wife Number Five decided to confront Donnie once and for all regarding his "wealth." During the confrontation, she told him if he was rich, he should write her a check for a million dollars. Donnie obliged by pulling out his checkbook and writing a check for the full amount. He handed it to his angry wife hoping it would prove to her that he had not lied. "OK," the wife said. "Let's go to the bank and cash the check."

Donnie had once again reached the end of the road of a long lie. True to form, he clasped his chest and collapsed claiming he was having a heart attack. Wife Number Five was finally facing the real Donnie. A very broke Donnie. A fifth divorce was in the works.

Sensing a deeper desire for some semblance of closure, Cindy and I flew to Houston hoping that perhaps something — anything — might add yet another piece to our still incomplete puzzle. We sat outside Donnie's apartment in Sugar Land and visited the homes of Wife Number Four and Wife Number Five. We even visited Mom's old house in Dallas, where we unashamedly trespassed by sitting poolside with our feet dangling in the water as we did so many times when Mom was sick. The trip was necessary for us, but ultimately fruitless as we had uncovered nothing new.

Shortly after we dropped off the rental car, Cindy received a call. She listened for a few minutes before she turned to me and whispered, "They are going to exhume Noreen!" After more than 40 years, the police had decided that Noreen's body may hold clues as to what happened. The police review of Donnie's life had taken a surprising turn. Instead of focusing on Loretta, the police were also now interested in what happened to Noreen. The differing stories about how the accident occurred and the inconsistencies of the massive head wound that caused her death warranted the drastic action of exhuming her body. The small cemetery where she was laid to rest in her beautiful wedding dress was now preparing for an unlikely event: the dramatic exhumation of Noreen Kumeta Rudd's body. Science would now have a chance to tell us what Donnie never did. What really happened to Noreen.

Cindy reached out to an unlikely contact when we returned from our trip to Dallas and Houston. She called Stephanie Tabak, Loretta's daughter. Although our stories are different, we shared a bond. The loss of a mom changed Stephanie's life just as it had changed ours. The deaths are all inextricably intertwined with the story of Donnie Rudd. Stephanie misses her mother every day just as we miss ours. We have a common bond in knowing the man who caused so much misery has still never been held accountable. Stephanie opened a Facebook site about Donnie and her mother's murder. She hopes that someone will leave a clue that will ultimately allow the police to make an arrest. She says she calls Donnie every year on the anniversary of her Mom's death to urge him to tell the truth. Sometimes he answers and listens quietly. Some years, the phone just rings.

Stephanie closed the conversation by saying, "I know he will answer for what he did someday to someone. Maybe after he dies … but I know he will."

CHAPTER TWENTY-FIVE
Did He do it?

D*o you think he did it?* There it is again. Are we talking about Noreen? Loretta? Eddie? Mom? If only there was order in the madness. Sometimes it reminds me of Rubik's Cube, where you spend hours twisting, turning, and spinning, and just when you think you got it ... one green square just won't line up. All of the facts are clear, but still nothing makes sense. That is how I feel when I think about our past and Donnie.

The new investigation as well as Cindy and my journey to Texas was making it hard for me to sleep. I am slowly realizing that I never left Donnie and the past behind. It is always there. Simmering right below the surface. It is why I am always running. I like to think I am running forward, but I think I am running away. Cindy is feeling the pull from the past as well. She calls me late at night and early in the morning. Cindy is increasingly obsessed with verifying everything we remember. She goes to the Cook County courthouse and pulls all of the legal filings against Donnie. And she is increasingly interested in relooking at every file and picture I have in the attic and in the basement. Still, while we now have verifiable documentation of almost every event we remembered, the police have not taken action on any of the deaths. Occasionally a tantalizing story will give us some hope that there has been a breakthrough in the investigation.

There was never any doubt that Donnie was a liar. A spectacular, convincing, consistent, deliberate liar. It is probably one of the few things we know for sure about him. He told big lies and small lies. He lied to cover up his lies. And he told lies with no purpose — lies that were sure to be uncovered. Lies so outrageous it was impossible not to believe him. I have this vaguely discomforting feeling that Donnie felt joy when the lies rolled off his tongue. He lied about his past, his education, his friends, and his accomplishments. He would talk about vacations he never took, people he never met, and jobs he never held. Donnie's lies extended to his family, his clients, and his friends. He manipulated us as each lie wore down our defenses and made us weaker whenever we believed him. He controlled us through his lies. Even our sympathy for his predicaments when his lies were uncovered was symbolic of his control over us.

Over the years, our family talked about whether Donnie was mentally ill. Mental illness seemed a logical conclusion. After all, he was diagnosed with manic-depressive disorder around the time that Loretta Bodtke turned up dead. However, he claimed the manic-depressive diagnosis as an excuse for his actions when it was convenient. But Donnie's behaviors did not always fit into a psychiatric diagnosis. He knew instantly when he was caught doing something wrong — which didn't support the conclusion that he had difficulty distinguishing reality from fantasy. He seemed to know the difference between right and wrong when he talked about what would happen if he were arrested. He used us, but had no emotional connection to us.

Donnie used illness — physical or mental — to explain why he acted or didn't act in a certain way. He told people he had cancer when he was in his early thirties. A cancer diagnosis and chemotherapy evoked a sympathetic reaction that directed attention straight to Donnie. Similarly, Donnie only sought treatment for his mental "condition" when he was under suspicion or pressure for one of his schemes. It made his diagnosis of manic depression suspect. Was it real or part of an elaborate scheme to avoid responsibility for a crime? Because no medication or therapy would change Donnie, it was hard to accept that mental illness precipitated his actions. "Sociopath" definitely seemed like a better diagnosis.

One thing was clear: Donnie acted with clarity unclouded by concern for others. Glory, didn't believe the maniac depressive diagnosis from the beginning. She always said Donnie was evil incarnate.

"We are living with the devil," she'd say. "He's not sick; he is ruthless and mean." That seemed to make more sense.

"I don't want to know," Jack said as he steadfastly held to his belief that we should put everything in the past. Although he believes strongly that Donnie killed Mom.

The chances of solving the Donnie mystery through rational thinking are about as likely as completing a puzzle by throwing all the pieces in the air and hoping that they come down in the right place. As hard as it is to find an ending to the Donnie years, I know that Cindy and I are slowing coming to the end of our personal search for the truth. The ending may not be conclusive, but it has left us with the sense that we have done all we could to determine the truth. And even from the dysfunction of our early life with Donnie, our family has found a positive ending to the Donnie years. We love each other and difficulties we have faced together have made us closer.

The one good thing about Donnie was that it made the four Hart kids more than just a family. The Hart kids were a team. It took a while, but eventually we decided we wanted to be the winning team. Dealing with Donnie built a toughness in us that would be difficult to replicate in anything but the most challenging of situations. I am not going to say the four of us are close all the time, but when there is a crisis, we have a way of putting aside our differences and acting in unison. We have grown up to be incredibly strong and resilient adults with a bit of an attitude. We have ended up a loving, interesting, and successful family.

In a strange way, I can't help but wonder what our lives might have been like today had Donnie not swept in with his cyclone of destruction. Would I have been a lawyer? If I wasn't a lawyer, would I have met my husband, had my daughters Amanda and Abby, and ended up with a wonderful home and a loving family?

And what about Dad? He has been married to Louann for more than 40 years — much longer than he was married to Mom. Cindy probably would not have married her first husband if not for Donnie. She married him to escape her family and start a perfect life. She dreamed of picket fences, normal families, and lots of children when she was way too young to get married. Her first marriage ended quickly. She later married her current husband, John, and lives happily with her boys Matt and Greg in Barrington, Illinois.

Jack's mechanical skills were honed during his time in the Navy. He has become a successful project engineer. He adopted a daughter who lives not far from him. And Glory is happily living in Houston, Texas. She's still the life of every party.

All of our children attend or have graduated from college. Glory's son, Christian, currently attends Yale University. Sam will start at one of the Texas colleges sometime in the next year. Amanda graduated from Auburn University and works for a large corporate firm as a financial analyst. Abby is currently attending the University of Alabama on a full engineering scholarship. Greg graduated from the University of Iowa with a degree in biomedical engineering. He just started his first sales job. Matt is a freshman at the University of Illinois and dreams of becoming a doctor. It is hard to believe that he was not born when Mom died.

And what would our lives be like without our stepsiblings? Eight of the Rudd and Hart kids flew to Dallas for my Dad's 80th birthday in 2015. Only we weren't kids anymore. We were grownups who have that special bond that only people who have endured something unique can share. As we sang happy birthday to Dad, I couldn't help but stare at my stepbrother. He looks exactly like Donnie did when I met him so many years ago at the little house on Flagstaff Lane. For a minute, it took me back. But he is everything Donnie is not. He is a fifth grade teacher with seven children of his own, an honest man whose life revolves around his children.

Today, Cindy and I are surprisingly content. I am no longer afraid. It is not that Donnie has changed. Every couple of months, an Internet story will pop up about some scheme he is selling, but we know now that time has not been kind to Donnie Rudd. His tousled white hair and big glasses give him a bit of a mad scientist look. At 70, his wild ideas and improbable inventions do not warrant much interest from investors. It may be that word of the Regenetech fiasco has tarnished his reputation far more than he believes. Or maybe he has just lost the fervor that always made his promises so believable. Occasionally, a post on his Facebook will announce his imminent death. Cindy always texts me his posts.

"The colon is gone," he writes. "Only a few more months to live." Or "tumor in leg pressing on muscle and nerve. Surgery within the hour …" Sound familiar?

The calls from the police come less frequently now. While they say they are continuing to work on the Bodtke and Kumeta cases, it is clear that the police files may once again be moved to the "cold case" warehouse. And my own Donnie files will slowly begin making their way back to my attic. Time is not a friend to solving the mystery of Donnie.

As I stated in the opening chapter, I want to say this is a true story. But all we can really say is it is *our* truth. It is what Donnie did to *our* family. When all is said and done, we feel we've done our part. We told the story as fully and as accurately as we could. We painstakingly retraced our steps. We've had dozens of conversations with law enforcement, logged hundreds of miles, and researched thousands of documents. We've been thorough and — we believe — objective. The facts are what they are.

In the end, I do know one thing for sure: Donnie Rudd never beat the Hart family. The devil may not have gotten his due, but the Hart family won.

And there is certainly some justice in that fact.

Epilogue

Cindy and I revisited Noreen's grave a couple of months ago. It had been nearly three years since the exhumation and we wanted to see if the headstone had been replaced. Indeed it had; the tombstone that was once engraved with the name *Noreen Rudd* for more than four decades now bore a much simpler design. The disturbed earth around the grave was settled now, with the growth of new grass blending into a seamless landscape. Everything looked as it had before … with one notable exception: The name on the stone now simply reads *Noreen Kumeta*.

* * * * * * * * * * * *

On Thursday, December 17, 2015, only a couple days after we had signed off on the final manuscript of what would eventually become this book, Detective Richard Sperando led a contingency of officers from the Sugar Land, Texas, and Arlington Heights, Ill., police departments to Donnie Rudd's apartment. After 40 years, the blood of Noreen Kumeta cried out for justice — and won — as Donnie was formally charged with her murder.

Donnie was flown back to Chicago the next day and bond was set at $4 million. The Cook County State's Attorney Cold Case Unit released several short statements to the media —

who pounced on the decades-old cold case — insinuating that they were also taking a long, hard look at the circumstances and evidence surrounding Loretta Tabak Bodtke's murder as well.

Is the devil getting his due? Is everything coming full circle? Is the house of lies, deceit, and corruption starting to crumble? I can't say for sure, but Donnie's last words as a free man were pretty telling.

When told he was being arrested for murder, Donnie's reply was simple and chilling.

"Which one?"

Author's Note: *Donnie is still awaiting trial for the murder of his second wife, 19 year old Noreen Rudd. He was released from jail after posting a $4 million dollar bond and is currently residing in the State of Illinois. The trial is expected to take place in 2018. The conversations in the book all come from our recollection, public records and writings of our mother. In some cases, the passage of time means that the words do not represent word for word transcripts. However, we have always written the words in a way that represents the feelings and meaning of what was said, the essence of the dialogue is true. In a few scenes, we combined recollections of events into one voice. We have not disclosed the names of women, friends and clients of Donnie. Most of the names can be ascertained through public records and court filings. This was a deliberate action on our part. While we chose to make our private life public, we wanted to give others the right to make that decision. The prologue is a compilation of stories regarding Noreen's exhumation. While we were there before and after, we were not at the cemetery the day Noreen's body was removed from the grave.*

Made in the USA
Lexington, KY
07 April 2018